THE REBUILDING OF ITALY

THE ROYAL INSTITUTE
OF INTERNATIONAL AFFAIRS
London: Chatham House, St James's Square, S.W.1.
New York: 345 East 46th Street, New York 17, N.Y.

Toronto *Melbourne*
Wellington *Bombay* *Karachi* *Cape Town*
OXFORD UNIVERSITY PRESS

THE REBUILDING OF ITALY

POLITICS AND ECONOMICS
1945–1955

BY

MURIEL GRINDROD

London & New York

ROYAL INSTITUTE
OF INTERNATIONAL AFFAIRS

First published 1955

PRINTED IN GREAT BRITAIN
AT THE BROADWATER PRESS, WELWYN GARDEN CITY
HERTFORDSHIRE

CONTENTS

INTRODUCTION

TILL recent times the Englishman's interest in Italy tended to be concentrated chiefly on all that that country had to offer in scenery, in climate, and in the sphere of art. From the wealthy young man of the eighteenth century for whom the Grand Tour was an essential part of his education, down to his less affluent but more comfortably travelling Edwardian counterpart, the main object of a journey to Italy was sun and sight-seeing. How the Italians themselves lived was largely incidental: they formed a background, whether quaint or picturesque, to the new panorama of sights and scenes that the traveller enjoyed, but he seldom stopped to consider how the country was run, how these smiling, cheerful people gained a livelihood, or why, amid all the wealth of magnificent architecture, there were so many signs of poverty. To the Northerner, Italy was warm and beautiful and 'different', and that was enough.

True, the élan of the Risorgimento had caught the imagination of many liberal-minded Englishmen who gave practical proof of their sympathies for Garibaldi and Mazzini. But once unification had been achieved political interest abroad waned again, and it was left to historians to record the less spectacular story of the building of a united Italy.

When the aftermath of the first world war brought with it first chaos and then the Fascist experiment, some English lovers of Italy were alienated by the authoritarian features of the new régime, while others found something to admire in its stern treatment of subversion. But the attitude to the country itself still remained much the same: you went to Italy—usually to Florence, Venice, or Rome—to see the galleries and the churches; or you went there—to the lakes or the Ligurian coast—to bathe and bask in the sun. It was a pity the Italians had this dictatorial régime—not that it made much difference to the ordinary traveller, but still . . .; or, alternatively, now that they had this new régime . . . and then would follow the usual inevitable remark about the trains running on time. As time went on some few convinced spirits boycotted Italian holidays; and indeed during the Abyssinian war and the sanctions period even the most abstracted English visitor could hardly fail to observe that things were not quite what they used to be. But right up to the summer of 1939 the English Italophiles continued, if in diminishing numbers, to visit the country of their affections; and for all their affection they remained for the most part aloof, uninvolved, drawn to the country for its natural and architectural beauties, yet unable or unwilling to penetrate below the surface to its real life.

There were, of course, exceptions. Among the English who made their homes in Italy, whether from choice or through intermarriage, many came to understand their second country as well as they did their own; and a writer such as Norman Douglas, for example, caused a region as remote as the then almost unknown Calabria to come to life for English readers. Yet even *Old Calabria*, *South Wind*, and *Siren Land* were read and enjoyed rather as literature, and for the tale they told, than for the penetrating light they shed on byways of Italian life.

There was, indeed, something to be said for those more spacious days of greater leisure and fewer sociological studies, when genuine knowledge and understanding of another country flowered either as a natural growth born of long intimacy, or not at all. Italians, at any rate, seem in those days not to have resented the Englishman's detachment; he came to their country, spent his money there, and enjoyed it, and that was enough. Resentment arose at a different level, and only penetrated to the people at large when Mussolini began to tell them that their country had all the makings of a great Power and was being deprived of its rights by more selfish and more fortunate nations.

The war put an abrupt end to this half-idyllic, half-artificial relationship between Italy and Britain. But one outcome of it was that many Britishers, coming from quite other walks of life than the earlier travellers, men who in normal circumstances would never have been able to afford to set foot in Italy, came to know the country at first-hand and both to appreciate its beauty and to realise something of the problems of its people. Moreover today, in a rapidly contracting world individual countries neither can nor may remain in quite such an ivory-towered ignorance about each other's way of life. Italy is now working side by side with the other countries of the West in wider communities and organisations. Her internal affairs are thus a matter of interest and concern for all her partners.

The ten years of Italy's life since the war ended are in any case an important and even dramatic chapter in her history. Her wartime experience was in some respects unique. She began the war in the Axis camp and ended it in the Allied; yet a part of the country remained bound to the last to the Axis allegiance. She suffered defeat, war in her own territory, and a division of the country as effective as at any time before the unification. Her change of camp had come about through the collapse of the Fascist régime, and for the last eighteen months of the war one half of the country was committed to an attempt to maintain that régime, while the other half embarked on the first tentative beginnings of a new democracy. She emerged from the war physically battered, economically bankrupt, and shorn not only of the more recent acquisitions of Mussolini's Empire but also of the older colonies which Italian money and energies had developed for more than half a century.

The Italian people, exhausted and often starving, were torn by conflicting emotions; while ardent anti-Fascists were exultant, buoyed up with the hope of building a new world, those who had been closely bound to the old régime viewed its fall as an unmitigated disaster and saw the end of all their hopes alike for Italy's greatness and for their own careers. Between these two extremes were the mass of ordinary people who had never concerned themselves much with politics, had contrived to tolerate the Fascist régime while heartily grumbling at it, and who now found themselves launched on an experiment in democracy without having any clear idea of what it involved. Among these people—who formed the vast majority of the population—many, while by no means nostalgic for the old régime, were deterred by two particular sentiments from wholeheartedly welcoming the new: one such sentiment was the bitterness aroused by Italy's defeat, by the circumstances of her change of camp, and by the 'unconditional surrender' terms of the Armistice; and the other was the feeling inspired by the monarchy which, despite the sorry part it had played in the Fascist story, still commanded sufficient allegiance to cause something approaching half the population to vote for its retention.

This is not to imply that the majority of Italians felt any particular regrets about the end of Fascism, as distinct from that of the monarchy. On the contrary: by mid-1943 practically the whole population was heartily sick of the régime which, in the person of Mussolini, had dragged them into a war they did not want. They therefore rejoiced at its collapse and prepared to welcome the Allies. What they had not bargained for was the prolongation for eighteen months of war and occupation in their own territory and of their own equivocal position in relation to the Allies. Yet such were the contradictions of the situation that those eighteen months provided Italians with the opportunity for what many of them still regard as their finest hour: the Resistance movement of anti-Fascist Italians against the Germans and remaining Fascists brought out all that was best in them, and afforded a justification for Italy to be regarded as an ally.

Even that genuine outburst of popular feeling against the oppressor was to become a source of dispute as time went on, and as its original motives became overlaid with new legends. It took its place among the legacies of that chaotic period when arbitrary brutality went side by side with valiant endeavour. The psychological as well as the material effects of that period of defeat and disorientation coupled with the violent explosion of long pent-up forces were to make themselves felt throughout the early years of the new Republic's life.

To the outer world, however, the immediate and practical task was to set Italy on her feet again and to ensure stable government there. In the international situation which developed from 1947 onwards Italy occupied a position of considerable significance, and one which made her internal stability a matter of moment to the Western Powers. First, owing to her geographical situation she constituted a key point in Mediterranean strategy. Secondly, she had the largest

Communist Party in Western Europe and the danger that the Communists might come to power in so exposed an outpost, whether by a coup d'état or by gradual infiltration and constitutional means, was not to be lightly dismissed. After the Election of 1948 that danger appeared to recede, but it could not be said to have been overcome; and for that reason alone, if for no other, Italian internal affairs have a special interest for other Western countries today.

Post-war Italian Governments were faced with tremendous tasks, some of them endemic to the country's new situation, others perennial such as had assailed every Italian Government since the unification. The immediate problems extended into all spheres of national life, whether of politics, economics, or foreign affairs. On the political side, the whole apparatus of the State had to be rebuilt; its very form had first to be decided on; once the decision in favour of a Republic had been taken, a new Constitution had to be evolved. Inexperienced parliamentarians had gradually to adapt themselves to democratic methods of discussion and legislation. They even had to learn that party strife, banned for nearly twenty years, must have its limits. Divergent views did not take long to develop. The forces of the Left, at first collaborators in the Government, soon became its fierce opponents; and as the parties of the Right gradually revived the Government was harassed from that quarter too. In economic affairs there were all the problems attendant on rehabilitation—the slow revival of industry, the restoration of a severely damaged agriculture, the building up of the country's shattered finances and of her foreign trade. In the sphere of foreign affairs, first of all the peace treaty had to be concluded. It bequeathed a fresh source of bitterness, as well as two particular problems, those of the colonies and of Trieste, which both took years of patient negotiation to settle. The treaty was barely ratified and the conduct of Italy's diplomacy once more in her own hands before she was called upon to make her choice in the cold war which was already developing. She had to weigh the rival claims of neutrality—with all its especial appeal to Italians since their war-time experiences—and of acceptance of American economic and eventually military aid, with all the commitments it involved.

In addition to all these immediate problems, the new democratic Government found that in the twenty-odd years since such an administration last held power little had altered in respect of such perennial stumbling-blocks to progress as the country's over-population, its basic poverty, and its inability to provide a livelihood for all its nationals: rather, indeed, had those difficulties emerged in aggravated form in consequence of war conditions. So, too, had the fundamental question of the disparity between the resources and living conditions of the North and those of the South which ever since the unification had retarded the development of the country as a whole.

Another problem of the past which again presented itself with added difficulties was that of political and administrative leadership. Since the unification Italy had produced a few outstanding political personalities such as Crispi and Giolitti, but the little more than fifty years between 1870 and the advent of Fascism in 1922 had barely sufficed to establish the habit of parliamentary method and to train a generation of politicians versed in democratic practice. Italy was, in fact, still a very young democracy, only gradually building up its traditions and experience, when Fascism came to alter the whole character of Parliament and arrest that development. During the Fascist interregnum non-conformist politicians either went into exile or took no part in public life. When after twenty years the survivors came into circulation again the period of enforced inactivity had inevitably had its effect, differing naturally in every individual case according to each man's temperament and his experiences while withdrawn from public life. All wanted to obliterate the traces of the Fascist period, but while the revolutionaries of the 'twenties now planned with renewed ardour to change everything and build afresh on new foundations, the more cautious and orthodox aimed instead at going back to the point where the 'wrong turning' had been taken and resurrecting the pre-Fascist State intact. Many of the difficulties which were to arise in building up the new State derived from this radical divergence of conception as to its form and functions.

Since those associated with the former régime were to be taboo, the choice of political leaders, and indeed also of politicians in general, was inevitably restricted either to men whose practical experience lay in the pre-Fascist past, or to untried men quite new to politics. The absence of the 'lost generation' of politicians was to be plainly seen during the first ten years of the new Republic's life in the gap between the older generation and the new. During those ten years many of the elder statesmen vanished from the scene—Croce, Orlando, Nitti, Sforza, and De Gasperi, to name no others; and new men, unheard of before 1945, were assuming responsibilities and beginning to make their name.

It is indeed impressive, looking back to the chaotic beginnings of those ten years, to realise how effectively many of the initial difficulties were overcome: that achievement is probably a tribute as much to the resilience and good sense of the Italian people themselves as to the wisdom of the politicians who guided them; and, it must be added, American aid also played a vital part in economic revival. It is by no means all a 'success story', as the vicissitudes recounted in the coming chapters will show. But at least by the end of that decade the new democratic State had successfully emerged from the formative stage and appeared to be firmly established; its Government had made serious efforts to tackle its gravest social and economic problems; it had regained a respected place among other nations and was playing an active part in the Western community; and it inspired sufficient confidence to justify the hope of outside assistance in the more positive phase of economic development on which the country was about to embark.

Part I

The Groundwork

CHAPTER I

ITALY AT THE END OF THE WAR

IN the last spring of the war events in Italy moved rapidly to their climax. The long-static military situation broke up and acquired a new impetus as the Fifth and Eighth armies advanced on Bologna and Ferrara. Strikes began in Milan and Turin. In the last days of April partisans seized and took over control in many of the main Northern towns. On 28 April the Republic of Salò, the last stronghold of Fascism, collapsed like a house of cards when Mussolini and a number of other leading Fascists met their end at partisan hands.

Italy emerged from these dramatic events to meet a host of problems. Some of them were common to all the countries which had been fought over and occupied by enemy forces: on the material side, war devastation, a wrecked economy, food shortage, and a dispersal of manpower; on the moral side, an overthrow or weakening of the recognised form of government, and a division within the country between those who had offered resistance to the enemy and those who had collaborated. But in Italy these problems were aggravated by special circumstances. During the last eighteen months of the war the country was not only a battlefield but was also occupied at either extremity by opposing forces—by the ex-enemy Allies in the South, and by the ex-ally Germans in the North. It was simultaneously under three different rules: the Italian Royal Government remained sovereign in the extreme South; Allied Military Government control gradually spread northwards as the armies advanced up through Central Italy; and Mussolini's Fascist Republican Government, under its German masters, dominated the North. Within each of these fluctuating areas communities and even families were divided between those who welcomed or tolerated the prevailing régime and those who repudiated it. Finally, the overthrow of Fascism in July 1943 had left the country uncertain as to its future political direction. On the one hand the monarchy had been seriously undermined both by its association with the Fascist régime during the past two decades and by King Victor Emmanuel's much-disputed action in leaving Rome for the South at the time of the Armistice. On the other hand, the reinstatement of Fascism in the North, following on Mussolini's rescue from confinement by German paratroops[1] after the Armistice, encountered severe opposition, both military and political, from the anti-Fascist groups which had begun to emerge during the forty-five days of Marshal Badoglio's Government between the overthrow of Fascism and the Armistice; and a considerable proportion of this anti-Fascist resistance was already demanding that the post-war Italian State should be a republic.

'THE WIND FROM THE NORTH'

Resistance in North Italy had become organised under local Committees of National Liberation (CNLs) which consisted of representatives of the main anti-Fascist political parties. A parallel development went on in the South, where, there being no need for military resistance, the CNLs' activities were entirely political. Five parties were represented on the CNLs in the North—Communists, Socialists, the Action Party, the Christian Democrats, and the Liberals—with the addition of a sixth, the small Labour Democrat party, in the South.

By the time the war ended these Liberation Committees, and the parties that composed them, had come to occupy an important position. In the North, they were the organising focus of partisan resistance to the Fascists and Germans, and their central Committee, the *Comitato della Liberazione Nazionale per l'Alta Italia* (CLNAI), was in close touch with Allied

[1] After the Fascist Grand Council meeting of 25 July 1943, at which Fascism was overthrown, Mussolini was at first put on the island of Ponza, a place of detention familiar to many of his anti-Fascist victims. He was subsequently transferred to the Gran Sasso, from which his spectacular rescue by German airborne paratroopers was effected on 11 September 1943. See his *Storia di un anno* (Verona, Mondadori, 1944).

Force Headquarters. When in the last days of April 1945 partisans freed many towns of North Italy, the local CNL took over in each town by agreement between the CLNAI and the Allied authorities and administered it until the arrival of the Allies.[1] In the Lombard provinces the period of CLNAI control lasted till the end of May, and thus during those first chaotic post-war weeks it fell to the CNLs to issue proclamations regarding the maintenance of order and the surrender of arms, and to appoint Prefects, mayors, and other local officials. Given the difficulty of communications at this time, they were for these weeks in virtual control of a series of autonomous city-states.

Meanwhile further south the CNLs had also exercised a powerful influence on events. The Allies had already discovered with some dismay when Rome was liberated in June 1944 that the pattern of government under Marshal Badoglio which they had approved while Italian rule was confined to the South would not meet the more stringent requirements of anti-Fascist leaders in Rome. They refused to serve under Badoglio, and instead Ivanoe Bonomi, President of the Rome CNL and a Prime Minister in pre-Fascist days (1921–2), headed the first anti-Fascist Government in Rome.

At the end of the war this situation was repeated even more forcibly. Though the country was still physically divided owing to the chaos of communications, the 'wind from the North' could now make itself felt, and in fact CLNAI leaders were flown down to Rome in the early days of May 1945 for discussions with the Rome Government. Out of these discussions, which were continued later in May in Milan, a sharp divergence of view emerged between the CNL parties themselves as to the future status and functions of the CNLs. The parties furthest to the Left—the Communists, Socialists, and Action Party—not only considered that the new Government which was to represent the now reunited country should be chosen by the CLNAI and should contain adequate CNL representa-

[1] The precedent for this collaboration was established during the battle for Florence in August 1944. A partisan who was there wrote later: '[In Florence] the Allies discovered that they needed the collaboration of the Liberation Committees. . . . They entered the town unprepared to collaborate with and recognise the Committees; they left it prepared to do so as a normal practice.' (Enzo Enriques Agnoletti, 'Dopo dieci anni', in *Il Ponte*, Florence, September 1954.)

tion; but they also demanded that the CNLs, in addition to acting as advisory bodies for the local authorities, should retain the wide legislative, executive, and judiciary functions which they had latterly been exercising. The Liberals, on the other hand, supported by the Christian Democrats and Labour Democrats, were strongly opposed to the continuance of even the local advisory powers of the CNLs, for they considered that this would mean a perpetuation of these resistance committees as institutional local organs of administration.

In this dispute as to the powers of the CNLs it is possible to see, in retrospect, the seeds of many future misunderstandings. On the one hand were the orthodox, traditional elements, exemplified by the Christian Democrats and Liberals, belonging to political groupings which had already existed in pre-Fascist days, who saw in a return to a familiar and recognised pattern of government the surest hope of stability for the future, and to whom that stability, and the law and order that went with it, represented the paramount need. On the other hand were the revolutionaries, whose whole past tradition was of opposition to the existing authority, who had suffered persecution and exile for that opposition, and who now considered that the time had come to discard all associations with the past and build a new society from the very foundations. Temporarily united during the war by their common resistance to Fascism and to Germany, once that danger was removed their different backgrounds and views as to the future inevitably asserted themselves.

The whole attitude towards partisan resistance, in Italy as elsewhere, has undergone profound changes in the years since the war. But it is necessary to think back into the climate of the Resistance period if we are to understand much that has happened since. Owing to the circumstances of the war organised military anti-Fascist resistance was confined to the North of Italy. This meant an accentuation of the already traditional difference of outlook between North and South. Of this deep-rooted difference more will be said elsewhere. Here it must suffice to say that in the last eighteen months of the war the North suffered experiences from which the South remained immune. The Northern provinces were occupied both by the Fascists—whom a large part of the population already repudiated—and by the Germans. To this occupation the partisans opposed organised military resistance which took the form of sabotage and harassing tactics which became increasingly effective as the Axis façade crumbled; but for which severe penalties had to be paid by the civilian population as well as by the partisans themselves. The partisans' efforts were crowned when in the last days of the war they themselves were able to evict the enemy from the main towns of the North before the Allies arrived. The summary execution which was meted out to Mussolini and other Fascist leaders is a measure of their feeling at that time.

All this had no parallel in the South. Southern Italy of course had its own difficulties, increasing as the Allied armies moved up towards the centre. But apart from air-raids and the German occupation of Naples in September 1943, events after the Allied landings in Sicily moved so quickly that the Southern provinces experienced little of the worst rigours of war; for the Allied occupation, though admittedly bringing its own problems of requisitioning, black marketing, and the like (especially in an already disrupted urban community such as Naples), did not on the whole bear hardly upon the local population. Moreover it must also be remembered that the remote South had suffered directly from Fascist oppression a good deal less than the North. It had been neglected—but that was also true under earlier Governments; and just because of its backward condition the Fascist régime had less to fear in the way of subversion from that quarter than from the much more politically conscious North. Thus it came about that while in 1943–5 anti-Fascist parties and CNLs were formed in the South, and provided the personnel for the first post-liberation Governments, their politics were often largely of a parochial character, and their views about the country's future less clear-cut than those of their Northern counterparts.

Thus when in May 1945 North and South were at last reunited and their representatives met to discuss their common aims, divergence was inevitable. On the immediate question of the powers of the CNLs a compromise was reached, hastened by the ending of CLNAI authority in North Italy on 1 June, when Allied Military Government took over control of the Lombard provinces. The six parties agreed on 2 June that the provincial and communal CNLs should continue for the time being to exercise local consultative functions, but only until the normal organs of local administration should be set up by democratic elections; otherwise, the CNLs were to confine themselves to purely political activities.

In the choice of a Prime Minister to lead the new Government the view of the CLNAI representatives prevailed. They proposed Ferruccio Parri, an outstanding CLNAI leader from Milan known to the partisans as 'General Maurizio', who enjoyed a prestige far beyond the limits of the Action Party to which he belonged. Though without previous direct experience of government, he was felt to have the stature needed to become the first post-war Premier of a reunited anti-Fascist Italy; and on 19 June he formed his Cabinet, which included representatives of all the six CNL parties, with the Socialist leader Pietro Nenni and Manlio Brosio (Liberal) as Vice-Premiers, the Christian Democrat leader Alcide De Gasperi as Minister for Foreign Affairs, and the Communist leader Palmiro Togliatti as Minister of Justice.

PARTIES AND LEADERS IN THE FIRST POST-WAR YEARS

Some of the anti-Fascist parties and leaders which emerged in the earliest months of the liberation are still prominent in the Italian political scene today. This is true, in particular, of the three 'mass' parties, the Communists, Socialists, and Christian Democrats, which from the first between them commanded the overwhelming majority of popular support. Apart from them the parties have experienced varying fortunes, new ones arising while others disappeared altogether. It was not till 1948 that the pattern became relatively stabilised. A brief survey of the immediate post-war groupings may be useful here, to be supplemented later on by an account of the more recent political alignments.[1]

Of the six parties represented in the Committees of National Liberation, the three furthest to the left, the Communists, Socialists, and Action Party, had in common a background of organised resistance to Fascism, mainly conducted from outside Italy; and they all envisaged a republic as the future form of the Italian State.

[1] See below, Part II.

The Communist Party. The Italian Communist Party, now the largest in Western Europe, came into being in 1921 as a result of a minority split from the Socialist party. A striking feature is the continuity of its leadership, which even then included Palmiro Togliatti, at that time 28 years old, and some others of the group centring round Turin (always a main stronghold), such as Terracini, who still figure among the Communist Old Guard. The founder and guiding spirit in the earliest days was Antonio Gramsci, who died in Rome after years of imprisonment in 1937.

The Communists were not at once suppressed in Italy after the Fascists came to power in 1922. Their daily newspaper, *Unità*, made its first appearance under Gramsci's editorship in 1924, and in that year eighteen Communist Deputies were returned to Parliament. They were deprived of their parliamentary mandate in November 1926, and most of the party's leaders were arrested and imprisoned, though nearly all of them survived their long sentences to reappear after the war. Togliatti himself went into exile, and spent the intervening years in Russia and elsewhere in Europe; he was a member of the Presidium of the Comintern from 1934 to 1943. He arrived in Southern Italy in April 1944, a legendary but little-known figure whose broadcasts from Moscow and underground name of Ercole Ercoli were familiar to Left-wing *conoscenti* but not to the masses.

His return brought about a complete reversal in the policy of the Communist Party in Southern Italy, which till then, together with the Socialists and Action Party, had refused to collaborate in the Badoglio Government. Collaboration involved taking the oath to the monarchy, and to this the republican-minded Left-wing parties would not agree. But Togliatti declared that, since the problem of the monarchy could not yet be solved, it should be waived for the time being in order to settle the more urgent question of creating a representative government. His action brought in the Socialists and Action Party too, and thus laid the foundations for Left-wing collaboration in all the Italian Governments till May 1947. This move of Togliatti's, welcomed at the time by non-Communist circles outside Italy as realistic, not to say public-spirited, was probably based on a far-reaching calculation that, by gaining a foothold in the Government, the Communists would be able to rally the other Left-wing parties under their aegis and so eventually acquire sufficient power to paralyse the whole party system.

The Communist following was at this time very much stronger in the industrial North than in the South. At the outbreak of war many of the party's exiled leaders in France were arrested, but between 1941 and 1942 propaganda groups and cells were established in Milan and Turin, and an underground press was started. The Communist-organised factory strikes which broke out in Milan and Turin in March and April 1943 marked the first open revolt against Fascism and did much to establish Communist influence among Northern industrial workers.

After the collapse of Fascism many Communists were released from prison and at once took part in the anti-Fascist struggle. Though the Communists subsequently made greatly exaggerated claims as to their own almost exclusive role in partisan resistance, it is probably true to say that the Communist ('Garibaldi') partisan brigades were numerically stronger than any others and attained a higher degree of organisation—as, indeed, was to be expected, given their leaders' much greater experience in clandestine action.

Thus the Communist Party embarked on the post-war period with three very considerable assets: an organisation which, more successfully than that of any other party, had maintained itself intact from an early stage in the clandestine period; an assured measure of support from the industrial working classes, already tested during the factory strikes of 1943; and the prestige of the Communist role in partisan resistance.

The Socialist Party. Socialism, whether of the extreme (Maximalist) or more moderate (Reformist) variety, played an important part in Italian politics from the 1890s onwards. Socialist Deputies put up a strong resistance to Fascism between 1922 and 1925, and were eventually, like the Communists, deprived of their mandate in 1926. The leaders were imprisoned or went into exile, among them Pietro Nenni who spent the intervening years till 1943 mainly in Paris. The Socialist and Communist parties in exile concluded a 'Unity of Action' pact in Paris in August 1934 which was to be revived with far-reaching consequences in the post-war era.

Meanwhile, the Socialists in 1943–5 lacked the underground organisation and experience of the Communists. The old Reformist leaders of pre-Fascist days, Turati, Treves, and Morgari, had died in exile. The new outstanding men, Nenni and Giuseppe Saragat (also an exile in Paris), were of such different temperaments and outlooks that a clash was inevitable sooner or later: the past history of Italian Socialism, divided between the Maximalist and the Reformist views, was to repeat itself. In the meantime the Socialist party after the war attracted a considerable if heterogeneous following among Leftist anti-Fascist elements unaware of the ties which were soon to bind it more and more closely to the Communists.

The Action Party. The Action Party was in some respects the most interesting, and at one time appeared the most vital, of all the anti-Fascist political groupings. Unlike the other CNL parties, it was the heir of no recognised pre-war political party; but it developed from the 'liberal-socialist' group of anti-Fascists which between 1929 and 1934 gathered round the exile Carlo Rosselli in Paris, and was known as the 'Giustizia e Libertà' movement. Like that movement, the Action Party based itself on the ideals of Mazzini and the Risorgimento, from which indeed it resurrected the name of Partito d'Azione. The party developed first as an underground group, mainly of intellectuals, in 1942, and brought out a clandestine newssheet, *Italia Libera*, from early in 1943. The programme which it issued during the Badoglio '45 days' embodied many of the ideals which were subsequently accepted by the 'mass' parties. Besides an uncompromising demand for a republic, these aims included regional decentralisation, the elimination of monopolies, some degree of nationalisation, factory councils, taxation of inherited wealth, agrarian reforms, freedom of worship, educational reforms, and the development of the South.

Though primarily the leading spirit in the realm of ideas, the Action Party played an active role in partisan resistance and, as we have seen, provided one of its main leaders in the future Prime Minister Ferruccio Parri. Count Carlo Sforza, a former diplomat and one of the most distinguished of the anti-Fascist exiles, who returned to Italy in October 1943, was at first associated with the Action Party, though he subsequently counted as a Republican.

Unfortunately the Action Party was to be shortlived: it lacked mass support, and as its ideas gradually came to be adopted by other parties it flickered out, and its members either joined other groups (usually the Socialists or the Republicans) or more frequently left the political scene. They are men of a quite especial stamp, recognisable in their different walks of life throughout the country today, and a serious loss to politics if a gain to their chosen professions.

The Christian Democrats. The Christian Democrat party was the direct heir of the Partito Popolare, the progressive Catholic party founded in 1919 by the Sicilian priest Don Luigi Sturzo. During the seven years of its existence the Partito Popolare had gained a very considerable following. Like the other Opposition parties it was disbanded in 1926. Its leader Don Sturzo had already been compelled to resign and left Italy in 1925, when he was succeeded as party secretary by the young Trentino Deputy Alcide De Gasperi.

A good many of the Partito Popolare leaders survived the years of Fascism and took an active part in the underground organisation in 1943–4 of a new Catholic progressive party, to be known as Christian Democracy. Foremost among them was De Gasperi, who after persecution and a term of imprisonment had spent the later years of the Fascist era working in the Vatican library. Don Sturzo was still in exile (he returned to Italy in 1946, then aged 74), so the party leadership naturally fell to De Gasperi, who was its main representative on the Rome CNL and became a Minister in the first Bonomi Government after Rome was liberated.

Being a confessional party, the Christian Democrats drew their following from a wide cross-section of the population; but among the working classes their main strength lay in the agricultural districts. Though the party's aims in these early days did not differ greatly from those of the other 'mass' parties, it naturally attached especial importance to safeguarding the religious life of the community and maintaining the agreements entered into with the Holy See—in relation to which, however, it was officially quite independent. On the question of the monarchy the party was at first divided.

The Liberals. The Liberal party, the furthest to the Right of the CNL parties, was, like the Christian Democrats, somewhat heterogeneous in composition, though from the outset it lacked the working-class support accorded to the three 'mass' parties. Its diversity arose rather from the different regional or professional backgrounds of its followers: on the one hand university professors, lawyers, and other professional men with a progressive outlook that was 'liberal' (and often anti-clerical) in the English rather than the Continental sense; and on the other hand landowners, particularly of the South, who, whatever their liberal beliefs, had tradition, not to say reaction, in their bones.

In its early stages of war-time revival the party's President was Benedetto Croce, whose philosophy of individual liberty was its watchword—if variously interpreted. At the same time the Liberals from the outset showed a more pronounced feeling for law and order, for legal and constitutional tradition and practice, than was to be found in some of the newer parties. This meant that a considerable proportion of its members favoured the retention of the monarchy,[1] and the party was seriously divided on this subject, as well as on land reform and other social questions where the conservative standpoint of the Southern landowners was in sharp contrast to the more progressive views of some of the Northern leaders.

The Labour Democrats. This small party, the sixth member of the CNLs in the South, had no counterpart in the North. It originated as a successor to the Reformist Socialists of pre-Fascist days, and centred largely round one or two prominent figures of that generation, notably Ivanoe Bonomi, the first Premier after the liberation of Rome, and Meuccio Ruini, a Minister in the first post-liberation Governments. It also had associations with Freemasonry. Its programme differed little

[1] It was the Liberal leader Benedetto Croce who in November 1943 made perhaps the most constructive proposal for a means of retaining the monarchy when he suggested that the King should abdicate, Prince Umberto should renounce his rights, and a Regency should be set up for the then six-year-old Prince of Naples. But owing to party disagreements this proposal was never followed up.

from that of the 'mass' parties, and, lacking popular support, it faded out after 1946.

Of the parties outside the CNLs (and thus outside the early Governments), the most important were the Republicans, the Monarchists, and for a brief period the Uomo Qualunque, or Common Man, party.

The Republican party combined a devotion to Mazzinian ideals with a definite anti-Communist bias. Its post-war leader, Randolfo Pacciardi, commanded the Garibaldi Brigade in the Spanish civil war. Its views in many respects resembled those of the Action Party, from which it gained some recruits after the Action Party began to dissolve. Uncompromisingly republican, as its name implies, its main *raison d'être* diminished after the question of the monarchy was decided in 1946, though, as will be seen, it still continued to play a part as a small unconfessional centre party.

Organised monarchist opinion in the early post-liberation years was chiefly focused in the Partito Democratico Italiano, whose leader, Enzo Selvaggi, edited its Rome daily newspaper, *Italia Nuova*. Up to the time of the referendum on the monarchy in 1946 this party strongly urged the view that the country's freedom and future prosperity was bound up with the monarchical institution, which, it was claimed, offered the best defence against totalitarianism. After the referendum monarchist views were taboo for some time, and the Partito Democratico Italiano disappeared, to be replaced in 1947 by the Partito Nazionale Monarchico.

The Uomo Qualunque, or Common Man, party was a curious and short-lived post-war manifestation which arose in 1945 under the leadership of a journalist and playwright, Guglielmo Giannini. With its slogan of 'We were better off when we were worse off!', it aimed at attracting the *piccolo borghese*, the disgruntled man in the street, who felt at sea in the chaotic post-war Italy and had no sympathy with the enthusiasms of the Resistance and anti-Fascist parties. It attracted a good deal of support in 1946, when it polled over 1,200,000 votes in the first post-war elections for a Constituent Assembly. But soon afterwards it lost its financial backing (which must at first have been considerable), Giannini lost interest, and its moderate supporters moved over to swell the

Christian Democrat vote in 1948, while its more extreme elements found a home when the neo-Fascist Movimento Sociale Italiano developed. At the time, this mushroom growth, and its equally rapid contraction, may have seemed difficult to explain; but in retrospect it can be seen as a relatively innocuous canalisation of the numerous elements whom the tide of enthusiasm for liberation from Fascism had failed to sweep along with it.[1]

Party programmes, in those first days of enthusiasm, were all-embracing. Every vestige of Fascist privilege and concentration of power in the hands of a few was to be swept away, and a new democratic State was to take its place. The anti-Fascist parties differed only in detail and in emphasis as to how this was to be achieved; moreover on the economic side the three 'mass' parties, the Communists, Socialists, and Christian Democrats, were already linked together—if uneasily—in the joint trade union, the Confederazione Generale Italiana del Lavoro (CGIL) founded at the CNL Congress in Bari in January 1944.[2] All wanted administrative decentralisation and regional autonomy, development of the neglected South, reforms in banking and taxation, in social assistance, and in education, and an extension of the co-operative principle in industry and agriculture. Industrial reforms were to include an end of monopolies, and the introduction of workers' representation on factory councils; in agriculture, landless peasants were to become smallholders on land acquired by breaking up the big estates. Nationalisation was already a bone of contention on which the more traditionalist parties, the Christian Democrats and Liberals, could not go the whole way with the parties of the Left. But the first thing to be settled was the form that the new State was to take; and so, amid the strains and stresses of reunification and a crippled post-war economy, and under the shadow of the peace treaty negotiations, the groundwork was prepared for the first democratic elections since 1921, which were to be coupled with a referendum on the monarchy.

[1] The word 'qualunquismo'—and the state of mind—remain. For instance, in the *Corriere della Sera* (2 March 1954) we find the phrase 'un certo fondo qualunquistico del Paese . . . di cui si deve tenere conto' (a certain Qualunquist element—or background—in the country . . . which must be taken into account)—'Qualunquist' being used in this connection to describe the wave of nationalism which swept the country in the autumn of 1953 at the time of the Trieste crisis.

[2] *Gli atti del Congresso di Bari* (Bari, 1944).

CHAPTER II

REBUILDING THE FRAMEWORK

FROM PARRI TO DE GASPERI

IN addition to the country's economic problems, many other difficulties confronted the Parri Government. The linking up between North and South went on slowly, hampered by restricted communications: control of the northern provinces was gradually transferred from Allied Military Government to the Italian Government, but it was not till the end of 1945 that the whole metropolitan territory except for Venezia Giulia and Udine came once more under Italian jurisdiction. Venezia Giulia, and Trieste in particular, constituted a first-class problem in itself—though it was little imagined then that it would still do so nearly ten years later: in the meantime its fate was discussed inconclusively at the London session of the Council of Foreign Ministers in September 1945,[1] together with other questions involved in the peace treaty. Sicilian demands for separatism suddenly flared up. The purge of Fascist elements, begun sporadically after the fall of Fascism in 1943 and systematically organised since May 1944 first under Count Sforza as High Commissioner and later under Pietro Nenni, was by mid-1945 practically completed in the South. But in the North, which presented a much more ticklish problem owing to the ramifications of the now-defunct Salò Republic[2] and the strength of feeling it had engendered, the whole business was still to be done. Petty officials and employees lived for months in a state of fear and uncertainty as to their ultimate fate, and it was not till mid-1946 that the purge process was virtually completed and the work of the High Commissioner's office wound up.

Nevertheless some progress was made towards deciding on the future form of the State. Ever since the earliest days of

[1] See below, p. 29.

[2] This was the name given to the neo-Fascist Republican Government of 1943–5, taken from the town on Lake Garda where it had its headquarters.

liberation the creation of a freely elected democratic parliament had been one of the main political aims of all parties, and since the Bari Congress of 1944 the Left-wing parties in particular had urged that some sort of interim parliament should be set up until a General Election could be held. Once the country was reunited it became possible to plan for a nation-wide election, but it was also realised that the compilation of electoral lists would prove a long and slow business in view of the chaotic state of the country.

It had therefore been decided in March 1945 to set up a provisional Consulta, or Consultative Assembly, to act as an interim parliament and, in particular, to prepare the new electoral law and the law governing the powers of the future Constituent Assembly. The Consulta held its first meeting on 25 September 1945. It consisted of 429 members nominated by the Government on the basis of lists put forward by the various political parties (CNL or otherwise) and trade union and professional associations, and also included some anti-Fascist former Deputies. Count Sforza was elected President.

The Parri Government of which such high hopes had been entertained lasted only five and a half months. Its fall was significant, for it can be seen in retrospect to mark the end of that brief period when a complete break with the past appeared to be a practical possibility.[1] But various forces opposed to such aspirations were already reasserting themselves. As far as the immediate present was concerned, the Parri Government fell victim to the opposing views within itself: disputes constantly arose between the progressives, who still hankered after maintaining as much as possible of the powers of the CNLs, and the traditionalists, anxious to revert at once to the orthodox organs of Government. Among the latter the Liberals were the most clear-cut in their views, and it was they who precipitated the Parri Government's fall by demanding a broadening of the Government to include some older statesmen such as Orlando or Nitti; they also took exception to the Government's action in enforcing a new purge law without first bringing it before the Consulta. Moreover Parri himself,

[1] For a description of this period see *L'Orologio* (Einaudi, 1950; English translation *The Watch*, Cassell, 1952), a novel by the artist Carlo Levi who was closely associated with the Action Party at this time.

always an idealist, and a man of action as well when faced with the emergencies of resistance, proved less adept when dealing with the intricacies of party disputes—a problem which might well have defeated a much more experienced politician, given the fundamental differences of view in his six-party team and their inexperience in democratic methods of government. He resigned on 24 November 1945, and on 10 December the Christian Democrat leader Alcide De Gasperi formed the new Government, thus entering on what was to prove an unbroken term of office until June 1953. His first Cabinet differed little in personnel from its predecessors: all six CNL parties were still represented in it, and Signor De Gasperi himself retained the post of Foreign Minister. A split in the Action Party at their Congress in February 1946, which was to prove the prelude to the party's disintegration, led to the withdrawal of two of its members from the Cabinet. One of them, Ugo La Malfa, broke away with Parri and others of the more moderate elements to form a Republican Democratic Alliance which soon merged with the Republican party.

LOCAL ADMINISTRATION

Meanwhile preparations were on foot for the elections to local administrative bodies, which, with the electoral lists at last compiled, were to take place in March 1946. It had been decided to revert to pre-Fascist methods, both in electoral procedure and in the organs of local administration. The provinces were retained as administrative units, with a Prefect at the head of each, as in both Fascist and pre-Fascist days. But the *Deputazione Provinciale* of pre-Fascist days was revived, varying in numbers from 6 to 14 or 15 according to the size of the province. At the communal level, the pre-Fascist *Consiglio Comunale*, or Communal Council, was revived, with 20 to 80 members according to the size of the Commune. This Council, whose members hold office for four years, in turn elects a smaller committee, or *Giunta*, and a *sindaco*, or mayor. According to the electoral law, which was voted by the Consulta on 23 February 1946, all citizens, other than proscribed persons, criminals, or persons closely associated with Fascism in the past, were eligible to vote, including, for the first time in Italy, women. Proportional representation was used in communes of over 30,000, the majority vote method in the smaller ones.

These local elections, though only a sort of dress rehearsal for the elections to the Constituent Assembly which were to follow in June, nevertheless held a certain interest as the first free expression of political opinion to take place in Italy since the advent of Fascism. The result, with a high poll of 80–85 per cent in most districts, was a foretaste of things to come: the three 'mass' parties already far outstripped the others. In the 5,596 communes in which voting took place (it was held over till the autumn in the remaining 1,704, including most of the larger towns), Communists and Socialists together won in 1,976 communes, Communists alone in 140, and Socialists alone in 140; Christian Democrats in 1,907; and all the other groups, including Liberals, Labour Democrats, Action Party, Republicans, and Right and Centre combinations, divided the remaining 1,433 places between them. When the other communes, including the larger towns, voted in the following November, there was a marked swing away from the Christian Democrats, by which the Communists profited heavily in the North and, to a lesser extent, the Uomo Qualunque party, then at the height of its short-lived popularity, in Rome and the South. But these autumn local elections aroused little interest, and abstentions were widespread; for in the meantime the electorate had had its fill of exercising its newly won voting powers in the much more significant General Election and Referendum on the monarchy.

THE FIRST GENERAL ELECTION AND THE END OF THE MONARCHY

Italians, though in many respects less time-bound than Northerners, have a habit of thinking in terms of dates. This has, indeed, become a form of shorthand, and certain dates, divorced from any context or explanation, will evoke in Italian minds the whole atmosphere of the particular event or epoch which they symbolise. Of these the 'due giugno'—2 June—is one. But while the dates of subsequent General Elections—the 'diciotto aprile' (18 April 1948) and the 'sette giugno' (7 June 1953)—have acquired a similar significance in general parlance, the 2nd of June stands alone, for it is also the day on which in 1946 Italy became a Republic; and as such it has been celebrated with varying degrees of conviction as a national holiday ever since.

The decision to hold the elections for a Constituent Assembly and the Referendum on the monarchy simultaneously was largely a matter of convenience. The actual voting processes were of course distinct from each other, the Referendum being taken by a single direct vote while the voting for the Constituent Assembly was carried out, in accordance with the new electoral law of 10 March 1946, by the method of proportional representation for a party list.

The truce on the question of the monarchy, agreed to in April 1944 when the Left-wing parties decided to collaborate in the Government,[1] had on the whole been observed. As was then agreed, King Victor Emmanuel withdrew from public life when Rome was liberated, and his place was taken by Crown Prince Umberto, with the title of Lieutenant-General. In the intervening two years party positions on the question had to some extent been clarified. The Christian Democrats had on the whole moved towards the republican view, and in April 1946 their Provincial Congress voted by a three-quarters majority in favour of a republic. The Liberals still remained divided, though the accession of Northern leaders had strengthened the republican wing. The Left-wing parties of course remained uncompromisingly republican.

On 9 May 1946, three weeks before the referendum was due to take place, King Victor Emmanuel formally abdicated and left Italy for Egypt. The Crown Prince automatically became King as Umberto II, and confirmed his undertaking to abide by the forthcoming vote of the people. This eleventh-hour abdication, which politicians of the Left interpreted as a last-minute piece of electioneering, may have influenced some waverers, for the Crown Prince was always regarded as being much less deeply involved with Fascism than his father, and indeed had at one time been the centre of some anti-Fascist hopes. But in any case the camps were already fairly evenly divided, and the result announced on 18 June showed a total of 12,717,923 valid votes in favour of a republic, with 10,719,284 for the monarchy. The North voted pretty solidly for the

[1] See above, p. 14.

republic, while in Rome and the South the preponderance of votes went to the monarchy, with a particularly large majority in Naples. Thus the regional division of the voting followed the anticipated lines. Some doubts were raised as to the validity of the voting: ardent monarchists alleged at the time, and have reiterated ever since, that votes in favour of their cause were suppressed. But a recount made after 10 June, when the results of the first count were made known, showed an increase of over 14,000 votes in favour of the republic, and there can be little doubt that the final figures represented pretty accurately the state of public opinion at the time. Ex-King Umberto left Italy on 13 June and has lived in Portugal ever since.

The question of the monarchy naturally had some influence in party alignments and in the voting for the Constituent Assembly. Here too, however, the results produced no great surprises. Voting was compulsory, so the very high poll (90 per cent in some of the larger constituencies) was to be expected. The three 'mass' parties far surpassed all the others. The National Democratic Union, a combined group of Liberals and Labour Democrats, came fourth, followed by the Uomo Qualunque party, the Republicans, the monarchist National Freedom Bloc, and the Action Party, now much weakened by internal splits. The many other small parties which presented lists (as many as 27 did so in Rome) together only obtained little over a million votes.

Elections for Constituent Assembly, 2 June 1946

Party	*Votes*	*Seats*
Christian Democrats	8,083,208	207
Socialists	4,744,749	115
Communists	4,342,722	104
National Democratic Union	1,559,417	41
Uomo Qualunque	1,209,918	30
Republicans	997,690	23
National Freedom Bloc	636,493	16
Action Party	333,758	7
Other lists	1,044,935	13
	22,952,890	556

The Christian Democrats, who probably profited most of all the parties from the access of women voters, now going to the polls for the first time, increased their vote considerably as compared with their results in the local elections of six weeks earlier. The Left-wing vote, on the other hand, fell, and moreover the Communists now dropped below the Socialists—for what was to prove the only time in post-war Italian elections, for the splits which were so greatly to weaken Italian Socialism began to emerge soon after. But in these first post-war elections it is already possible to discern the even balance between the Christian Democrat Centre and the Communist-Socialist Left which has provided the major problem of Italian politics ever since. The nucleus of resurgent Right-wing opinion was already finding temporary expression in the Uomo Qualunque party and the monarchist National Freedom Bloc; while the Liberals and Republicans, later to provide, with the yet unformed Social Democrat party, the much-needed support for a greatly weakened Christian Democrat Centre, already tipped the balance away from the Left.

The Constituent Assembly held its first meeting on 25 June and elected the leading Socialist Giuseppe Saragat as its President. On 28 June Senator Enrico De Nicola, a much-respected Neapolitan lawyer who with Croce had played an active part in attempts to find a solution for the monarchical problem in 1944, was elected provisional Head of the State.[1] He called upon Signor De Gasperi, as leader of the largest party, to form the new Government. The Cabinet which De Gasperi announced on 12 July no longer reproduced the pattern of the six CNL parties. It was instead a four-party coalition including representatives of the three 'mass' parties, Christian Democrats, Communists, and Socialists, now joined by the Republicans who had hitherto refused to participate in any Government owing to their opposition on the question of the monarchy. The Liberals, on the other hand, stayed out, partly, apparently, in protest against the methods they alleged to have been used in the conduct of the Referendum; and the Action Party was by now so much reduced that its collaboration was out of the question.

The key posts in the Government still eluded the Communists. Signor De Gasperi became his own Minister of the Interior, as well as retaining the Ministry of Foreign Affairs

[1] Provisional, since the title of President of the Republic did not become effective till after the Constitution came into force.

until the conclusion of the peace treaty negotiations, when he was replaced in October by Pietro Nenni. For the first time since 1944 Togliatti himself remained outside the Cabinet. In November he came near to causing a Government crisis through his unsponsored attempts to reach an agreement with Marshal Tito on the subject of Venezia Giulia, whose fate had by then been virtually decided at the Paris Peace Conference. Togliatti visited Belgrade and as a result of conversations with Marshal Tito suggested a barter arrangement whereby Yugoslavia should receive Gorizia in exchange for renouncing claims to Trieste. The Italian Government took no responsibility for this suggestion, which was not pursued further.

CHAPTER III

THE PEACE TREATY

THE shadow of the peace treaty loomed large over Italy throughout the months following the end of the war, for till it was concluded Italy could not regain freedom of action in her foreign policy, while uncertainty as to its provisions hampered political and economic reconstruction.

The Italian treaty was first discussed by the four-Power Council of Foreign Ministers at meetings in London in the autumn of 1945, and again in Paris in April-May and June-July 1946. The Council's recommendations were incorporated in a draft peace treaty[1] which was presented for consideration to the Peace Conference of twenty-one nations which met in Paris from 29 July to 15 October 1946. The Paris Conference discussed the draft clause by clause and proposed amendments, and the final draft was approved by the Council of Foreign Ministers in New York in November-December. The Ministers' deputies then drew up the final texts[2] for signature on 10 February 1947. Both in London and in Paris Italy's case was strongly stated by Signor De Gasperi, the leader of the Italian delegation. But the final result was a bitter disappointment to Italy, who had been led to hope that her renunciation of her Fascist past, given practical expression in her declaration of war on Germany on 13 October 1943 and in anti-Fascist resistance, would receive fuller recognition. Moreover, membership of the United Nations, which was expected to follow automatically once the treaty was signed, has ever since been denied owing to the Russian veto.

The treaty covered three main aspects—territorial (including colonial); naval, military, and air; and economic. Of these, the two latter proved both the easiest to settle and the less far-reaching in consequences. Under the military clauses Italy was required to cede a considerable portion of her fleet, renounce the possession of certain types of offensive weapons

[1] Cmd. 6892 (1946). [2] Cmd. 7022 (1947).

such as submarines and bombers, and to limit her army to 250,000 men, her navy to 25,000, and her air force to 25,000. On the economic side, the Western Powers renounced all claim to reparations, but Russia insisted on the handing over of specified Italian vessels and the payment of $100 million,[1] to which a further $260 million was added in reparations to Yugoslavia, Greece, Ethiopia, and Albania. Italian property in Allied territory was to be seized, retained, or liquidated, though here some countries (e.g. France and Egypt) agreed from the first not to press their claims to the full, and in several cases the matter was settled by means of special agreements with Italy. Damage to property in Italy belonging to countries of the United Nations was to be compensated for at the rate of two-thirds of the agreed value of the property damaged.

Under the territorial and political clauses of the treaty Italy was required to cede four small frontier areas to France, the Dodecanese Islands to Greece, and her Adriatic islands and most of Venezia Giulia to Yugoslavia; and she undertook to 'respect the sovereignty and independence' of Albania, while renouncing all claim to former Italian State property there. Contrary to the expectations of some, she retained the disputed South Tyrolese province on her Austrian frontier, Bolzano.

The questions of South Tyrol and, more especially, of the Yugoslav frontier were the major territorial problems at issue. In both cases the disputed territories had been ceded to Italy after the 1914–18 war in consequence of promises made in the secret Treaty of London of 1915. In both a good proportion of the population could be considered as ethnically and linguistically Italian, and both had therefore been regarded as *terre irredente* and made the subject of Italian claims since the time of the Risorgimento. Unfortunately for Italy—and for the populations concerned—the Fascist régime followed close upon the recognition of these claims in the Treaty of St Germain (1919) which after the break up of the Hapsburg Empire transferred both the South Tyrol and Venezia Giulia to Italian rule. During the Fascist era the regions were subjected to an intensive process of Italianisation; the rights of the local popu-

[1] An Italo-Soviet agreement regulating the method of payment was signed on 11 December 1948.

lation to maintain their own language, schools, and press and to be adequately represented in local and central government were increasingly disregarded; and throughout the twenty years between the wars protests were constantly raised by Austrian and Yugoslav publicists against the alleged injustice of the transfer and the oppressive methods of its implementation, as well as against the continued infiltration of Italians who threatened to swamp the original ethnic structure of the regions.[1]

THE AUSTRIAN FRONTIER

In 1945 the two regions found themselves in somewhat different situations. In South Tyrol, during the last eighteen months of the war the provinces of Bolzano, Trento, and Belluno had been incorporated in the Reich as the operational zone 'Alpenvorland' and had been overrun by German officials who introduced measures for the Germanisation of the whole area. It had, in fact, been invaded and occupied by the Reich at a time when Italy was officially at war with Germany. Moreover the rival claimant for the South Tyrol, Austria, was technically an ex-enemy, even if by compulsion rather than of free choice. A further complication arose from the fact that in July 1939 Hitler and Mussolini had agreed to permit the transfer to the Reich of any German-speaking citizens of South Tyrol who might opt for it, and some 185,000 had chosen to emigrate. Under wartime conditions the transfer proved a slow business, but at the end of 1943 (by which time the South Tyrol had come under German control) it was estimated that probably some 75,000–80,000 persons had migrated to the Reich, the majority of them townspeople and officials. In the changed conditions after the war some of these eventually decided to return to South Tyrol.

On ethnical grounds it was recognised that Austria had a

[1] Both the South Tyrol and Venezia Giulia were the subject of a considerable propaganda literature between the wars. On the Austrian side see, for example, Hans Fingeller, ed., *Die Wahrheit über Südtirol 1918–1926*, a collection of documents drawn up by a committee of Tyrolese citizens (English edition, C. H. Herford, ed., *The Case of German South Tirol against Italy*, London, 1927); Dr E. Reut-Nicolussi, *Tyrol under the Axe of Italian Fascism* (London, Allen & Unwin, 1930). On the Yugoslav side see, e.g., L. Cermelj, ed., *Life and Death Struggle of a Minority* (Yugoslav Union of League of Nations Societies, Ljubljana, 1936). Numerous Italian publications argued the question from the other side.

strong case as far as the northern province, Bolzano, was concerned. On the other hand the Italian character of the southern province, Trento, was never in doubt. Italy based her arguments for retention of the whole region partly on the strategic need for the Brenner frontier and partly on economic grounds such as the extensive development of hydro-electric power which Italian money and labour had initiated in the South Tyrol between the two wars. The Italian case won the day—perhaps as much as a result of power politics at a high level as on its own merits. A separate bilateral agreement, concluded on 5 September 1946 between Signor De Gasperi for Italy and Dr Gruber for Austria and written into the peace treaty,[1] provided for complete equality of cultural and economic rights for the German-speaking inhabitants of Bolzano and the bilingual areas of Trento, with elementary and secondary education in both languages, equal right of entry into the public services, and a measure of local autonomy. This last provision was given effect in 1948, when on 29 January the Regional Statute for Trentino–Alto Adige was approved by the Constituent Assembly.[2]

The Austro-Italian treaty was regarded as an outstanding example of the way in which agreement could be achieved in difficult circumstances given the goodwill of both sides. It has on the whole worked well. The Regional Statute has given the South Tyrol provinces a considerable degree of local autonomy, and the rights of the German-speaking minority have in general been observed, if not in particular instances as fully as the minority could wish. South Tyrol sends nine Deputies and six Senators to the central Parliament in Rome, of whom three Deputies and two Senators are representatives of the Südtiroler Volkspartei. It was not till the autumn of 1953, when during the agitation concerning Trieste a plebiscite for that region was suggested, that there began to be any serious suggestion that the German-speaking South Tyrolese might be dissatisfied with their lot and might also desire a plebiscite on the grounds that the De Gasperi-Gruber agreement of 1946 had not been fully implemented and that Italian immigration into South Tyrol was swamping the German minority. This contention, probably in part at least the result of artificially-

[1] Annex IV. [2] See below, p. 62.

aroused agitation in Austria itself,[1] was refuted by Italy.[2] It was claimed that 42 per cent of officials in the region spoke German, so that every office could transact business in that language (the Südtiroler Volkspartei Senator Raffeiner contended that the figure was much lower).[3] As to Italian immigration, this was largely explained by the natural shifting of labour from the poorer regions of unemployment to a province like Bolzano where unemployment hardly exists and where the execution of important hydro-electrical works creates a demand for labour.

The signature of the Austrian State Treaty in May 1955 was made the occasion for a further recrudescence of agitation for greater autonomy by some members of the Südtiroler Volkspartei. An Italian Foreign Office statement at that time[4] emphasised that the attitude of these agitators was 'in contrast with the objective and consistent attitude' displayed throughout by the Austrian Government. It was necessary, in fact, this statement went on, to distinguish between the representatives of the German-speaking minority in national, provincial, and municipal bodies who loyally recognised the Italian State, and the few who refused to recognise it and wanted separation for the Alto Adige, or at least the creation in the Region of a state within a State.

VENEZIA GIULIA

With the South Tyrol question settled, the treaty-makers went on to the more difficult problem of Venezia Giulia. Here the rival claimant was in a much stronger position, for Yugoslavia was an ally who had suffered direct invasion and occupation by Italian troops, Tito's partisans had for eighteen months offered effective resistance to the enemy, and—most cogent of all—Yugoslav forces had been the first to enter and occupy Trieste at the beginning of May 1945 and only with difficulty had been induced to surrender control to the joint Allied authorities after forty-three days of occupation.[5] This posses-

[1] Yugoslavia had been trying during the autumn of 1953 to enlist Austrian opinion on her side in the Trieste dispute.

[2] See *Data on Immigration in the Alto Adige . . . 1947 to 1953* (Rome, Istituto Poligrafico dello Stato, 1954); and Italian Green Book, 1952.

[3] See his speech in the Italian Senate, 26 February 1954.

[4] *Il Messaggero*, 19 June 1955.

[5] For a first-hand account of conditions during this period see 'Trieste Diary', in *The World Today*, October 1945.

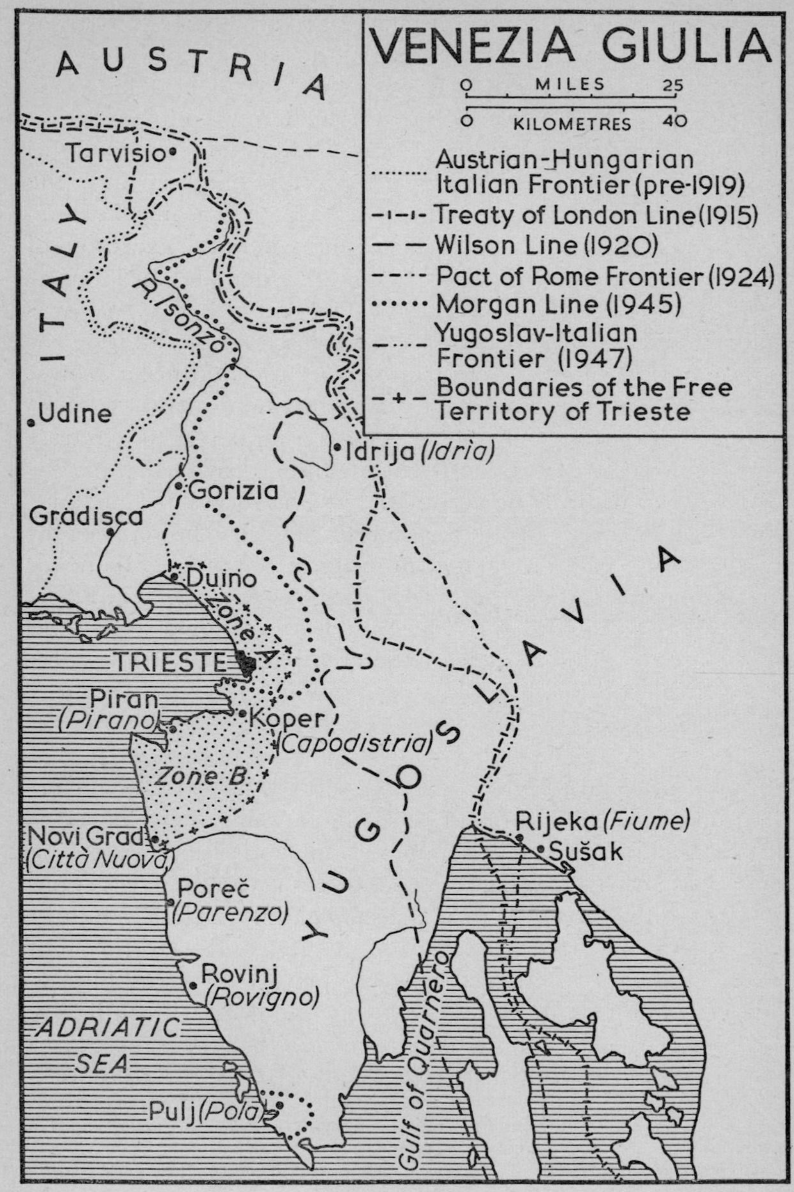
VENEZIA GIULIA
0 MILES 25
0 KILOMETRES 40
Austrian-Hungarian Italian Frontier (pre-1919)
Treaty of London Line (1915)
Wilson Line (1920)
Pact of Rome Frontier (1924)
Morgan Line (1945)
Yugoslav-Italian Frontier (1947)
Boundaries of the Free Territory of Trieste
AUSTRIA
ITALY
YUGOSLAVIA
Tarvisio
R. Isonzo
Udine
Idrija (Idrìa)
Gorizia
Gradisca
Duino
Zone A
TRIESTE
Piran (Pirano)
Koper (Capodistria)
Zone B
Novi Grad (Città Nuova)
Rijeka (Fiume)
Sušak
Poreč (Parenzo)
Rovinj (Rovigno)
ADRIATIC SEA
Gulf of Quarnero
Pulj (Pola)

sion seemed indeed to the Yugoslavs to constitute nine points of the law—the more so as they had throughout been led to believe that in liberating Trieste and Venezia Giulia from the Fascists and Germans they were at the same time reclaiming what was by right their own; and in default of precise prior agreement to the contrary they proceeded to set up their own (Communist) form of government there.

Eventually, under an agreement concluded on 20 June 1945 between the Generals on the spot, Generals Morgan and Jovanović, Yugoslav forces withdrew behind a line of demarcation (subsequently known as the 'Morgan line'—see map, p. 34) and Allied Military Government assumed control of the portion of Venezia Giulia including Trieste and the roads and railways north through Gorizia to Carinthia and also over Pola and the west coast anchorages south of Trieste. The line ran westwards towards the coast to the north of Capodistria.

This was the position when the peace treaty negotiations began. Both Italians and Yugoslavs came to the conference table with a strong sense of injustice; the sufferings of the Triestini during the forty-three days' occupation were fresh in Italian minds (and they were still remembered ten years after), while the Yugoslavs were smarting from what they regarded as their unjust eviction. The two viewpoints were poles apart, and a compromise solution seemed wellnigh unattainable. A four-Power boundary commission sent out in March 1946 failed to reach agreement on its recommendations. Each investigating Power proposed a different line, the Russian line lying furthest to the west and including roughly the maximum Yugoslav claims; the American line furthest to the east, followed fairly closely by the British, allotting a large part of the Istrian peninsula to Italy and dividing the region's coal and bauxite deposits between Italy and Yugoslavia; and the French line being the one most nearly approximating to the 'ethnic' frontier, but leaving Trieste with only a very narrow hinterland.

It was this French line, with some minor modifications, which the Council of Foreign Ministers eventually decided to adopt. Trieste, as the main port and city of the whole region, was to be treated separately: it was proposed to create a Free Territory of Trieste, to include the city itself and the region immediately surrounding it.

The proposed settlement satisfied neither party. The Italians had hoped for a line further to the east, approximating more nearly to the 'Wilson Line' proposed, though never adopted, after the 1914–18 war; while the Yugoslavs remained intransigent in their claims to the whole territory. The Western Powers inclined towards the Italian standpoint, while the USSR supported Yugoslavia. But in default of any other solution which would satisfy both the claimants and the four Powers, it was agreed to. The Governor of the new Free Territory was to be appointed by the United Nations Security Council, and only after his appointment was the Statute, or Constitution, of the Free Territory to come into force. Until that time, a provisional régime was to be carried on under Allied military occupation: the Free Territory was temporarily to remain divided by the Morgan line into two zones, 'A' and 'B', under British-United States and Yugoslav occupation respectively.

The seeds of discord thus sown were to bear fruit during the next eight years. For the four Powers failed to reach agreement on the initial step of appointing a Governor, so the provisional régime, designed as a stop-gap administration of a few weeks or months at most, remained in force until October 1954[1].

But all this lay in the future. In the meantime the Italian delegates affixed their signatures to the treaty. It was ratified by the Constituent Assembly on 31 July 1947, and came into force on 15 September.

THE EX-ITALIAN COLONIES

Though the ultimate fate of the former Italian colonies was not settled under the peace treaty, but merely postponed, it may be convenient to complete the story here. Under the treaty it was agreed that Italy should renounce all claim to her possessions in Africa—the colonies of Libya, Eritrea, and Italian Somaliland; their final disposal was to be determined by the four Powers within a year of the coming into force of the treaty, i.e. by 15 September 1948. In the event the question took much longer to settle, and it was not until the end of 1950 that the final decision was reached.

A commission of investigation visited the colonies in the

[1] See below, pp. 147 ff.

winter of 1947–8 and the four Powers met in September 1948 to consider its Report but failed to reach agreement concerning the future of the colonies. The question was therefore referred to the United Nations, where in the spring of 1949 proposals sponsored jointly by Mr Bevin and Count Sforza failed by one vote to obtain the approval of the General Assembly.[1] Discussions were resumed in the following autumn (by which time the Italian view had veered towards independence for the colonies), and resulted in agreement as to two of the three territories. It was decided that a unified Libya should achieve independence by 1 January 1952, and that in the meantime administration should be carried on by a United Nations Commissioner with an Advisory Council composed of representatives of Egypt, France, Italy, Pakistan, Great Britain, the United States, and four representatives of the local population. All this worked out according to plan, and on 24 December 1951 Libya was proclaimed an independent State. Special agreements covered the questions of Italian property and the position of Italian nationals. At the November 1949 meeting of the United Nations it was also decided that Italian Somaliland should be placed under Italian trusteeship, with a three-Power Advisory Council, for ten years, with a view to eventual independence; at the end of that period the General Assembly is to review the situation.

Eritrea, Italy's oldest colony, proved an even more difficult problem. Its fate was eventually decided at the General Assembly in December 1950 when a plan for the federation of Eritrea with Ethiopia was approved, Eritrea to have full domestic autonomy within the federal Government. A United Nations Commission was appointed to supervise the transfer of authority, which took place on 15 September 1952. Italian State property was handed over to Eritrea but Italian private property remained exempt.

[1] These proposals differed from the eventual settlement in two main particulars. As to Libya, while independence in ten years was envisaged, an interim trusteeship period was proposed, with Tripoli under Italian, Cyrenaica under British, and the Fezzan under French trusteeship. Eritrea was to be divided between Ethiopia and the Anglo-Egyptian Sudan, with treaty safeguards. Italian Somaliland was to come under Italian trusteeship.

CHAPTER IV

THE ECONOMIC BACKGROUND TO RECOVERY

THE SITUATION AT THE END OF THE WAR

At this point we must pause to consider briefly the economic background against which the first efforts towards building up the new Italy were being made.

Conditions when the war ended were, to say the least of it, extremely unfavourable. For the past twenty months the country had been divided in two, with dual administrations in every department of affairs. Damage to national territory and property was reckoned to have reduced it to about two-thirds of its pre-war value.[1] Air-raids and destruction during the fighting had been responsible for vast-scale damage to buildings, roads, railways, ports, and electrical installations. The disruption of internal communications for many months after the war aggravated local shortages of food and other supplies. Damage to shipping had reduced the active merchant fleet to about a tenth of its pre-war tonnage (though recovery of ships and repairs had already brought the fleet up to a third of pre-war strength by the end of 1946). In terms of available foreign currency to cover essential imports of food and fuel Italy was bankrupt. Prospects for agriculture were particularly gloomy: shortage of fertilisers throughout the latter part of the war had exhausted the soil, livestock was seriously depleted through war demands, German looting, and lack of fodder, thousands of acres of olive groves, vineyards, and orchards had been destroyed, while much of the land normally under cultivation was requisitioned or in a dangerous state because of uncleared minefields. To make matters worse, in 1945 Italy suffered one of the worst droughts within living memory.

There were, however, one or two brighter spots. Contrary

[1] See *Lo Sviluppo dell'Economia Italiana* (Rome, Istituto Poligrafico dello Stato, 1952), p. 3. See also UNRRA, Italian Mission, *Survey of Italy's Economy* (Rome, June 1947), from which many of the following details are derived.

to expectation, damage to industrial plant proved much less serious than had been feared. It was in fact estimated that some 20 per cent of the country's industrial capacity had been destroyed as a result of the actual fighting, bombing, and sabotage or removal of plant to Germany. The damage was very unevenly distributed—the worst areas were in the two central belts between Naples and Rome, and between Florence and Bologna, where fighting had been more or less static during the winters of 1943–4 and 1944–5. Factories in Campania and Tuscany suffered severely—damage to the textile industry (reckoned at 10 per cent of output capacity) was virtually confined to this area, while output capacity of the iron and steel industry here was reduced by 90 per cent.

In the industrial North, on the other hand, owing to the rapid advance of the Allied armies in the last weeks of the war and, more especially, to the partisans' action in taking over and safeguarding factories and installations, damage was relatively slight. Reduction of capacity in the Northern iron and steel industry was estimated at 15 per cent; the textile industry escaped practically unscathed. The preservation of the electrical installations in the North, once again largely due to partisan action, was of vital importance in rebuilding the post-war economy. In this respect the Centre and South suffered much more severely; in 1945 power production in the Centre was 67·5 per cent, in the South 41·71 per cent, below the 1941 level.

Yet industrial recovery could be only a slow business, retarded by shortage of coal and other raw material stocks, of merchant shipping, and of foreign currency, as well as of internal transport and food supplies. Moreover the plant in many factories had not been renewed for years. In these circumstances the provision of employment for discharged soldiers and returning prisoners of war presented a very serious problem. Inflation threatened to become a real danger, especially in the North, and the uncertainties of the future until the peace treaty was signed produced a general lack of confidence. The estimated Budget deficit for 1945–6 was 300,000 million lire. The black market flourished, both in currency and in goods.

BASIC FEATURES OF THE ECONOMY

Despite the changes wrought by the Fascist régime and by

the circumstances of war, the major structural features of the Italian economy emerged but little altered in 1945.

Italy was relatively a late comer among European countries in the industrial field. Nevertheless, though agriculture still plays a very important part in the life of the country, industry, concentrated mainly in the North, by the outbreak of the second world war contributed 34 per cent of the national income (as against 36 per cent for agriculture) and provided employment for 33 per cent of the total working population, as against 48 per cent employed in agriculture,[1] while semi-manufactured and finished goods together accounted for nearly 60 per cent of pre-war exports. Industrial development in Italy has throughout been handicapped by her lack of most of the basic raw materials essential to her economy, and her consequent high degree of dependence on imports. It was to counter this situation that Mussolini initiated the autarkic experiment in the 1920s, in an attempt to make Italy as nearly as possible self-sufficient in raw materials and foodstuffs. To this end some elements of the country's economy were artificially stimulated by means of State subsidies. But Italy's poverty in raw materials, and even in the type of soil suitable for widespread intensive cultivation, made the success of any such scheme highly problematical.

Among Italy's limited mineral resources, mercury, sulphur, and marble are available in excess of domestic requirements, while she is self-sufficient in zinc and manganese. She has only small supplies of solid fuel and that of poor quality; the main sources are in Sardinia (the Arsa mines in Istria went to Yugoslavia under the peace treaty). Till the recent discoveries of oil in Sicily and the Abruzzi, the extent of which cannot yet be gauged accurately,[2] she was entirely dependent on

[1] 1936 census. See UNRRA, *Survey of Italy's Economy* (Rome, 1947). By 1952 the proportion employed in industry had risen to 31·6 per cent, while that for agriculture had fallen to 42·4 per cent (1951 census figures). But the ratio of agricultural to other types of employment still remained high (cf. 31·8 per cent in France).

[2] The American Gulf Oil Corporation struck oil near Ragusa, in Sicily, in October 1953, and by the end of 1954 had two wells in production. Prospecting had been carried on since 1950 in various parts of Sicily by a number of companies, mainly American but also including latterly the D'Arcy Exploration Co., which had been granted concessions under the Sicilian Regional Government's law of 20 March 1950. This law, more favourable to prospectors than Italian legislation, facilitated concessions to private enterprise and foreign capital. The whole question of foreign investment, as well as of State participation, in oil

imported supplies of crude liquid fuels, which form a heavy item in her balance of payments; other imports essential for her industrial activity are iron ores and scrap, phosphates, copper, nickel and other non-ferrous metals, cotton, wool, cellulose, wood-pulp, hides and skins, and even timber, of which domestic sources have suffered severely through unsystematic deforestation.

Nevertheless, to offset her poverty in coal and liquid fuels, Italy possesses a most valuable asset in her sources of hydro-electric power, already extensively developed before the war and by 1953 producing more than twice as much as in 1938. Another important asset, and one which indeed may well revolutionise the Italian economy, is the post-war discovery and development of large deposits of methane, or natural gas, which by 1953 had already reduced by a third the country's dependence on imported coal.

In foodstuffs Italy is more nearly self-supporting, at any rate as far as the staple foodstuffs, wheat, maize, and rice, are concerned. Though Mussolini's claim that the 'Battle for Wheat' of the 1930s had made Italy practically self-sufficient was exaggerated and based on precarious premises, she did in certain of those years reduce her imports of wheat to about 5 per cent of her needs. Of olive oil, too, another basic item in Italian diet, Italy is one of the largest producers in Europe; but she is by no means self-supporting in edible fats, and if her low consumption of meat and dairy products were to increase materially these too would have to be added to her import list.

Italy's economy in fact still possesses certain inherent structural weaknesses from which it is hard to break loose. In addition to the inadequacy of her natural resources, other geographical factors, as will be seen later on in discussing the impoverished South, militate against a sound and balanced economy—the wide extent of land that is mountainous or unsuitable for cultivation, the difficulty of communications, the unbalance between the relatively prosperous and highly industrialised North, easy of access to the rest of the Continent, and the backward and isolated South. Some of the other

development became the subject of heated controversy once oil had been actually found, and received a further impetus when a fresh source was struck (once again by American prospectors) in the Abruzzi early in 1955.

factors contributing to this inherent weakness will be touched on later: the population pressure, the low income structure, and the low degree of capitalisation.

ACTION FOR RECOVERY

Against this background it can easily be understood that the country's economy sustained a severe shock from wartime destruction and the crippling of normal activities, from which recovery could only be slow and difficult. Yet how resilient the Italian economy has in fact proved may be conjectured from the 1951 industrial and agricultural census, which showed no material variations, as compared with the census of 1937–8, in the number of concerns or their distribution among the various sectors of industry. This would seem to indicate that the Italian economy had already before the war achieved a certain stability to which it has since returned and on which it can now build.

Recovery can be seen in retrospect to have fallen into three main phases. In the first phase, which lasted from 1945 to 1947, the predominant need was to feed the country and to emerge from the prevailing state of economic paralysis—in fact, to repair damage and get the means of production moving once more. This was largely a hand-to-mouth struggle, characterised by mounting inflation, but greatly assisted by the aid received under the UNRRA, AUSA, and Interim Aid programmes.[1]

During the second phase, from 1947 to 1950, inflation was checked and financial stability achieved, while trade began to flow more freely and industrial production improved considerably. Early in this period Marshall aid began to bring the country much-needed supplies of foodstuffs and industrial raw materials.

By 1950 the phase of immediate post-war recovery could be said to be over, and Italy could embark on a third stage, that of long-term plans for tackling the major structural economic weaknesses. It was at the beginning of this stage

[1] UNRRA aid to Italy between January 1946 and its termination in June 1947 totalled \$589·4 million. In the early stages foodstuffs were the main imports, especially wheat, otherwise the bread ration could not have been maintained even at the low figure of 200–225 grs a day per person; but latterly more than half the imports consisted of raw materials.

that plans were initiated for developing the South and providing fresh opportunities for employment. Despite the Korean crisis financial stability remained unimpaired, and a long-term policy of furthering productive investment was initiated, together with reforms in the taxation system. When Marshall aid ended in 1952[1] its place was to some extent taken by aid under the MSA programme and by 'offshore' orders. Finally, increased foreign investment was also hoped for in connection with the ten-year plan for economic development announced by Signor Vanoni, the Budget Minister, early in 1955,[2] which aimed at eliminating one of the major handicaps, that of unemployment.

The action taken by the Government to deal with these various basic economic problems will be described in detail later on. But the presence of those problems, and the controversy engendered by divergent views as to how they should be treated, runs like a thread through the whole story of Italy's post-war political development. The overthrow of the Fascist régime could not in itself alter the fact that they existed; for such problems as over-population, unemployment, extreme unevenness in the distribution of wealth, and the unbalance between North and South had for long been endemic to the structure of the whole economy. But the end of the régime could, and did, engender the hope that they would be treated in a more dynamic way than in the past. It was soon seen, however, that efforts towards radical reforms were being constantly curbed and impeded by opposition from those elements in Italian social life, and in particular the propertied elements, which stood to lose their traditional privileged position should the structure of society alter fundamentally. The dead weight of such opposition played its part even as early as the autumn of 1945 in bringing down the Parri Government and with it all hopes of a complete break with the forces of the old tradition of privilege; and eight years later the same thing was to happen to the De Gasperi Government, and over the specific question of land reform.

[1] ERP (Marshall) aid received by Italy between 1948 and 1952 totalled $1,515 million. Total net U.S. aid to Italy between 1945 and 1952 under both the various pre-ERP and the ERP programmes was $2,390 million (see U.S. Department of Commerce, *Survey of Current Business*, October 1952, p. 10).

[2] See below, p. 188.

The problems were, in fact, social at least as much as economic. The tardiness of industrialisation in Italy, and its virtual confinement to the North, had resulted in a perpetuation of backward and indeed almost feudal conditions in certain regions, particularly in the South, long after they had been swept away, or at any rate very considerably modified, in more advanced countries. But for a few outstanding exceptions, the aristocracy and the landowners had never concerned themselves much with political life and lacked a tradition of public service. The industrialists were primarily business men concerned to run their factories successfully, with little time for the intricacies of politics. Thus the classes of society from which leaders might have been expected to develop were all, in a sense, disengaged and indifferent, anxious only to maintain the conditions most favourable to their own prosperity.

The explosion of new ideas released at the end of the war shattered their possibility of remaining aloof. Peasants who had hitherto been subservient if discontented, urged on by political agitators, assailed the landowners with demands for land for themselves. In the factories the rapidly developing power of the trade unions and the constant threat of strikes compelled industrialists to take increasing account of social and political factors. Resistance to these demands, even if based on sound economic reasons (as for example in the case of dismissals of supernumerary factory workers), was liable to be interpreted in a political sense. The parties of the Left, and the CGIL, the Communist-controlled trade union, enunciated their own extreme panaceas for the country's economic ills and by their very intransigence provoked landowners and employers of industrial labour into taking a more rigid stand.

The Left, in fact, wanted to alter the whole framework of the liberal economy which had been restored after the war under the aegis first of Italy's future President, Professor Luigi Einaudi,[1] and subsequently under such orthodox economists as Giuseppe Pella and Ezio Vanoni. As, short of a seizure of power, the Communists could not bring about wholesale changes, they instead adopted guerrilla tactics, constantly attacking both existing institutions and the Government's efforts towards reform. They found some vulnerable

[1] See below, p. 182.

targets, for example in such an institution as the IRI, the organisation for State financing of industry (a survival from Fascist days),[1] and in the monopolistic character of some branches of industry. But their attacks on the Government's plans for reform in such spheres as those of agrarian questions, taxation, and Southern development merely had the effect of hampering and retarding parliamentary discussion of vital progressive measures.

Thus in the passage through Parliament of practically every major economic reform the Government had to fight its way through a double barrage of criticism, the Right blaming it for going too far and too fast, whereas the Left accused it of dilatoriness and of going nothing like far enough. In these circumstances it is not surprising that one of the main reproaches levelled against all the post-war Governments was that of *immobilismo*—of failing to get a move on. There was nothing particularly new about this reproach, which indeed is one that Italians, with their innate scepticism in relation to governmental authority, have made against their Governments for generations. But it had a new cogency now, both because of the fresh hopes of action that had been aroused since the war and because of the consciousness of the alternative should the forces of legitimacy fail to bring improved conditions to the country.

It was in part this fear that the Communist alternative might gain strength which prompted the United States to extend lavish aid to Italy throughout the years of the Marshall Plan's operation—and without that aid the story of the past few years might have been a very different one. It at first seemed natural to believe that, in a country of poverty and mass unemployment such as Italy, the mere creation of conditions tending towards a greater material prosperity would suffice to turn the balance against Communism. Yet the fallacy of that theory, if held in its simplest form and applied in regions that were backward in education at least as much as in social conditions, was demonstrated to American dismay in the Election of 1953. The Communists' advance had, it is true, been held in check, but their promises still exercised a strong appeal, and their progress had been greatest in those

[1] See below, p. 157.

very regions of the South where the Government, backed by American aid, had made its most strenuous efforts to introduce material improvements. It was, in fact, as coming chapters will show, the need to achieve a just balance between the claims of social and economic progress and the claims of political necessity that was to provide the ultimate test for Italy's democratic Governments.

Part II

Political Developments 1947–55

CHAPTER V

1947: THE YEAR OF EMERGENCE

THE signature of the peace treaty on 10 February 1947 brought with it the end of Allied tutelage. Italy could now emerge once more as a free and independent State, able to conduct her own internal, commercial, and foreign affairs. From the administrative point of view the most immediate task was the drafting of the Constitution, which occupied the Constituent Assembly from 4 March until the year's end. On the economic side the most urgent need was to secure loans from abroad to aid in the rebuilding of the country's industry, agriculture, and foreign trade. UNRRA aid had sustained Italy through the first eighteen months after the war, furnishing not only foodstuffs and medical supplies but also raw materials for industry, and in particular coal.[1] But this aid was to end in June 1947, and in the meantime Italy was in serious need of foreign exchange against the day when she would have to pay for essential imports herself. Consequently great importance was attached to the visit which Signor De Gasperi paid to the United States in January 1947, at Mr Byrnes's invitation, together with Dr Menichella, Director-General (later Governor) of the Bank of Italy, and the Minister for Foreign Trade, Signor Campilli.

This was the first time since the war that an Italian Prime Minister visited an Allied country on a footing of equality, and the effects were to be far-reaching. An immediate result was that the Italians succeeded in obtaining a $100 million loan from the Export-Import Bank, as well as other aid in the matter of shipping, coal supplies, etc. But also on a long-term view this visit laid the foundations for the special

[1] See below, p. 156.

interest which the United States subsequently took in Italy's welfare; and it is probably not too much to say that Signor De Gasperi's masterly presentation of his country's situation played an important part in convincing the American authorities of the need for continued aid to war-torn European countries after UNRRA should come to an end, thus preparing the way for General Marshall's offer of aid in the following June which Italy was among the first to accept.[1]

THE SOCIALIST SPLIT

Meanwhile the political situation at home had not stood still during Signor De Gasperi's absence. For some time the more moderate Socialists had been increasingly alarmed at the strengthening ties between their party and the Communists. A second 'Unity of Action' pact, had been concluded between the parties on 25 October 1946, which went further than the first in providing for co-ordination of joint decisions on all problems and at all levels;[2] and Socialist (as opposed to Communist) losses in the November local elections[3] were thought to have been a direct result of the electorate's dislike of this policy. Moreover the growing tension between Russia and the Western Allies was already making the 'neutralist' attitude cherished by so many socialist-minded Italians increasingly difficult to put into practice. The choice, in fact, was not only between independence and subservience to Communism but between West and East. This was realised by Saragat and some of the group known as 'Iniziativa Socialista', which included Matteo Matteotti, whose father had been murdered by the Fascists in 1924; and on the occasion of the Socialist Party's National Congress in Rome on 9 January 1947 they abstained from the main meeting and staged a rival congress of their own in Palazzo Barberini at which was founded a secessionist Socialist party, the Partito Socialista dei Lavoratori Italiani, thus reviving the name of the pre-Fascist reformist Socialist party of Turati and Giacomo Matteotti. Some fifty of the 115 Socialist Deputies went

[1] See Adstans, *Alcide De Gasperi nella politica estera italiana (1944–1953)* (Milan, Mondadori, 1953), p. 84.

[2] For the earlier pact see above, p. 16. See also Paolo Emiliani, *Dieci anni perduti* (Pisa, Nistri-Lischi, 1953), p. 59.

[3] See above, p. 24.

with them, including such veterans as Modigliani and D'Aragona.

This secession inevitably led to the withdrawal from the Government not only of the two PSLI Ministers, Saragat and D'Aragona, but also of Signor Nenni himself. The Socialist party split necessitated extensive reorganisation for both sides—new party executives and committees at every level, a new party organ, *Umanità*, for the PSLI, and intensive propaganda to convince the working-class electorate that each of the now rival parties was the true heir of Socialism in its purest form. After the Socialist withdrawals Signor De Gasperi offered his Government's resignation on 20 January, and on 2 February formed a new Cabinet. As the Republicans stayed out, this was a three-party coalition of the Christian Democrats, Socialists, and Communists, but without either the Socialist or the Communist leader.[1] Signor Nenni, who since October had been Foreign Minister, was now replaced by Count Sforza, who thus at last achieved once more the post for which he was fitted and from which he had earlier been excluded by Allied suspicions of his outspoken republican views.[2]

GOVERNMENT WITHOUT THE LEFT

But the withdrawal of the moderate Socialists and the Republicans brought into sharp relief the ideological divergences between the Christian Democrats and the two Left-wing parties. Numerically these two forces were practically evenly balanced in the Cabinet, with the result that firm governmental action, especially necessary in the economic sphere, was virtually paralysed. Togliatti summed up the situation in February as an alternative between a perpetual crisis or a Communist programme. After three months of stalemate Signor De Gasperi cut the knot and on 13 May resigned. Attempts on the part of the veteran statesmen Nitti and Orlando having failed, he was again asked to form a Government, and since he could not secure the collaboration of the Left-Centre parties (the PSLI and the Republicans) the Cabinet

[1] Signor Togliatti never held Cabinet office again after the end of June 1946.

[2] This was in November 1944, when the Allies were still inclined to support the monarchy, and were in any case not in a position to do otherwise until after the referendum. Britain, in particular, at this time vetoed the assumption of high office by Count Sforza. He had already been Foreign Minister for a brief period in 1920–21.

he announced on 31 May was formed entirely of Christian Democrats except for some independents.[1]

Thus ended the period of Communist collaboration in the Government which had lasted since April 1944. Almost simultaneously the same thing had happened in France, when early in May 1947 the Communists were dismissed from M. Ramadier's Government as a result of their opposition to the official policy on wages. At the time perhaps neither departure was seen as irrevocable. But in fact the post-war collaboration between such different allies, prolonged while the community of aims engendered during the Resistance period still had some influence, was bound to weaken as conditions gradually became more normal. Moreover the increasing tension between East and West, as exemplified in the Moscow Conference of February 1947, inevitably had its counterpart in the domestic politics of the two Western countries which possessed the strongest Communist parties. The collaboration experiment of 1944–7 had paid at the time, by giving the Communist parties an aura of legitimacy and enabling them to have some say in the framing of immediate post-war policies. But in Italy the Communists never succeeded in obtaining any key posts in the Government, and given the balance of political forces in 1947 it seemed probable that the Left parties had at least as much to gain as to lose by going into opposition. Thus while the immediate break arose from the Christian Democrats' realisation of the impossibility of prolonging the impasse of tripartite collaboration, it seems likely that the Left-wing parties too felt that its usefulness to them was over. The further divergence of view which arose within a few weeks around the Marshall offer was to make the split irrevocable.

In the meantime, however, in one respect at least the appearances of collaboration were to be preserved for some time longer. The three mass parties had since 1944 combined in a common trade union, the CGIL.[2] Though from the beginning the Communists were the largest group in the Confederation, responsibility at the top was at first supposed to be equally divided among three secretaries, Giuseppe Di

[1] The PSLI and Republicans joined the Government after a reshuffle in December, their respective leaders, Saragat and Pacciardi, both becoming Deputy Prime Ministers.

[2] See above, p. 20.

Vittorio, Oreste Lizzadri, and Achille Grandi, representing respectively the Communist, Socialist, and Christian Democrat workers. Of these, Di Vittorio was throughout the dominating personality; the Christian Democrat representative, Grandi, already a sick man, died in 1946 and was replaced first by Rapelli and then by Giulio Pastore. Di Vittorio came of an Apulian family of *braccianti*, or day-labourers. He was born in Cerignola, a town where the poverty and unemployment of the landless Southern peasant could be experienced in its most acute form. He had come early to Communism through the part he played in social and syndical organisation in his own region, had been imprisoned by the Fascists, and eventually escaped abroad to become a political commissar in the Garibaldi Brigade in Spain. After the fall of Fascism he took an active part in syndical and Communist organisations in the South. Under him the Communists, through their continuous sponsorship of labour's interests and their effective placing of their own men in factories and in key trade union jobs throughout the country, kept the leading role in the CGIL throughout the whole period of tripartite collaboration in the Government; and even when this ended, in the face of increasing Communist control the façade was maintained until October 1948, when the Catholic and some other non-Communist elements at last broke away from the CGIL to form a free trade union.[1]

THE CONSTITUTION

Against this background of political vicissitudes, for nine months from March to December 1947 the Constituent Assembly debated article by article the new Constitution which had been drafted by a parliamentary committee under the chairmanship of the lawyer and elder statesman Meuccio Ruini. It was finally approved in the Assembly on 22 December by 453 votes to 62 (the adverse votes coming mainly from monarchists) and came into force on 1 January 1948.

The Constitution represents a gallant attempt to combine in a single document all the aspirations which were burgeoning after twenty years of repression, and at the same time to reconcile a variety of already highly divergent views. Its predecessor dated from 1848, when King Carlo Alberto granted

[1] See below, p. 59.

a 'Statute' to the Kingdom of Sardinia (then including Piedmont and Sardinia) which was later extended to cover the whole Kingdom of Italy after the unification. During the Fascist régime considerable changes were introduced, tending towards an increase in the powers of the Executive, especially the Head of the Government, and a curtailment of civil liberties.

The new Constitution consists of 139 Articles, subdivided into 'Fundamental Principles' (Arts. 1–12), a First Part on 'The Rights and Duties of Citizens' (Arts. 13–54), and a Second Part on the 'Organisation of the Republic' (Arts. 55–139). It opens with the statement that Italy is a democratic Republic based on work. Sovereignty belongs to the people, who exercise it in the forms and within the limits prescribed by the Constitution.

Among the Fundamental Principles are listed the 'inviolable rights' of the citizen to equality before the law, irrespective of race, language, religion, or political opinions, and his right to work. It is 'the duty of the Republic' to remove economic and social obstacles restricting his liberty and equality. Local autonomy and decentralisation are to be furthered. All religions are equally free before the law, but (here we have the much contested Article 7, agreed to by the Communists only after long debate[1]) 'The States and the Catholic Church are . . . independent and sovereign, and their relations are regulated by the Lateran Pacts'. Finally (Art. 11), 'Italy repudiates war as an instrument of offence against the liberty of other peoples and as a means of resolving international controversies' (the Italians' post-war longing for neutrality got the upper hand here).

The sovereignty of the people is exercised through their parliamentary vote and, if need be, through a Referendum which can be taken in particular circumstances, among which is the possible revision or modification of the Constitution. Parliament is bicameral, consisting of the Chamber of Deputies and the Senate, freely elected for terms of five and six years respectively. The legislative functions of Parliament are outlined in detail. The Head of the State, i.e. the President of the Republic, is no longer, as was formerly the case under the

[1] The Socialists and Republicans voted against it.

Crown, the Head of the Executive: executive functions now belong to the Government. The President is elected by both Houses of Parliament for a seven-year term. Special laws define the position of judges (usually permanent appointments in Italy) and ensure their independence and freedom from interference by the Executive. An innovation in local government is the creation of the 'Region' as an autonomous local administrative unit: the Constitution provides for the division of the country into nineteen such Regions and outlines their functions.

Certain special bodies are to be set up to carry out the provisions of the Constitution in particular spheres. In that of law, a Constitutional Court (*Corte Costituzionale*) is to be the organ competent to judge whether laws are constitutional, with power to invalidate any laws that do not conform to the Constitution (Arts. 134–7), and a *Consiglio Superiore della Magistratura* is to be the independent organisation determining all nominations and provisions affecting the careers of judges. In the economic sphere, a National Economic and Labour Council (*Consiglio nazionale dell'economia e del lavoro*), composed of representatives of all categories in economic life, is to be 'the advisory organ for Parliament and the Government', with power to promote legislation on economic and social questions.

From the foregoing short summary it will be seen that the Constitution contained a good many unimpeachable sentiments and aspirations as well as some very comprehensive legislation. Unfortunately it is precisely in the implementation of the clauses designed to 'put teeth into' this document, to give it a more practical application, that subsequent practice has been least successful. In fact, in 1954, six years after the Constitution came into force, the necessary legislation to bring into effect several of its provisions had not yet been passed. As one of its more severe critics, Professor Gaetano Salvemini, put it: 'The Italian Republic has a written Constitution as long as a Christmas night . . . drafted according to the philosophical and deductive method dear to the Latin genius', but 'the structural crowning touches indispensable for the normal functioning of democracy are lacking':[1] the Constitutional Court, the *Consiglio Superiore della Magistratura*, the National

[1] Gaetano Salvemini, 'Coronamenti Strutturali', in *Il Ponte*, March 1954.

Economic and Labour Council, and the measures regarding the referendum had not yet come into being.[1] Nor, incidentally, had the provisions concerning regional autonomy, except in the particular cases of the peripheral regions—Sicily, Sardinia, Trentino–Alto Adige, and the Val d'Aosta, but that is another story which will be discussed elsewhere:[2] the decentralising tendencies of 1946 have in the meantime given way to an understandable unwillingness to expand the already top-heavy bureaucratic machinery still further.

In the meantime, however, partly owing to party dissensions, partly to the pressure of parliamentary business, to Parliament's slowness in dealing with it, and to the feeling that there was always more urgent legislation to be got through, these 'structural crowning touches' of the Constitution were still lacking at the beginning of 1955: and, in the absence in particular of the Constitutional Court, no decision had yet been reached as to the official abrogation of Fascist laws—indeed, as Professor Salvemini pointed out, a law was still theoretically in force condemning to fourteen years' imprisonment any anti-Fascist exile who spread abroad 'false and tendentious rumours' about the Fascist régime!

[1] The law establishing the Constitutional Court was passed after years of discussion in March 1953. But of the fifteen judges who composed it five had to be nominated by Parliament, and though these were in theory non-political appointments the parties could not agree about them, and the first attempt to elect them, in July 1954, failed for this reason.

The draft Bill on the setting up of the National Economic and Labour Council came up for debate in the Chamber in January 1955.

[2] See below, pp. 59–62.

CHAPTER VI

1948: THE CHRISTIAN DEMOCRATS IN THE SADDLE

THE GENERAL ELECTION OF 18 APRIL

THE coming into force of the Constitution necessitated the holding of elections for the new Chamber and Senate, and the early part of 1948 was taken up with the electoral campaign. This was the Left's last chance for the next five years, to obtain power by constitutional means and as election day, 18 April, approached tension increased and the party groupings on both sides redoubled their propaganda efforts.

Several factors contributed to make the issue by now a clear-cut one between non-Communism on the one hand and Communism on the other. The coup d'état of February 1948 in Czechoslovakia had shocked public opinion into an awareness of what might happen in Italy too in the event of an outstanding success for the Communist Party, which since September 1947 had also been a member of the Cominform. On the other hand the post-war dream of neutrality, of an Italian bridge between West and East, was being gradually abandoned by the more realistic elements of the public (it had probably never been seriously entertained in official circles), and Italy had in fact effectively made her choice by her enthusiastic adherence to the Marshall offer of June 1947. Aid under the European Recovery Programme was due to begin in April 1948, and in the meantime Italy was already receiving Interim Aid to bridge the gap since the cessation of UNRRA. These benefits were not to be lightly jeopardised.

A further factor which undoubtedly influenced the outcome of the elections, and which was to have far-reaching consequences, concerned the problem of Trieste. By the spring of 1948 it had become apparent that there was little prospect of four-Power agreement on the appointment of a Governor for the Trieste Free Territory envisaged under the peace treaty.[1]

[1] See below, pp. 136–7.

This deadlock, coupled with the situation in Zone B of the Free Territory, where Yugoslavia had been carrying on a policy of gradual assimilation, caused the three Western signatories of the treaty, Great Britain, France, and the United States, to issue on 20 March a Declaration recommending the return of the whole Free Territory area to Italy, in view of the unworkability of the original scheme. This statement (partly, no doubt, timed to strengthen the hand of the anti-Communist parties in the imminent Election) was greeted with tremendous enthusiasm in Italy, where it was taken as the basis for all subsequent negotiations—with what results will be seen later.[1] Its immediate effect was to enhance the prestige of the Government parties as the upholders of an Italian Trieste, and to emphasise the advantages of the Western alignment for which they stood. The Communists, on the other hand, were by this time identified with the Soviet line of strict adherence to the letter of the peace treaty.

The Election, with a very high poll reaching over 90 per cent in some Northern districts, resulted in a sweeping victory for the Christian Democrats, who obtained 48·5 per cent of the total votes, as against 31 per cent for the Popular Front, the name under which the Communist and Socialist parties fought the Election on joint lists.[2] The Christian Democrats obtained an absolute majority in the Chamber, with 305 seats out of 574. In the Senate, though they won more than half the elected seats, obtaining 149 seats out of 344, they lacked an absolute majority, as in this first post-war full Parliament provision was made for the appointment of 107 Senators 'by right', in addition to those elected. These Senators qualified by virtue of past services to the State, and included post-war ex-Premiers and ex-Presidents of the Chamber, and Deputies who had been imprisoned for more than five years under Fascism; of the latter the largest proportion (45) were Communists or Left-wing Socialists.

The Christian Democrats' poll increased by over 4½ million as compared with 1946, whereas the Popular Front vote fell by over a million. They undoubtedly owed their success first and foremost to the fact that public opinion regarded them as

[1] See below, Chapters XIII and XIV.
[2] For the detailed results, see below, pp. 88–9.

the main rallying point against Communism. Fear of wasting their vote caused many potential adherents of the smaller Centre parties to vote instead for the Christian Democrats. Moreover in the absence of more confidence-inspiring parties on the Right a good deal of amorphous conservative opinion became grouped under the Christian Democrat aegis for the next five years—thereby storing up some complications for internal party management in the future. The Liberals, in particular, suffered from this mass swing towards the Christian Democrats. The true Right-wing parties, the Monarchists and the newly-founded neo-Fascist Movimento Sociale Italiano, were still only insecurely established in 1948; they gained some recruits from the virtually defunct Uomo Qualunque party, but on the whole in this election they were viewed askance by the majority and remained the home of the extremists.[1]

Of the smaller Centre parties, the Social Democrats, fighting the election under the name of Unità Socialista, did well enough, with over 1,850,000 votes, and 33 seats in the Chamber, to appear to justify Signor Saragat's gamble in breaking away from the Nenni Socialists in 1947. The Liberals were reduced by internal divisions as well as by losses to the Christian Democrats, while the Republicans, though they gained some recruits from former Action Party members, had by now lost much of their *raison d'être* and were henceforth to survive chiefly in certain traditional strongholds such as the Marche.

Signor De Gasperi, as leader of the largest party, was once more called upon to form a Government, and on 23 May announced a Cabinet consisting of eleven Christian Democrats, three Social Democrats, two Republicans, two Liberals, and two Independents. This four-party Centre coalition represented the De Gasperian ideal, which he strove, with varying success,

[1] The MSI had begun to develop during 1947–8 under the leadership of some former Fascists of Mussolini's Republican Government and with a programme based in part on that Government's 'national socialist' tenets. Its adherents at this time were drawn mainly from among ex-servicemen and returned prisoners of war. But the climate was not propitious for an extensive revival of Fascism; the party lacked well-known leaders, and was moreover hampered in the Election by the ban debarring persons prominently associated with Fascism from voting or standing as candidates. Right-wing votes went rather to the Monarchists, who before the election campaign had united to form the Partito Nazionale Monarchico, with Signor Alfredo Covelli and the well-known Neapolitan shipowner Achille Lauro as its leaders.

to maintain intact throughout the next five years. In this he succeeded up to a point, for though at different times one or other of the smaller parties withdrew from collaboration in the Government they still remained united in their opposition to the extremes whether of Left or Right. Signor De Gasperi attached great importance to the coalition as a combination of Centre democratic opinion, both Catholic and secular: he felt that the presence of the three secular parties could counteract the inevitable tendencies towards clericalism within his own party. As far as the immediate present was concerned, it was hoped that these parties would also serve as a counterpoise to the conservative wing of the Christian Democrats which had gained strength through the circumstances of the Election, and would, in particular, be of special assistance in setting on foot the plans for social and economic betterment on which the Government must now embark. With the prospect of five years in power (and given the Centre's overwhelming majority this was a fairly safe reckoning) these plans could afford to be comprehensive. They included agrarian reform, housing measures, the alleviation of unemployment, and greater administrative decentralisation.

There remained yet another election to complete the framework of the Republic under the new Constitution: that of the Head of the State. President De Nicola, elected after the Republic was proclaimed in June 1946, had expressed his wish to continue in office only for the lifetime of the Constituent Assembly. On 11 May 1948 Professor Luigi Einaudi was elected President for a seven-year term. An economist of international repute who, as Professor of Economics and Finance at Turin, had influenced several generations of Italian students, he had always been known for his liberal and anti-Fascist views, and while in exile in Switzerland during the last year of the war had continued to lecture on economics at Geneva. On his return to Italy in January 1945 he was appointed Governor of the Banca d'Italia, and played an important part in guiding the reconstruction of the country's economy. In June 1947 he became Finance and Treasury Minister, and initiated effective measures for combating inflation.[1] His calm and steadying influence behind the scenes was invaluable

[1] See below, p. 182.

during the difficult early years of the Republic, and his eightieth birthday, which fell in March 1954, during his sixth year of office, was the occasion for widespread expressions of affection and regard from all parties.

In the meantime the Communists and Socialists, far from resigning themselves to their defeat, set out to sabotage the Government's efforts in every possible way, not only by continuous criticism and propaganda, but also through strikes and the fomenting of unrest. Three months after the Election, in July, an unsuccessful attempt on Togliatti's life by a student was made the reason for a nation-wide general strike called for in protest by the Communist-dominated trade union, the CGIL. The Government took swift action and the strike soon ended, but other strikes for higher wages and improved conditions among both industrial and agricultural workers hampered the country's economic progress throughout the year, while in November a more insidious and long-term method of sabotage was introduced in the form of 'non-collaboration' or 'go-slow' strikes in factories. One result of this policy, and in particular of the demand for a general strike in July, was the decision in August of the Catholic and some other non-Communist trade union elements at last to break away from the CGIL and create a separate union, which was formally instituted in October as the Libera Confederazione Generale del Lavoro (soon to become the Confederazione Italiana dei Sindicati Lavoratori—CISL) with the Christian Democrat Giulio Pastore as its Secretary-General.

REGIONAL ADMINISTRATION

This is perhaps the point at which to outline what had been accomplished in the sphere of regional decentralisation by the end of 1948. By that time Statutes had been granted to all the four peripheral Regions, and elections for the Regional Councils had been held. Nothing had been done about implementing the Constitution's provisions for a country-wide regional decentralisation, and in mid-1955 the position was virtually still the same—for though a law of February 1953 established measures for introducing a wider regional organisation, they had not yet been carried out. Thus in 1948 the basis, for the next seven years at least, had already crystallised.

As has been mentioned earlier, the idea of regionalism, or a division of the country into a number of 'Regions' with a degree of administrative and legislative autonomy, had figured in all the main party programmes after the fall of Fascism. The conception itself was not new: Cavour, one of the main authors of a united Italy, was himself a firm believer in decentralisation, and it was at his instigation that the earliest schemes for regional government were drafted. Though they never came into effect, there were always some advocates of a greater degree of local autonomy who could support their views by pointing to the tremendous differences of geographical, social, and economic conditions in the various regions of the peninsula.

By the time the new Constitution came to be framed the original post-war enthusiasm for widespread decentralisation had been damped by practical contact with the difficulties encountered in reuniting the country after its wartime divisions. But though the draft articles on regional autonomy were among the most fiercely argued in the Constituent Assembly they eventually went in, if considerably whittled down to reconcile varying opinions. One of the 'Fundamental Principles' with which the Constitution opens states that 'The Republic . . . recognises and promotes local autonomy' and . . . 'gives effect to the widest administrative decentralisation . . .', and Articles 114–33 outline the provisions for local government in the Regions, Provinces, and communes. Nineteen Regions are envisaged, and under the terms of the Constitution should have been formed and have held their first elections for Regional Councils by 30 October 1949. The four peripheral Regions of Sicily, Sardinia, Trentino–Alto Adige, and Val d'Aosta are each to have their own special Statute. Their legislative and administrative powers are to extend over a wide field of local affairs, including urban and local police, public health, professional and technical instruction, public works of regional concern, communications, and agriculture. The Region has a degree of financial autonomy: it is itself the owner of its own domain and patrimony and can impose local taxation and retain the proceeds thereof together with a quota of the taxes imposed on the Region by the Treasury in Rome. It cannot, however, levy import or export duties.

Each Region has an elected Regional Council with an Executive Committee and President, and elections to the Council (or Assembly) are conducted according to an electoral law enacted by the Region but in conformity with the law of the Republic. The Central Government's control over regional affairs is exercised through a resident Commissioner who has to approve the laws passed by the Regional Council. These laws must be framed within the limits of the State laws, and can be brought before the Constitutional Court if their legality is questioned.

The Statutes granted to the four peripheral Regions follow these broad outlines, with some difference of detail according to the locality. For example, in the two bilingual regions of Val d'Aosta and Trentino–Alto Adige, the Statutes include provision for the equality of rights of all citizens irrespective of their language group; and since both these Regions contain some of the most important hydro-electrical stations in Italy their Statutes also contain provisions about water concessions.

All four Statutes were passed by constitutional laws of 26 February 1948 and came into effect in March.[1] But regional autonomy had in fact been legally recognised and put into practice for much longer in three of the four Regions in question.

In Sicily, the Region with the longest experience of local autonomy, it was decided during the war to provide for some degree of decentralisation in order to counter the demand for separatism which arose soon after the Allied landings in 1943. High Commissioners of the Royal Government were installed in Sicily and Sardinia early in 1944, and a Royal Decree Law of 1946 granted a Statute for Sicily which was converted unchanged into constitutional law when the other three Regions received their Statutes in 1948. An amendment to the 1946 law also extended autonomy to Sardinia, and the Statute for Sardinia was approved by the Constituent Assembly on 28–9 January 1948.

In the Val d'Aosta, too, local autonomy was early granted in order to counter some tentative attempts at separatist agitation which arose at the end of the war. On 19 August 1945

[1] Texts of all the Statutes are given in the *Manuale Parlamentare* of 1948 (Rome, Tipografia del Senato, 1948).

two decrees were passed establishing a régime of autonomy there,[1] to which the Statute of 30 January 1948 gave definitive constitutional form.

The granting of a measure of local autonomy was regarded as especially important in the case of the disputed frontier of South Tyrol, combining the two Provinces of Trentino and Alto Adige; it had indeed been expressly stipulated in the De Gasperi–Gruber agreement of September 1946 which was annexed to the peace treaty.[2] In the Statute for Trentino–Alto Adige, which was approved by the Constituent Assembly on 29 January 1948, provision is made not only for regional autonomy but also for separate, and relatively autonomous, administration in each of the two Provinces within the Region. The Regional Council, elected for four years, has its seat for two years in Trento and two in Bolzano, with a President elected for the first two years from the Italian-speaking group and for the second two years from the German-speaking one. Equal citizenship rights for all language groups are guaranteed.

Regional autonomy in these four outlying Regions (each of them rather special cases) seems on the whole to have worked well. In Sicily, for example, the land reform question has been tackled with vigour by the Regional authorities. Particular local difficulties have, of course, arisen in each Region. In Sicily and Sardinia there have been the problems of a backward economy (especially acute in Sardinia, without the same attractions of tourism as in Sicily to alleviate it) and of banditry; and the discovery of oil in Sicily brought into relief the contrast between Sicilian Regional and national law concerning mining rights.[3] In the Val d'Aosta the competing claims of Regional and State finance have raised difficulties, especially in connection with the taxation of some of the big hydro-electric and industrial concerns situated there. Similar problems arise in the Trentino–Alto Adige, where the position is further complicated by the constant need to satisfy the claims, reasserted in 1953 and again in 1955,[4] of the large German-speaking population. But on the whole the decentralisation principle has been fully justified in these four Regions.

But there has been markedly little inclination to argue from

[1] See 'Autonomy in the Val d'Aosta', in *The World Today*, June 1946.
[2] See above, p. 32. [3] See above, p. 40. [4] See above, pp. 32–3.

this success that the principle should be extended in full, with all its paraphernalia of Regional Presidents and Councils, to the rest of the country. Greater decentralisation would no doubt be generally welcomed—probably even more warmly than in 1948, given the increasing tendency to draw all the threads towards Rome which the State machine has manifested since then. But while centralisation is attacked, so too is the swollen bureaucracy, to which a separate Regional machinery would only add another series of cogs. The regional principle has also since 1948 become something of a political question: Liberal and Right-wing trends have strongly opposed it, and there has been a widespread fear that were the regional Parliaments to come into being the Communists might make use of them to strengthen their own position. The Communists, incidentally, have become ardent advocates of regionalism and blame the Government for the delay in putting it into effect.

CHAPTER VII

PARTY TRENDS WITHIN THE COALITION

THE five years 1948–53 during which the Government under Signor De Gasperi's leadership enjoyed a strong majority can be seen in retrospect to fall into three phases. The first two years were ones of consolidation and preparation, during which, with the advent of Marshall aid, the foundations were laid for the Government's major social and economic reforms. Foreign affairs played an important part during this period, especially in 1949, when the main discussions on the disposal of Italy's former colonies took place and when Italy, in the face of strong opposition from the Left, joined the Atlantic Pact and the Council of Europe.[1] The second phase opened in 1950 when the major reforms began to be put into effect: in January Signor De Gasperi announced the ten-year plan for Southern development, in May land reform came into operation in the Sila, and in October the new taxation reform was introduced.[2] The Korean war, besides affecting the economic situation, brought with it the need for increased expenditure on defence, and the Left's opposition to the Government's rearmament policy, together with the adjustments needed to balance the rival claims of defence and the newly-inaugurated reforms, were outstanding features of 1951. In the third phase, 1952–3, the Government found itself increasingly on the defensive. Its term of office was running out: the Southern administrative elections in the spring of 1952 sounded a warning note, and preparations for the coming General Election, which included the launching of the new electoral law, dominated the winter of 1952–3.

Politically, the five years witnessed a continuous struggle on the part of Signor De Gasperi to maintain the four-party Centre coalition, and on the part of the small allied secular parties to achieve a *modus vivendi* with the predominant partner, Christian Democracy. This struggle was to an appreciable

[1] See below, pp. 122–3. [2] See below, p. 183–5.

extent conditioned by the vicissitudes of Italian Socialism and their repercussions among the Social Democrat allies in the coalition. It was also sharply reflected among the different trends within the Christian Democrat party itself. But it was the Liberals who were the first to leave the coalition, in January 1950, nominally because of disagreements concerning land reform and the wider application of regional administration, though in part too because of their uneasiness at the alleged increasingly 'clerical' trend of the Christian Democrats and of their influence in the sphere of education. The question of collaboration in the Government figured prominently throughout the discussions on reunification of the different non-Communist Socialist groups which went on throughout 1948–51; but it was not till April 1951 that the Social Democrats finally quitted the Government. This left only the small Republican party, who for the last two years of the De Gasperi Government's life continued as its sole partner. But the other Centre parties did not withdraw their support in Parliament, and the four parties, or various combinations of them, presented allied lists in many constituencies in the local administrative elections of 1951–2. Finally, in the autumn of 1952 the four parties once again reached agreement to stand together in the General Election of 1953.

The policy of maintaining a coalition between Christian Democracy and the small secular parties raised considerable difficulties for Signor De Gasperi: his hoped-for allies proved carping and often unwilling partners, and sections of his own party would prefer to have done without them. This, from a parliamentary point of view, could easily have been managed, for the Christian Democrat majority during 1948–53 was so great as to have no need of allies. But collaboration between the confessional and the secular forces in the country was a cardinal point in Signor De Gasperi's vision both of Italian democracy and of the Christian Democrat party's role within it. He wished above all things to guard against a revival of the rift between Catholic and lay forces, between Church and State, which had created so many problems for Italy in the past: and he reverted to this point only a few days before his death, when in a letter to Fanfani which has come to be regarded as in some sense his political testament he spoke of Christian

Democracy's need to avoid becoming anew 'involved in the toils of the traditional choice between Guelphism and Ghibellinism.'[1] He felt that Christian Democracy, to maintain its rôle as a Catholic party of the masses, must on the one hand, like its predecessor the Partito Popolare, keep itself free from pronounced affiliations with the Holy See and the ecclesiastical authorities, and on the other hand must maintain positive and strong links with the forces of secular democracy. Any rift between these two sections of the democratic whole could only work in favour of Communism, by helping to build up an 'anti-clerical' front.

This view of Signor De Gasperi's was allied to his fundamental belief in the future of democracy and in Parliament as its instrument. Time and again he outlined this belief in his speeches. For example, at the Christian Democrat party National Council in August 1949, speaking of the party's relations with its allies, he said:

> Our own experience and that of the Socialists and Liberals can all be of use in the service of our country and for the consolidation of democracy. But democracy itself constitutes an essential and homogeneous framework, with its own propulsive dynamism, and with sufficient autonomy to carry it far. . . . The Constitution . . . affords the legal basis for our common effort, excluding intolerance and providing for mutual respect of each other's faiths. . . . We are aiming at a collaboration which is necessary for the consolidation of democracy.[2]

TRENDS WITHIN THE CHRISTIAN DEMOCRAT PARTY

But if the desirability of the coalition was crystal-clear to Signor De Gasperi, it was not accepted with such enthusiasm by the whole of his party. Within the heterogeneous forces now grouped together under the Christian Democrat aegis there were a number of trends which throughout the five years tended to pull in different directions and which it needed all Signor De Gasperi's consummate political skill to reconcile.

[1] Letter of 9 August 1954, published after De Gasperi's death in *Il Popolo*, 21 August 1954—see below, p. 112. The words 'Guelphism' and 'Ghibellinism' may lack force to non-Italian ears; but the terminology of the dispute which in Dante's day split the country between the factions of the Papacy and the Empire has long survived its original context, and still has a vivid meaning in Italy today in denoting the contrast between ecclesiastical and temporal forces.

[2] Quoted in Giorgio Tupini, *I Democratici Cristiani* (Milan, Garzanti, 1954), pp. 253 ff.

In the Centre was the bloc surrounding Signor De Gasperi himself. Many of these were older men, survivors of the Partito Popolare, while others were officials in the party machine. Not many were outstanding, though among the younger generation some few, such as for example Signor Scelba, the Minister of the Interior, were already making a name for themselves. But on the whole the Centre tended to concentrate on party interests rather than on wider issues and, as time went on, to fear encroachments on their own positions.

On the Right were Southern landowning elements, some with monarchical leanings, men with business interests, and rigid Catholics from the middle and upper bourgeoisie. Some of these elements in 1951 became known as the 'Vespisti', from the name of their meeting-place, the Vespa motor-scooter club in Rome—perhaps a somewhat incongruous nomenclature for a group which inevitably became regarded as the conservative wing of the party, though they themselves repudiated any suggestion of reactionary tendencies. Support for them was probably stronger among the electorate than among party leaders—though 74 Deputies and Senators subscribed to the manifesto they issued in December 1951, under the title *Problemi dell'ora e azione di governo,* criticizing the Government's policy in social and economic spheres.

Similar criticisms, but from a different angle, came from the various Left-wing trends within the party which throughout the five years of supremacy provided some of its most vital elements, and which were eventually (after 1953) to gain the upper hand in its counsels. The composition of these trends has varied from time to time, but they may be said to have fallen into three main groups, all adopting a progressive line on social reforms, and each, in the early days, making known its views and criticisms through a newspaper or periodical of its own.[1] These were: (i) a group round Signor Giovanni Gronchi, President of the Chamber, which in November 1948 began to publish a daily paper *La Libertà*, and which stood for greater collaboration with the forces of socialism and adopted a line verging on neutralism concerning Italy's adherence to

[1] The various 'trend' publications of the Christian Democrat groups were eventually suspended early in 1952 when the Party Secretary, Gonella, called for party unity in preparation for the Southern administrative elections.

the Atlantic Pact;[1] (ii) syndical elements, grouped at first round the trade unionist Deputies Ravaioli and Rapelli and later round the Catholic trade union leader Giulio Pastore; (iii) the group which in its early stages might be termed the 'academic' or 'corporativist' Left, whose leaders were Giuseppe Dossetti, Amintore Fanfani, and Professor Giorgio La Pira (later Mayor of Florence), and who between 1947 and 1951 published the review *Cronache Sociali*.

It is this last group which has throughout proved the most interesting and important among the Christian Democrat Left-wing trends. It includes the party's younger and more progressive elements, has consistently laid great stress on social reform, and in its early days, under Dossetti's leadership, showed decided leanings towards a form of Catholic corporativism. Dossetti himself, a Professor of Ecclesiastical Law at the Catholic University in Milan, was something of a visionary, and his constant efforts to associate the party with a tendential Catholic interpretation of social reform came into direct contrast with Signor De Gasperi's own views concerning the desirability of collaboration with the secular elements in the State. No less a visionary, though in some ways a very practical one, was Professor La Pira, who later as Mayor of Florence became a byword throughout Italy for his efforts on behalf of the poor of Florence and for his open championship of workers dismissed from the Pignone factories in the autumn of 1953.[2] These two and the group surrounding them exercised a function of active criticism within the party until towards the end of 1951, when La Pira became Mayor of Florence, Dossetti resigned from the party Directorate and withdrew from political activities, and *Cronache Sociali* suspended publication. At the time a good deal of mystery surrounded the reasons for Dossetti's withdrawal from active politics, which was variously attributed to his own ill-health or to his personal wish for a period of study and meditation. But it also seems likely that the curbing of the effervescent Left-wing trend was felt to be in the interest of the Christian Democrat party as the critical pre-election period approached.

[1] Five years later Signor Gronchi was to be the foremost among the few Christian Democrats who seriously believed in the possibility of an alliance with the Nenni Socialists—see below, p. 100.

[2] See below, p. 104.

There remained the third of the trio of Left-wing progressive leaders, Amintore Fanfani. Of more practical stamp than his companions, but no less dynamic, Fanfani became actively associated with some of the Government's main plans for social reform. As Minister of Labour between 1947 and 1950, he put through the housing scheme associated with his name.[1] In mid-1951, when the *Cronache Sociali* grouping was already going into eclipse, he became Minister of Agriculture and was thus closely concerned with a vital phase of the land reform policy. At the same time he still played an active part within the Christian Democrat party as leader of the Left-wing trend, now known as Iniziativa Democratica, which had succeeded the *Cronache Sociali* grouping. In the years after 1951, and in particular after the salutary shock of the 1953 Election and Fanfani's subsequent failure to form a Government,[2] the group became less intransigent in its views, while at the same time gaining ground. By the time of the Party Congress in Naples of June 1954 it had come to be the strongest current within the party, capturing over two-thirds of the seats on the National Directorate, and Fanfani himself then became party Secretary on Signor De Gasperi's resignation.[3]

These party divisions are a complicated story. But they represented a very important aspect of Italian political life during the five years of Christian Democrat supremacy, inasmuch as the policies of both Right and Left wings of the party were constantly, in varying degrees, pulling in opposite directions from the Centre line of secular collaboration advocated by Signor De Gasperi. To the intransigent Catholics of either wing collaboration with the lay parties was not fundamentally welcome, or regarded as a prime necessity: and both wings at different times tried to urge the advisability of a single-party Christian Democrat Government. The extreme tendencies of either wing, stigmatised as over-clerical, were equally distasteful to the secular parties—quite apart from the constant jockeying for ministerial position that went on between the smaller parties and their predominant ally. It took all Signor De Gasperi's skill as a politician to reconcile these warring trends both between the allied parties and between the factions in his

[1] See below, p. 214. [2] See below, p. 104. [3] See below, p. 112.

own party. As to the latter, a well-known commentator[1] writing after his death suggested that Signor De Gasperi probably regarded as the greatest success of his life as a party man the transformation of the old Dossettian Left into something more moderate—'the grafting of the fundamentally democratic and constitutional spirit of the Partito Popolare on to the intransigents' zeal as social reformers.'

THE PROBLEM OF THE SOCIALISTS

So much for the Christian Democrats' internal difficulties. On the other side of the picture of Centre collaboration, the most problematical yet in many ways the most essential of their allies were the Social Democrats, or PSLI (Partito Socialista dei Lavoratori Italiani), as they were then still called. Essential, because it was in them that the coalition's best hope of enlisting greater support from among the working masses appeared to lie. This had been the basic dream and intention of Signor Saragat's Socialists in effecting their break-away from the Socialist party of Signor Nenni in 1947: to provide a focus for non-confessional and non-Communist working-class opinion. Unfortunately that split proved to be only the first of many dissensions and fragmentations—some of them perpetuated in the name of reunification—which were further to erode the core of Italian Socialism. No small part of these dissensions concerned the question of the PSLI's collaboration in the Government.

Doubts and questionings as to their future course existed on both the Nenni (PSI) and the Saragat (PSLI) sides of the Socialist fence, and on each side there were some who still hoped to effect a bridge between the two. Prominent among these on the PSI side was the well-known Socialist Senator Giuseppe Romita, a Minister in all the post-war tripartite Governments, who at the time of the split in January 1947 had remained in the PSI. In November 1948 he combined with some Centre-Left members of the PSLI and certain prominent independent Socialists (including some former Action Party members) who had not yet taken the step of joining the PSLI[2]

[1] Giuseppe Spadolini, in *Corriere della Sera*, 29 August 1954.

[2] They included the writer Ignazio Silone, the Florentine lawyer Avv. Piero Calamandrei (editor of *Il Ponte*), Professor Ernesto Codignola, and others.

to produce a 'Document for Unification' of the non-Communist Socialist forces. This document proposed that these forces should unite in a party which, to avoid giving the country the impression that it was too closely associated with the Christian Democrats, should go over to the Opposition. A few months later further weight was lent to the idea of unification by the action of the International Socialist Conference (Comisco) which in March 1949 expelled the PSI from Comisco and made known its favourable attitude towards a unification of the non-Communist Socialist groups in Italy.

By this time another source of disagreement had come to the fore in the question of Italy's adherence to the Atlantic Pact, which was being fiercely debated in Parliament during the spring of 1949, and on which the PSLI itself was divided, its Left-wing elements being opposed to the Government's policy as were also the groups of Silone and Romita (who had by now been expelled from the PSI). Yet another dispute centred round the question of trade union affiliation: in June 1949 the PSLI representatives, together with the Republicans, broke away from the Communist-dominated CGIL to form a free and non-confessional trade union, the Federazione Italiana del Lavoro (FIL).

It was in this atmosphere that a Congress for Socialist Unification took place in Florence on 4–8 December 1949. This was planned as a full-dress affair leading up to a merger between all the non-Communist Socialist groups. But before it took place Signor Saragat made known his refusal to take part, while at the same time tendering his own resignation and that of the two other PSLI Ministers from the Government. The Right-wing trend of the PSLI also held aloof from the Congress, which was consequently attended only by the Romita–Silone groups and by the Left and some Centre elements of the PSLI. Far from achieving unification, it resulted in the formation of yet another Socialist party, the Partito Socialista Unitario (PSU), which for some time to come was to contest with the PSLI for the blessing of Comisco.

The PSLI, shorn of its Left wing, affirmed at its congress in January 1950 its 'conditional confidence' in the Government, and PSLI Ministers were therefore included in the new

Cabinet which Signor De Gasperi formed, without the Liberals, at the end of January 1950. Ironically enough, it was at about this time, when the Liberals were already quitting the coalition and the non-Communist Socialists were providing a remarkable display of disunity, that a good deal was heard of the need for a 'third force' in Italian politics. This 'third force' was to consist of an alliance of the three lay democratic parties and should stand between the two extremes of Communism and 'clerical' Christian Democracy. Its advocates included such men as the prominent Republican Minister Ugo La Malfa and the Left-wing Liberal Count Niccolò Carandini (who was Italian Ambassador in London at the end of the war). The latter, in an article in *Il Mondo* (5 November 1949), outlined the need for such a 'third force'. Democratic Socialism and Liberalism, he said, could not hope by acting separately to exercise a normalising influence on Italian life:

> It is useless to conceal from ourselves that, failing an agreement between the minor democratic forces, there will be nothing left for them but a prolonged state of dependence on one or other of the two most powerful Italian parties. In Italy today the institutions of democracy exist but the spirit is lacking. The great mass of Italian democratic opinion lives entrenched against Communism, seeks of Christian Democracy the right of asylum, and grows flaccid in an atmosphere of tepid liberty.

The need for a 'third force' plainly existed, but the parties who should have composed it continued to go their own ways. In the Socialist camps, in particular, bickerings and uncertainties continued throughout 1950. Unification of the non-Communist forces was still discussed, and was repeatedly urged by Comisco; but to the other groups outside the continued presence of the PSLI in the Government, which implied approval of the Atlantic Pact policy, seemed to constitute an insuperable barrier. There was also trouble in the labour field: in April a split arose in the newly-formed free trade union, the FIL, one section joining the hitherto largely Catholic union, the CISL, while the other formed a new union, the Unione Italiana del Lavoro (UIL) in collaboration with the PSU syndicalists who meanwhile had left the CGIL. But at least the waverers were all gradually burning their boats and moving away from the Nenni party, in whose eyes they had of course become the arch-traitors. The PSU's leanings towards European federalism gradually gained the upper hand over their objections to the Government's foreign policy in relation to the other Western combination, NATO, and by October 1950 they were stating that Socialism must now 'continue the struggle for peace from less advanced positions such as those constituted by the Atlantic Pact.'[1] This was a far cry from their earlier intransigence.

In January 1951 an event occurred which, while it may not have greatly influenced the now growing trend towards unification, undoubtedly provided a fillip for non-Communist Socialism. This was the withdrawal from the Communist Party of two Communist Deputies, Aldo Cucchi and Valdo Magnani, both former prominent Resistance leaders, who resigned on the ground, among other reasons, of their objection to the Communist line that, in the event of a war in which the Soviet army was forced to follow the aggressor on to Italian soil, it would be the people's duty to support the Russians.[2] The resignation of these two Communists did not have the far-reaching political effects which some optimistic foreign observers anticipated. But it, and the reasons for it, encouraged the democratic Socialist trends and intensified their detachment from the fellow-travelling wing.[3]

The long-discussed unification of the PSLI and PSU was at last effected on 1 May 1951. Each side had to make some compromise, the PSLI agreeing to withdraw from the Government, while the PSU reluctantly abandoned its opposition to the Atlantic Pact policy. The new unified party was at first given the cumbersome name of Partito Socialista (Sezione Italiana dell' Internazionale Socialista); in the following January the name was changed to the present title of Partito Socialista Democratico Italiano (PSDI). The position of the

[1] *Pace e Libertà. Quaderni socialisti*, 1 (PSU, Rome, 1950), p. 12.

[2] This line was first enunciated by Togliatti (following a similar statement by the French Communist leader Thorez) in February 1949 at the time of the debate on Italy's membership of NATO (see, e.g., interview in *Corriere della Sera*, 27 February 1949). It came into prominence again in the autumn of 1950 during the Left campaign against the Korean war.

[3] Cucchi and Magnani did not, as was at first thought likely, join the democratic Socialists, though they were in close touch with Signor Silone. Instead they formed a movement known as the Unione dei Socialisti Indipendenti.

Social Democrats was at last stabilized, but at the sacrifice of their collaboration in the Government. As matters turned out, they were not to return to it for the next three years. Until the June 1953 Election the Christian Democrats' sole ally in the Government was the small Republican party.

CHAPTER VIII

LOCAL ELECTIONS OF 1951–2 AND THE RISE OF THE RIGHT

Though only two of the original four coalition parties remained in the Government after the spring of 1951, the Social Democrats and Liberals continued to support the Government in Parliament. The four parties also presented a fairly united front in the local elections which were held throughout Northern Italy in May and June of 1951 (the second round, in Rome and the South, being held over till 1952), and for which the system of 'related' electoral lists was for the first time adopted.

This was the first trial of strength between the parties since April 1948, and though the elections were only for local bodies —Provincial and Communal Councils—they could be regarded as a provisional verdict on what the Government had hitherto accomplished; and international as well as domestic issues played a considerable part in the election campaign. By this time, despite delays concerning which the Left parties hotly accused the Government but for which their own obstructive tactics in Parliament were to a considerable extent responsible, a serious beginning had been made with some of the most important reforms. The land reform, begun in the Sila in 1950, was now under way throughout Southern Italy; the Cassa per il Mezzogiorno was working out long-term plans for the development of the South; and the new taxation reform was to come into effect in the autumn.[1] Moreover financial stability had been securely achieved and industry was making good progress. On the other hand defence expenditure was being stepped up to enable Italy to meet her obligations under NATO, and this and the rearmament policy as a whole came under heavy fire from the Left; while no serious impression had been made on such perennial long-term problems as unemployment and even housing.

[1] See below, pp. 200, 204, 183–5.

Nevertheless the election results, though they sounded a warning note, were not yet alarming to the Government. Indeed the Christian Democrats in combination with the other Centre parties succeeded in winning over a number of communes from the Left, including such important strongholds as Turin, Venice, and Florence. But the number of votes polled showed no perceptible decline in Communist strength and an unexpected increase for the PSI, while the Christian Democrat vote was considerably reduced by comparison with the sweeping successes of 1948. Thus it seemed that despite the various assaults on the Left during the past three years—the trade union split, the draining away from the PSI to the non-Communist Socialists, the Cucchi–Magnani defection, Signor Scelba's sternly repressive measures, and the excommunication decree pronounced by the Vatican against members of the Communist Party in mid-1949—there had been no serious weakening of Communist-Socialist strength in the North.

The counterpart of these local elections in Rome and the South, held a year later (May-June 1952), was to provide a further shock, and from a different quarter as well. Here in the South the impact of the land reform had been little short of explosive. The reforms initiated were still in a transitional stage, and their benefits were by no means universally apparent. They had been ridiculed and belittled by the Communists, who claimed, first, that nothing of significance would be done, and later, when the reform's serious intent began to emerge, that the Government would never have moved but for the fright it received from the (Communist-inspired) occupation of land by the peasants in the autumn of 1949. The peasants, who in many cases were receiving from the Communists the first form of political education they had ever experienced, were in no position to assess the truth of these statements. The Left vote in the South, instead of falling as a result of the Government's efforts there, increased by more than 200,000 over the 1948 figure.

But this was not all. If the peasants were still suspicious and uncertain what to make of the new efforts on their behalf, the landowners' verdict was swift and definite. The land reform meant an attack on all their traditional privileges and position, and they uncompromisingly condemned it. The votes of the

Right-wing parties, the Monarchists and the MSI, more than doubled the 1948 figure, reaching over 1,600,000, or 23·4 per cent of the total. This gain was almost entirely at the expense of the Christian Democrats and Liberals, who lost respectively 1,400,000 and 230,000 votes.

This striking resurgence of the Right was not of course to be attributed solely to the effects of the land reform. Southern Italy is by tradition much more closely attached to the monarchy than was ever the case in the much more politically conscious North, and it was from here that a large proportion of the votes for the retention of the monarchy came in 1946. The reasons that prompted that vote had not been greatly attenuated in the intervening years; rather, indeed, the reverse. They had been difficult years of hard struggle and small immediate benefits for most of the populace except a few fortunate speculators, and it was easy for Southerners to listen to the propaganda of the Monarchist leader Achille Lauro (himself one of the fortunate), who, backed by his own immense resources, proclaimed up and down the countryside that the past glories of the *patria* must be revived and that the present Republican Government was not the one to do so. The emotional appeal of this nostalgic oratory evoked a ready response. Moreover Southerners had a lurking admiration for Lauro himself: he was one of themselves, and they basked in the reflected glory of his success, while his prolific spending recalled the traditional magnificence of the Bourbon courts. Neapolitans forgot that now, as then, they could expect little share in the magnificence beyond the free spaghetti which Lauro distributed—and voted for him. The Monarchist vote in the South in fact rose from 5·9 to 9·7 per cent of the total. The advance of the MSI, hitherto the lesser partner in the Right-wing alliance, was even more spectacular. From 276,000 votes in 1948, their poll increased in 1952 to 790,000, or more than 11 per cent of the total.

During the electoral campaign a curious episode had occurred which, while probably over-dramatised at the time, served to emphasise the difficult situation in which Christian Democracy now found itself, assailed from both Left and Right. Fears of Communist gains in the election, coupled with a realisation of the weakness of the smaller Centre parties in the South, had caused the Christian Democrat party Secretary, Gonella, to consider the possibility of forming alliances, in certain constituencies, with the Monarchists. The idea was viewed with strong distaste by the Republicans and Social Democrats; and it was in any case to be made conditional on the Monarchists' repudiation of their alliance with the MSI. In fact it came to nothing because Lauro eventually refused to renounce the MSI alliance. But further in the background another and less official attempt was being made to link up Right-wing Catholic opinion with the Monarchists (who in the minds of many represented not so much a positive desire for the restoration of the monarchy as an outlet for Conservative views) and even with their neo-Fascist electoral allies. Manoeuvrings in this direction went on during April 1952, closely linked with the name of Professor Luigi Gedda, President of Catholic Action, and supported by the well-known preacher Padre Lombardi. The Christian Democrat party never lent its approval to these overtures (Signor De Gasperi himself had by now openly repudiated any alliance with the Monarchists) but the projected Right-wing grouping got so far as to put forward, on the eve of the poll, a proposal for an anti-Communist 'civic list' of candidates for the election in Rome to which no less a person than Don Luigi Sturzo was at first persuaded to lend his name.

Once again the proposal came to nothing, for Don Sturzo realised in time the dangers of the situation and withdrew his support. But the episode served to underline how Signor De Gasperi's desire for a middle-of-the-way policy was not necessarily shared by all shades of Catholic opinion. Christian Democracy had always had to move carefully to maintain a just balance in its relations with Catholic Action, the Church's lay arm. Catholic Action had in the past played a considerable role in keeping Christian Democrat forces together during the clandestine period, and later through its political action committees, the *comitati civici*. But Signor De Gasperi had always striven to maintain a strict distinction between the political and the religious spheres and hence to keep the Christian Democrat party free from undue dependence on religious authorities—a distinction not welcomed by Professor Gedda, in whose view the *comitati civici* which he organised were justified in embarking if necessary on direct political intervention for the 'Christian reconquest of Italy'. This whole question of the relations between the Christian Democrat party and Catholic Action, and of Christian Democrat independence of the religious authorities (including also the degree of approval accorded to the Christian Democrats by the Vatican), is of course an ever-present one. It came up in acute form at this particular moment of pre-election tensions, and soon died down again; but it is inevitably a constant preoccupation of Christian Democrat leaders.

One of the reasons why the proposed combination was widely viewed with alarm was because it seemed likely, via the Monarchist–MSI alliance, to involve closer contact with the neo-Fascists. The MSI had in fact by 1952, aided by a few powerful backers, built up some sort of status for itself.[1] The climate in the country had changed perceptibly since the immediate post-war days, and while in ardent anti-Fascist circles the whole subject of the former régime was still anathema, there was in general a greater tolerance towards its lesser adherents. This did not mean that in the country as a whole there was any widespread desire to return to Fascism: on the contrary, most people seemed to regard it as a sort of disease from which, once cured, Italy would in future be immune. But former Fascists were now no longer boycotted to the same extent as formerly. Practically all of those imprisoned after the war had by now been released; the initial embarrassments of their return to circulation had worn off, and though they occupied no important posts, and indeed often found it difficult to make a living, Italian tolerance had reasserted itself and they were no longer generally regarded as pariahs. Among the few surviving 'big shots' most were now elderly and lived in retirement. Count Grandi, the most prominent surviving member of the Fascist Grand Council, continued to live in Brazil, whither he had gone from Portugal in 1946; but—once again a sign of the changed climate—he now sometimes openly visited Italy on business.

The absence of prominent leaders undoubtedly handicapped the MSI: in a movement based on totalitarian ideas the *Führerprinzip* still counted. But no new Duce emerged on

[1] For its origins see above, p. 57, note.

whom his mantle could naturally fall, and the only well-known figures of the past whom the MSI succeeded in enlisting proved but inadequate substitutes. After Marshal Graziani's release from prison under various amnesty provisions in August 1950, when he was nearing 70, the MSI tried to build him up as the party's main figure; but his chequered relations with it proved an embarrassment rather than an asset. In the spring of 1952 he played some part in the attempt to form a Right-wing Catholic–Monarchist–MSI bloc; but he periodically resigned from the party owing to disagreements, and during the 1953 election campaign even appeared on a Christian Democrat platform in his home town of Arcinazzo to proclaim that Fascism could not revive and the present Government had done miracles.[1] The MSI were not much more fortunate in their other would-be leader, Prince Valerio Borghese. This much younger man, known during the war as Commander of the Tenth MAS Submarine Flotilla, was elected President of the MSI in December 1951; but he proved lukewarm and at times unorthodox, and resigned from the Presidency in 1954.

Lacking an outstanding leader, the chief moving spirits in the MSI were the party Secretary, Augusto De Marsanich (a former Vice-Secretary of the Fascist Party) and a few other former Fascists such as Giorgio Almirante and the journalists Giorgio Pini and Concetto Pettinato. But the party suffered from constant divisions arising out of the different backgrounds and views of its members: former Fascists of the North, originally basing their aims on the 'Social Republican' programme of Salò[2] (though this soon became outdated), were of tougher calibre, and held more extreme views, than the nostalgics of the South who might on occasion be lenient towards the monarchy.

Though the line of descent was never in doubt, the MSI was careful not to stress its provenance publicly. This discretion was dictated as much as anything by tactical reasons: an MSI Congress arranged to be held in Bari in October 1950 was prohibited by the chief of police on the ground that some

[1] Marshal Graziani died in January 1955. His memoirs, a turgid defence of his actions during the period of Fascism and of the Salò Republic, were published in 1948 (*Ho difeso la Patria*, Milan, Garzanti).

[2] As framed in the Verona Manifesto of November 1943 (text in Muriel Grindrod, *The New Italy*, 1947).

of the party's members were known to have defended Fascism, and a month later a law for the suppression of Fascist activities was introduced in Parliament and approved the following year. At this period some alarm was felt at the advances which the MSI was said to be making among university students, though elections to their representative bodies showed that the proportion of neo-Fascists was no higher than that in Parliament. The party had its own youth movement, and it later formed a trade union, the CISNAL, which advocated the socialisation of factories but does not seem to have gained much effective adherence among the workers.[1] From May 1952 it had the support of a Rome daily newspaper, *Il Secolo*, edited by Bruno Spampanati, formerly editor of *Il Messaggero* under the Fascist régime, and with Almirante and the ex-diplomat Filippo Anfuso among its political directors. At the time of the party Congress which the MSI was at last permitted to hold in July 1952 at Aquila, in the Abruzzi (not far from the Duce's former place of confinement in the Gran Sasso), membership was claimed to have reached over 600,000. After its success in the Southern administrative elections the party proceeded cautiously and the Congress passed off without fireworks, black shirts, or Fascist canticles. It passed a resolution advocating a national State based on labour—'which only a Republic can guarantee'—with a corporative socialised economy, and even announced that it was now in favour of the Atlantic Pact.

[1] By early in 1955 the CISNAL had made some headway in a few individual concerns—e.g., in the factory committee elections at the Dalmine works (Massa) in January 1955 it obtained 197 votes and 1 seat, as against the CGIL's 393 votes and 3 seats and the CISL's 212 votes and 2 seats (*Il Tempo*, 12 January 1955).

CHAPTER IX

THE GENERAL ELECTION OF 7 JUNE 1953

By the autumn of 1952 the General Election due in mid-1953, when the Chamber's statutory five-year term of office ended, was already the main preoccupation. To the Centre parties, and to the Christian Democrats in particular, the administrative elections had shown that they could no longer count on an overwhelming vote such as they obtained in 1948. They had behind them, moreover, years of bitter experience of frustrations and delays in Parliament due to the wilfully obstructive tactics of the Left. The Christian Democrat leaders therefore sought to discover some method whereby, in the next Parliament, such obstruction should be minimised and the governing parties should be assured of a stable working majority. With this end in view it was decided to replace the electoral law of 1948, which provided for a modified form of proportional representation, by a new law compromising between the majority and the proportional systems. Its main feature was that any party or group of parties obtaining more than half (i.e. 50·01 per cent) of the total votes should be awarded a bonus of seats bringing their total number of seats up to nearly two-thirds of the entire House: this meant in practice that the successful party or group of parties would be entitled to 380 out of 590 seats.

From the outset this proposal aroused widespread opposition. From the non-Government parties this was inevitable, for it was at that time considered practically as a foregone conclusion that the Christian Democrats with their lesser allies would obtain the necessary majority, and the other parties, both of Left and Right, condemned the new law as a barefaced attempt to perpetuate Christian Democrat predominance: the Communists at once christened it the *legge truffa*, or swindle-law, and the name stuck. The Centre parties themselves were far from happy about the law. Even its Christian Democrat promoters seemed sometimes, by the very frequence and plausibility of their explanations of the need for it and by their stress on its constitutional character, to show signs of inward uncertainties. It was constantly argued that the new law would benefit the smaller parties, who would receive their share of the bonus of seats. But the Liberals and Republicans, though acquiescent, were unenthusiastic, and the Social Democrats at one time seemed likely to jeopardise the whole Centre alliance by their vacillations. At their Party Congress in Bologna in January 1953 they had continued to oppose collaboration in the Government and voted in favour of 'pure' proportional representation in the next Election; but at a further Congress in Genoa in October Signor Saragat's more moderate centre faction gained the ascendancy and the Bologna decisions were virtually reversed. It thus became possible for the four Centre parties to reach an agreement, on 15 November, to present 'related lists' in the General Election, as they had done already in the earlier administrative elections. The Communists and Socialists, on the other hand, each decided to stand separately, abandoning the 'Popular Democratic Front' tactics of 1948; and the Monarchists and MSI also abandoned their earlier electoral alliance.

Discussion of the electoral law Bill began in the Chamber on 8 December and at once ran into heavy weather. Opposition came not only from the usual quarters but also, and more cogently, from seven dissident members of the PSDI on whose behalf Avv. Piero Calamandrei spoke forcibly against the Bill on 12 December. He and his fellow-rebels were suspended by the PSDI executive and resigned from the party to form a new group known as Unità Popolare which stood as an independent party in the following June.[1] But despite this setback and the delaying tactics employed by the Opposition, who tabled no less than 220 amendments, the Bill was passed by the Chamber on 21 January 1953 by 339 votes to 25. The adverse votes came from the Monarchists, the MSI, and the dissident PSDIs,

[1] The Unità Popolare group included some of the most outstanding individual figures among the non-Communist anti-Fascists of the Resistance period, several of them formerly members of the Action Party. Senator Parri, Italy's first post-war Premier, became its leader, and besides Avv. Calamandrei the new party included such men as Tristano Codignola, Avv. Antonio Greppi, the former Socialist Mayor of Milan (he eventually reverted to the Nenni Socialist Party in November 1954), and Professor Arturo Carlo Jemolo, the well-known author of *Chiesa e Stato in Italia negli ultimi cento anni* (Rome, 1948).

while the Communists and Socialists walked out before voting took place.

After this tussle it was generally thought that the Bill would have an easier passage through the Senate. But this optimism proved mistaken. The Left, relatively stronger in the Senate than in the Chamber, used every conceivable method to prolong the debate until it should be too late for the Bill to come into effect (for technical reasons the Election had to take place by early June, and the date had been already postponed from 31 May to 7 June). These tactics culminated during the last week in March in sittings so stormy that free fights took place. Parliamentary prestige was gravely compromised, and the elderly President of the Senate, Giuseppe Paratore, tendered his resignation. The final vote was taken on 29 March in conditions of such chaos that the Left failed to vote at all because, as one correspondent put it, they were too busy fighting their colleagues. Consequently the Bill was passed by 174 votes to none, out of a total of 350.

As a result of this attack on the authority of Parliament Signor De Gasperi decided to recommend the dissolution of the Senate as well as the Chamber. The Senate would normally have continued in office till 1954, since under the Constitution it is elected for a six-year term. Its unforeseen dissolution in 1953 created a fresh problem, for the new electoral law applied only to elections for the Chamber. The Senate elections therefore had to be carried out under the old law of 1948, and thus by a quite different procedure for which the contemplated electoral alliances might prove less well suited. There was, moreover, the still unsettled question of the 'Senators by right'—those Senators, eighty-seven in number, who under a temporary provision appended to the Constitution had been nominated to the first Parliament of the Republic either because they had already held office as Senators or anti-Fascist Deputies in earlier Parliaments or because they had suffered long terms of imprisonment under Fascism. This provision, framed in the first ardour of anti-Fascist regeneration, not unnaturally had the effect of increasing the proportion of Left-wing Senators: in fact thirty-nine of the eighty-seven were Communists. Were they to be automatically reappointed or not? There was no time for fresh legislation on the subject, so as far as the 1953 Election was concerned these former Senators 'by right' had to stand for election in the ordinary way. The eventual decision concerning the office of 'Senator by right' was left over for discussion by the next Parliament, which was also to deal with the reform of the Senate as a whole; but the subject had not yet been debated by mid-1955.

However, the electoral law had struggled through Parliament in the nick of time, and if some of its sponsors began to feel qualms as to its wisdom in view of the opposition it had aroused in the country no less than in Parliament, the ardours of the electoral campaign allowed of no display of doubts. The campaign followed its inevitable course. More and larger posters were displayed each day on every available wall, to be torn down at night and replaced at dawn by a willing army of small boys with ladders and paste-pots. Election speeches were made in every town and hamlet, often several of them on the same night as election day approached, with the rival politicians competing for the best position in the piazza, or, if there was only one good platform available, succeeding each other like Jacks-in-the-box. The Government's posters and speakers sought to persuade by lengthy citation of statistics as to the benefits it had brought—so many kilometres of new roads in the South, so many peasants given land under the reform. The Opposition attacked anything and everything the Government had done, including, of course, the *legge truffa*. The crowds stood and listened to it all, giving nothing away. There were remarkably few 'incidents', and from their demeanour it was impossible to tell which way their votes would go.

Certain external episodes, dropping like pebbles into this already seething pool, created ever-widening circles. Sir Winston Churchill's 'Locarno' speech of 11 May intensified the hopes that many Italians were already beginning to entertain about the possibility of an international détente: should these prove founded, they argued, should a change in Russian intentions really come about, where was the need for all this intensive rearmament, for the too close association of Italy with the United States and the other Western Powers, for the Government's insistence on speedy ratification of the EDC treaty? Such questionings all provided grist for the Communist mill. So too did a reference in a speech of 18 May by the United States Ambassador in Italy, Mrs Clare Luce, to the 'grave consequences' to Italo-American co-operation which might ensue should the Italians fall victim to 'totalitarianisms of Right or Left'. For the Right, even the coronation in Britain of Queen Elizabeth II provided a talking point, and this event, taking place only five days before the Election, undoubtedly had some effect in stirring up nostalgic memories and in emphasising the contrast between the panoply of monarchy, especially dear to Southern Italian hearts, and the seeming drabness of life under a Republic.

But behind these occasional focusing-points of criticism there was a more abiding discontent, arising from both domestic and foreign causes. On the external side, it was obvious that the Election was taking place in very different conditions from those of 1948. It will be recalled that the main issue at that time concerned Italy's relations with the outer world: was she to remain within the Western orbit (thus qualifying for Marshall aid) and stand firm against Communism? Czechoslovakia's fate was then still fresh in men's minds; while the Western Powers' tripartite statement concerning the return of Trieste to Italy[1] undoubtedly played a part in influencing voters in favour of the Western orientation. In 1953 these external considerations no longer had the same force. The choice for the West had been made, bringing with it the undoubted benefits of Marshall aid which, however, had come to be taken rather as a matter of course by most of the populace. Familiarity had come to breed a mistrust of Italy's close association with the United States as a beneficiary, which carried with it the obligation of rearmament and gave the Americans the opportunity to interfere unduly, as the critics argued, in Italian affairs. In this feeling of impatience at tutelage there was a tendency to overlook the invaluable assistance which Italy had derived from American aid in carrying out post-war reconstruction, in the revival and re-equipment of industry, and in embarking on her ambitious long-term plans for the development of the South. To the Left, of course, the Western orientation, the 'subservience' to America and all that it entailed, was a perpetual subject for attack; and the Right too, while paying lip service to the Atlantic alliance,

[1] See above, p. 56.

reproached the Government with lack of independence and initiative in its foreign policy, pointing as an example to the still unsettled question of Trieste.

But on the whole domestic issues were the more important in 1953. Here again, though specific points of controversy existed, for the ordinary elector objections to the existing Government arose as much as anything from a vague malaise and a weariness of any Government that had been in power for five years. People had grown tired of the Christian Democrats with their rather humdrum and pedestrian virtues, and they tended to ignore the benefits they had brought: the country's financial stability under their régime, the revival of its industry and commerce, the unprecedented attention now being given to the neglected South—and the fact that Italy had survived the post-war years without major upheaval, had evolved a system of normal democratic and parliamentary government, and had regained a respected place among the other nations of the world. All this—and the possible alternatives—seemed for the time being unimportant in comparison with the drawbacks of the régime. Among the more specific reproaches made against the Christian Democrats (for they, as the predominant partners, inevitably came in for most of the blame) were the Government's slowness in initiating much-needed social reforms and in implementing the legislation required by the Constitution; their alleged tendency to plant their own supporters in all the best jobs; their too strongly marked clerical associations; the swollen bureaucracy; the repressive methods of Signor Scelba's police; and, above all, the general feeling that they were becoming too high-handed, too *prepotente*—and were seeking to perpetuate their predominance by means of the *legge truffa*.[1] Yet another weapon turned against the Government was its most outstanding innovation in the sphere of social reform, its policy of land reform: it has been seen how this policy virtually operated against the Government in the Southern administrative elections of 1952. A year later its effect was to be no less critical.

[1] In the words of some of its most articulate critics, those of the Unità Popolare group, Christian Democracy was 'aiming solely at ensuring for itself in both Houses of Parliament that fictitious exclusive majority which it well knows it no longer commands in the country' (Unità Popolare election manifesto, published in the party's fortnightly news-sheet *Nuova Repubblica*, Florence, 20 April 1953).

ITALIAN ELECTIONS, 1953 and 1948

CHAMBER

7 JUNE 1953

Parties	Votes	Seats	Per cent of Total
CENTRE			
Christian Democrats	10,834,466	261	40·08
Social Democrats (PSDI)	1,222,957	19	4·52
Liberal Party (PLI)	815,929	14	3·14
Republican Party (PRI)	438,149	5	1·61
Sard Action Party	27,231	—	0·1
South Tyrol Christian Democrats	122,474	3	0·3
Val d'Aosta Christian Democrats	27,607	1	0·1
TOTAL	13,488,813	303	49·85
LEFT			
Communist Party (PCI)	6,120,709	143	22·7
Socialist Party (PSI)	3,441,014	75	12·7
			35·4
Unione Socialisti Indipendenti (Cucchi–Magnani)	225,409	—	0·8
Unità Popolare (Parri)	171,099	—	0·6
Alleanza Democratica Nazionale (Corbino)	120,685	—	0·4
			37·2
RIGHT			
Monarchist Party (PNM)	1,854,850	40	6·85
Movimento Sociale Italiano (MSI)	1,579,880	29	5·83
Others	85,142	—	0·27
OPPOSITION TOTAL	13,598,788	287	50·15
TOTAL SEATS		590	

18 APRIL 1948

Parties	Votes	Seats	Per cent of Total
CENTRE			
Christian Democrats	12,712,762	305	48·5
Social Democrats (Unità Socialista)	1,858,346	33	7·1
Liberal Party (Blocco Nazionale)	1,004,889	19	3·8
Republican Party	652,477	9	2·5
Sard Action Party	64,201	1	0·3
South Tyrol Christian Democrats	122,781	3	0·5
TOTAL	16,415,456	370	62·7
LEFT			
Democratic Popular Front (Communist and Socialist)	8,137,047	183 (131+52)	31·0
RIGHT			
Monarchist Party (PNM)	729,174	14	2·8
Movimento Sociale Italiano (MSI)	526,670	6	2·1
Others	383,947	1	1·4
OPPOSITION TOTAL	9,776,838	204	37·3
TOTAL SEATS		574	

Senate

7 June 1953

Parties	Votes	Seats	Per cent of Total
CENTRE			
Christian Democrats	9,894,754	116	40·7
Social Democrats (PSDI)	988,778	4	4·1
Liberal Party (PLI)	720,698	3	3·0
Republican Party (PRI)	225,611	—	0·9
Others (S. Tyrol CDs, Sard Action Party, etc.)	366,317	2	1·5
TOTAL	12,196,158	125	50·2
LEFT			
Communist Party (PCI)	5,080,143	54	20·9
Socialist Party (PSI)	2,929,906	28	12·1
Socialist-Communist joint lists	418,940	4	1·7
Alleanza Democratica Nazionale	197,482	1	0·8
Unità Popolare	230,370	—	1·0
RIGHT			
Monarchist Party (PNM)	1,734,275	16	7·1
Movimento Sociale Italiano (MSI)	1,482,101	9	6·1
Others (Right-wing independents)	30,171	—	0·1
OPPOSITION TOTAL	12,103,388	112	49·8
TOTAL SEATS		237	

18 April 1948

Parties	Votes	Total Seats	Seats Elected	Seats by Right*	Per cent of Total
CENTRE					
Christian Democrats	10,740,131	149	131	18	48·1
Social Democrats (Unità Socialista)	1,580,722	22	10	12	6·2
Liberal Party (Blocco Nazionale)	1,364,741	31	9	22	5·4
Republican Party	637,433	10	5	5	2·6
S. Tyrol CDs / Trentino independents	278,351	3	3	—	1·6
Sard Action Party	65,242	1	1	—	0·2
TOTAL	14,666,620	216	159	57	64·1
LEFT					
Democratic Popular Front (Com. & Soc.)	6,955,229	117	72	45	30·8
RIGHT					
Monarchist Party (PNM)	436,597	6	3	3	2·0
Movimento Sociale Italiano (MSI)	244,646	1	1	—	1·6
Others		4	2	2	1·5
OPPOSITION TOTAL	7,636,472	128	78	50	35·9
TOTAL SEATS		344	237	107	

* i.e. the Senators appointed 'by right' on a basis of pre-Fascist parliamentary service or anti-Fascist record—see above, p. 84.
(SOURCE: *Relazioni Internazionali*, 20 June 1953.)

By the time the election day, 7 June, was reached it was realised even in Government circles that the outcome was going to be a very near thing: though even then a Centre majority, if of only 52 or 53 per cent, was widely expected; and it was in that expectation that many people, as a last if probably useless gesture of defiance, cast their votes for one of the smaller Opposition parties. The results proved that such gestures had their cumulative effect. In the voting for the Chamber the Centre parties obtained 49·85 per cent of the total number of votes, thus failing by a mere 57,000 votes to reach the required majority which would have brought into operation the electoral law's promised bonus of seats.[1] The votes given to either of the main splinter parties which came into being largely in protest against the electoral law (the Unità Popolare of Senator Parri and the dissident PSDIs, and the Alleanza Democratica Nazionale led by the former Liberal Senator Epicarmo Corbino) would have more than sufficed to make up this deficiency. The law had in fact proved completely *controproducente*, to use that most expressive Italian word which can perhaps be translated as self-defeating. Ironically enough, in the voting for the Senate, under the old method, the Centre parties obtained just over half the total votes —50·2 per cent.

The Christian Democrats still remained the largest party; but, though their total poll was higher than in the administrative elections, they had lost over 2 million votes since 1948. Proportionately, their smaller allies, the lay democratic parties, had sustained even heavier losses—the Republican party, in particular, achieved only half its 1946 poll, and lost ground even in its traditional strongholds of the Marche and Tuscany. On the Left, the joint Communist-Socialist vote had increased by over 1,400,000, with Socialist gains accounting for a considerably larger proportion than in 1948. The small splinter parties (classified above with the Left, though none of them was in outright sympathy with the Left-wing mass parties)

[1] There were over 1½ million spoilt votes—votes defaced or disqualified for some other technical reason. After the Election it was widely thought that among these votes were far more than enough in favour of the Centre parties to have ensured them the majority needed to bring the bonus into operation. But the Government, sensing the temper of the country, decided to do nothing about them.

obtained no seats at all in the Chamber and only one, for the Alleanza Democratica Nazionale, in the Senate. That party and, more especially, Unità Popolare had had their effect, as has been seen, in detracting votes from the Centre; but their breakaway meant virtual political suicide for their leaders, and those of Unità Popolare were of a calibre that could ill be spared from Parliament. On the Right, both the Monarchist party and the MSI greatly increased their vote. Monarchist gains, mainly at the expense of the Christian Democrats and Liberals, brought their poll for the Chamber to two and a half times that of 1948, while the MSI vote trebled, and the increases in both cases were even greater in the voting for the Senate.

In the main, the causes which had produced the advance of the PNM and the MSI in the Southern administrative elections of 1952 were still valid in 1953, when the South was responsible for a major proportion of their votes. Opposition to the Government's land reform policy probably remained the greatest single factor in their success, though the nationalistic character of their propaganda also evoked some response. As far as the MSI, in particular, was concerned, the Election of 1953 was of course fought in quite different circumstances from those of 1948: not only had the party had five years in which to consolidate itself but also the ban forbidding prominent former Fascists from voting or standing for election now no longer applied. The result was the emergence in the 1953 Parliament under the MSI aegis of several former Fascists who had remained under a cloud in the early post-war years, such as, for example, the ex-Fascist diplomat Filippo Anfuso and the well-known propagandist Ezio Maria Gray; while some more moderate ex-Fascists stood as PNM candidates. While in the North the MSI improved its position as compared with the vote in the administrative elections, in the South its poll was lower than in 1952, largely owing to losses to the PNM, whose votes rose 9·71 to 13·64 per cent of the total Southern poll. An interesting pointer which suggested that young people were not, as had sometimes been feared, being attracted in large numbers to the MSI was the fact that this party's increases were proportionately much greater in the voting for the Senate (where the minimum voting age was 25) than in that for the Chamber (minimum age 21). This was also true of the Monarchist vote.

On the other hand estimates suggested that the proportion of young people voting for the Communist and Socialist parties was relatively high.[1] But the major responsibility for the Left's advance lay, as subsequent analyses of post-war election results showed,[2] in the South. In the industrial North, regarded in the early post-war years as the main stronghold of Communism, and in the Centre, the Left vote reached its highest point in 1946, with a total of some 7¼ million, representing just over 50 per cent of the electorate in those regions; in 1948 it dropped by about 1½ million votes, and though it recovered some 600,000 in 1953, it still remained more than 900,000 votes below the 1946 figure. In fact, it seems possible that in these more highly developed regions of Italy the Left may have reached its limits of expansion.

In the South, on the other hand, the picture is very different. The gradual awakening of political awareness and consequent strife in the remote Southern villages has been well described by Rocco Scotellaro, himself from Lucania, in his *Contadini del Sud*, a book which rivals Carlo Levi's in its portrayal of peasant life in the South.[3] He tells how in 1946 his own district of Lucania, the Alto Materano, largely succumbed to the Uomo Qualunque party, and after its eclipse was bitterly contested between Christian Democracy and Communism:

> In those hamlets there reigned at first a sort of poor 'Qualunquismo', made up of disorganised impulses and reactions. The peasants continued to till the soil; the landowners, the elementary school teachers, the former local Fascist officials, critical of the new liberty, were waiting to see how things would go before committing themselves. In these small places . . . the petty and medium bourgeoisie consists chiefly of farmers and professional men, and is eminently lacking in leaders: public office is always carried out by

[1] See, e.g., Elio Caranti, *Sociologia e statistica delle elezioni italiane nel dopoguerra* (Rome, Editrice Studium, 1954), p. 120.

[2] e.g. Francesco Compagna and Vittorio De Caprariis, *Geografia delle elezioni italiane dal 1946 al 1953*, published by the periodical *Il Mulino* (Rome, 1954).

[3] Rocco Scotellaro, a young Lucanian poet and writer who after the war when still in his early twenties became Socialist mayor of his village of Tricarico, near Matera, died in December 1953 while preparing an inquiry into Southern peasant life, based on interviews with typical local characters. His *Contadini del Sud* (Bari, Laterza, 1954), which was published posthumously with a preface by Manlio Rossi-Doria, contains some of these interviews.

the same two or three people, and becomes a burden even to them. . . .

The stagnant calm of Fascism was broken by the return of the first prisoners of war. Mostly peasants and artisans, they were the first to combine together in the face of their country's defeat and of the eternal misfortunes of their own hamlets which, though untouched by the war, were becoming more and more poverty-stricken and neglected. They wanted work and help at the expense of the well-to-do, but they also wanted to revert to the peace and quiet of the pre-war order, and therefore they rejected the exhortations alike of Communists and Christian Democrats. . . . Their bitterness . . . produced a conflict between the age-old scepticism and the new need for struggle and organisation.

Even before the failure of the Uomo Qualunque party had become apparent, the Communists had stepped in to fill the void with their propaganda. In the seven years between 1946 and 1953 the Left vote increased by nearly a million (from 1,350,000 to 2,345,000), rising from 21·75 to 30·21 per cent of the total Southern electorate. This was the result of a clear-cut policy, for the Communists immediately after the war had been quick to grasp the immense possibilities of winning adherents for their cause in the neglected South. In this they showed themselves far shrewder and more speedy in action than the Christian Democrats. In the pre-land-reform years they increasingly advocated such a reform, and encouraged the peasants to occupy land, proclaiming that the Government would never take the initiative and that only a completely revolutionary policy could bring about the radical changes needed. When, in 1950, the land reform was introduced, Communist propaganda fastened on every shortcoming and magnified every local squabble. At the same time the Communists showed tremendous energy in penetrating to the most remote hamlets, in setting up their own local organisations throughout the South, and in organising Congresses for the 'renaissance of the Mezzogiorno'. The peasants, without previous political education and lacking, in many instances, adequate guidance from the authorities as to the real scope and purpose of the land reform, tended to believe what the propagandists told them. The Elections, in both 1952 and 1953, came at too early a stage for the land reform to have conclusively proved its worth. Its promises had thrown the South into a ferment, but progress was inevitably slow in this difficult and long-neglected terrain, and while the fortunate peasants who had received land supported the Government, there were enough jealous and disappointed ones to form fertile soil for Communist aspersions against the reform. The Government's long-term plan for Southern development under the Cassa per il Mezzogiorno naturally came under much less heavy fire than did the land reform; but it, too, was at too early a stage to provide, in the peasants' minds, a clinching answer to their own innate scepticism skilfully fostered by the Communists.

Thus the scene of the Government's greatest initiative in the sphere of social reform became a battleground in which it was assailed from both Left and Right. Among the many stocktakings that subsequently went on among Christian Democrat leaders in an effort to account for the failure of their Southern policy to bring in votes, Signor De Gasperi himself blamed not the peasants but the landlords. The 'bitterest pill', he said,[1] was the irresponsible behaviour of some groups in the South—not the people, but the leaders who had failed to recognise the Government's efforts. The Monarchists' votes 'could not alter the institutions of Italy', and their intervention had merely aided the Left: 'A last poster should really be set up in Southern Italy to make these irresponsible gentlemen who claimed they wanted to save the monarchy aware of how much they have put the nation in peril'.

Yet if the immediate cause of the Government parties' reverse could to a considerable extent be attributed to the reassertion of Right-wing opinion in the South, the abiding problem nevertheless still remained that of the Left. Despite all the measures taken during the past five years of Christian Democrat supremacy, both to maintain the check administered to the Communists in 1948 and to counteract their further advance by the improvement of social conditions, the Left-wing parties had continued to attract supporters—to the tune of 1,400,000 new votes.

The success of the Communist Party in Italy is of course in part due to the skill of its organisers, and in particular of Signor Togliatti. He is a man of education, and his ability in

[1] In an interview in *Il Messaggero*, 11 June 1953.

argument, and his apparent moderation, are very considerable assets in maintaining his party's appeal to wider circles than those of the proletariat alone. The Communists have, in fact, been at pains to enlist and retain the sympathies of 'intellectuals', both of well-known personalities such as, for example, the painter Renato Guttuso, and of university professors or writers such as Professor Concetto Marchesi and Francesco Flora. Such names, and those of the borderline sympathisers among the intellectuals who can be persuaded to lend their support to broadly-based 'peace' moves, give an air of respectability to the party and breed confidence in waverers. Among the bourgeoisie, more timid towards revolutionary innovations and preoccupied with their own material cares, the Communist Party has not obtained much following—they are said to be among the targets for the future.

But it is naturally from the working classes that the Communists have drawn their greatest support; and once enlisted, the various subsidiary organisations—the youth movement, the Women's Union, the ex-partisans' association, and so on—keep a watch against backsliding. Trade union influence is considerable, exerted both through the factories and through the category associations. A factory or shipyard worker under a Communist foreman is hard put to it not to become a Party member or at least sympathiser himself, for fear of losing his job. Similar pressure can be exercised through the agricultural co-operatives in the regions (Emilia in particular) where they have to a large extent come under Communist control.

Such reasons may go some way to explain how the Party operates to retain its sympathisers—who are, of course, far more numerous than the actual membership of some 2¼ million. But the question still remains: how is it that in Italy, a Catholic country, more than a third of the electorate now votes Communist or fellow-travelling Socialist?

It is often said that Communism, if it came to power in Italy, would be 'different', and that the Italians who vote Communist have no conception of what a thoroughgoing Communist régime on the Soviet pattern would be like. While both these statements may be true as far as they go, it has to be remembered that there is a wide gulf between the average Italian worker's conception of a Communist State and the

State which the Moscow-trained or -influenced leaders of the Italian Communist Party have in mind to impose. The Italian worker listens to the promises of better conditions expounded from the platform or in *Unità*, but he interprets them according to his lights, with no thought for the straight jacket within which his utopian Communist State would confine him. There is reason to suppose that the Italian, a highly individual being, would not make a particularly good Communist—he made a pretty poor Fascist and does not, in the long run, take kindly to totalitarian régimes; it was, indeed, the suspicion of a tendency towards authoritarianism, or at least towards over-paternalism, that alienated many votes from the Christian Democrats in 1953.

But that, precisely, is the crux. Highly individual though Italians may be in their own personal affairs, they are still only gradually and painfully acquiring the political experience to enable them to make a wise choice in public matters—it was, after all, only in 1919 that the Vatican's edict of *non expedit*, forbidding Catholics to take part in parliamentary elections, was entirely abandoned. Conditioned by their whole tradition and training to listen to the voice of one supreme authority, the Church (and this is subconsciously true of lapsed or lukewarm Catholics as well as of the devout), if they begin to secede from that authority they move into a vacuum—and there they find the Communist Party waiting with promises to help them to find a new *terra firma*.

Among those promises, the hope of better material conditions—in employment, housing, land tenure, and living standards—is bound to play a great part among people who often lack the barest necessities of life. But the Communists can appeal on other grounds as well. They are as capable of emotional oratory as any other Italians, and their picture of a State in which the hitherto insignificant workers acquire a new and respected position (at the expense, of course, of all those who have 'exploited' them in the past) cannot but arouse a response in the minds of simple peasants who have never heard anything like it before. It is, in fact, through their ideological appeal—through their offer of a new and non-priest-ridden heaven as well as of a new earth—that the Communists have succeeded in inspiring the confidence of many Italians.

That confidence is often still half-sceptical; but its progress as evidenced in the 1953 Election results was the measure of the Christian Democrats' failure till then, for all their efforts at reform, to meet the challenge on its own ground—on the ground of faith as well as of works.

CHAPTER X

THE SEARCH FOR A GOVERNMENT

THE Election had shown a draining away of strength from the Centre to both Left and Right; and, apart from the Right's increase, a general Leftward trend was apparent among most of the other parties. Some Socialist votes had moved over to the Communists (the latter had increased their poll from 20·3 per cent of the total in 1951–2 to 22·7 per cent in 1953, while the PSI vote fell from 13·1 to 12·7 per cent); the PSDI had lost votes both to the PSI and to Unità Popolare; and within the Christian Democrat party itself the Left-wing Iniziativa Democratica group had emerged considerably strengthened, a tendency further demonstrated in that group's successes in the voting for the party's National Council at the end of June. This indication of a Leftward trend among the non-conservative sectors of the electorate clearly had to be taken into account in the formation of the new Government and in giving it an intensified policy of social reform.

At the same time the change in the balance of forces within Parliament—the *mutata topografia parlamentare*, as Signor De Gasperi expressed it—made it far from easy to decide on the Government's composition. As the strongest party in the country the Christian Democrats must obviously still form the backbone; and Signor De Gasperi's leadership remained uncontested. But who were to be their allies? In the new circumstances all the possible combinations had to be taken into account, excepting collaboration with either of the two extremes, the Communists or the neo-Fascists; and it at once became clear that both the Nenni Socialists and the Monarchists felt they had a claim to be included. Signor De Gasperi was thus faced with four possible choices: (i) a renewal of the four-party coalition with the now much reduced lay democratic parties; (ii) a three-party coalition to the Left, with the PSDI and PSI; (iii) a three-party coalition to the Right, with the

Liberals and Monarchists; and (iv) a single-party Christian Democrat Government.

Numerically, the Left-wing coalition would have been the most advantageous—the PSI would bring with it 75 seats in the Chamber, making 94 with the PSDI's 19. A Monarchist-Liberal coalition would have added 54 seats to the Christian Democrats' 261; whereas a revival of the Centre coalition meant an addition of only 38. But the problem was far from being one of simple arithmetic alone, though given the Christian Democrats' reduced lead this had to come into it too.

Signor De Gasperi himself had repeatedly made it clear that he was most unwilling to move either to the Left or to the Right: his ideal remained, as it had always been, a collaboration between the Catholic and the lay democratic forces of the Centre. This opinion was shared by the Centre group in his own party, which however included some who, according to their different trends, favoured each of the other alternatives.

On the other hand among the PSDI, the most important of the small lay democratic parties, the Leftward trend shown in the Election had been interpreted as an indication that the country felt the need for that more active policy of social reform which they themselves had constantly advocated; and at the same time it had revived their longings to draw the Nenni Socialists back into the 'democratic' fold. The PSDI, along with the other lay Centre parties, had been bitterly disappointed at the failure of the electoral alliance to produce better results for themselves, a failure which they tended to attribute to faults in Christian Democrat propaganda. They therefore now welcomed the possibility of giving a more pronouncedly Socialist tinge to the Government and diluting Christian Democrat predominance, and maintained that a trial should be given to the *apertura a sinistra*, or 'opening to the Left', as the experiment of collaboration with the Socialists was termed.

Signor Nenni himself claimed that the Election results provided the justification for including the PSI in the Government, and declared his willingness to collaborate—on his own terms. These included, in domestic policy, the abolition of the electoral law (this was in any case tacitly agreed to by all parties); the passing of all the still outstanding legislation required by the Constitution; and a social policy calculated to improve living standards and production; while in foreign affairs he asked for a less rigid application of the Atlantic policy. At first no mention was made of the PSI's 'Unity of Action' pact with the Communists,[1] which was of course the real crux of the matter. But in discussions between Signor De Gasperi and Signor Nenni early in July it became obvious that Signor Nenni had no real intention of abandoning the Communist alliance. The *apertura a sinistra* was therefore ruled out; but it continued to haunt subsequent discussions on party combinations throughout the following winter, finding some favour, if with increasing disillusionment, among the PSDIs and among a few Left-wing Christian Democrats, notably Signor Gronchi, the President of the Chamber.

Signor De Gasperi's soundings with the Monarchist leader Achille Lauro showed equally clearly that an alliance with the Monarchists would jeopardise the future, for though less specific then the Socialists as to preliminary conditions the Monarchists plainly held in reserve their intention to revive the whole question of the monarchy when they thought the moment suitable.

With these alternatives eliminated, there remained only the possibilities of a revival of the four-party coalition or a single-party Christian Democrat Government. The latter would numerically be extremely precarious, and though advocated by some of his party was in complete contradiction to Signor De Gasperi's own view of the function of Christian Democracy as only one among the central and moderate forces, both Catholic and secular. But the PSDI, though its attempt to form a bridge between the Christian Democrats and Socialists had failed, still refused to join the Government, 'in order', as Signor Saragat said, 'not to compromise a swing to the Left on the part of democracy'. Doubts and hesitations were also felt among the Liberals and Republicans. So, faced with the impossibility of reconstructing the Centre coalition, Signor De Gasperi on 21 July put forward his eighth Ministry, composed for the first time since 1947 of Christian Democrats alone.

In his speech introducing his Government's programme Signor De Gasperi stressed the need for a more positive policy

[1] See above, p. 48.

of social reforms aimed at combating the abiding problem of unemployment. The land reform was to be carried out in full within the framework of the existing laws, and there was a rather vague reference to another law to be worked out with a view to testing the capacity of landowners themselves to carry out improvements on their estates—should they fail to do so the State would have to intervene. In foreign affairs, Signor De Gasperi emphasised Italy's intention to fulfil her commitments under the Atlantic Pact (here he pointed out, for Signor Nenni's benefit, that Italian policy was no more 'extreme' than that of France or Britain); and he included a strongly worded reference to Italy's claims regarding Trieste which was the only part of the speech to win applause. Otherwise the reception was unenthusiastic: in trying to please all Signor De Gasperi had satisfied none, and there was a general feeling that the new programme did not go far enough in taking account of the country's changed mood. On 28 July he sustained the first defeat of his post-war parliamentary career when his Government was rejected by 282 votes to 263, with 37 abstentions. Only the Christian Democrats had voted in favour; the three small Centre parties abstained, and all the rest opposed.

This adverse vote probably caused greater dismay abroad than in Italy itself, for outside his own country Signor De Gasperi enjoyed tremendous prestige for his known integrity and sincerity, for the part he had played as the outstanding post-war statesman under whom his country had rebuilt its democratic institutions, and for his ardent advocacy of European integration. Yet there was also a feeling of inevitability about the rejection of his Government: the vote of 7 June already seemed to mark the end of an epoch—the epoch of post-war reconstruction under Christian Democrat rule—and its author must go with it. New men and new methods were being asked for; but in what direction were they to be sought? Parliament and the country itself at this stage had no clear idea of the answer: they had rejected the old, but there was no corporate consensus of opinion as to what form the new should take.

This did not of course mean that the parties were without ideas; on the contrary, they all, and especially those untried in

Government, had their solutions. But in the general feeling of bewilderment prevailing after the Election they were still feeling their way, and in the meantime the business of government had to go on. The search for a workable combination continued well into the normal parliamentary recess. Throughout a sweltering August Deputies and Senators were kept in Rome. On 2 August another leading Christian Democrat, Signor Attilio Piccioni, Deputy Prime Minister in earlier Governments, was invited to form a Ministry and attempted to reconstruct the four-party coalition; but he was unsuccessful, largely owing to Social Democrat objections to the proposed inclusion of certain Christian Democrats of the Right. President Einaudi then called on Signor Giuseppe Pella, the former Budget Minister, and he put forward a Cabinet composed, with one exception, entirely of Christian Democrats which on 22 and 24 August obtained a vote of confidence from an exhausted Senate and Chamber. He had won the approval of the Monarchists, who together with the Christian Democrats, Liberals, and Republicans voted in favour; the Communists and Socialists opposed, while the PSDI and MSI abstained. His Ministry, of a more Right-wing tinge than had yet been attempted, was described as a 'caretaker' or 'business' Government which would merely tide over till the autumn when the budgets of the various Ministries had to be approved. It was regarded as a temporary affair, likely to be replaced as soon as this essential business was done. But this proved a miscalculation. External events were soon to take a hand in Italian domestic affairs and involve the Pella Government in a stormy episode for which it had not bargained.

In the meantime the parliamentarians hastened to join their long-deserted families in their *villeggiature* on the beaches or among the mountains. Normal routine had been quite sufficiently disturbed, and everyone felt entitled to a period of undisturbed calm. Barely a week had passed before this illusion was shattered, and Italy found herself in the midst of what appeared to have the makings of a first-class crisis on the subject of Trieste.

The story of that crisis, which lasted throughout the autumn of 1953, is told elsewhere.[1] It will suffice here to recall that the

[1] See below, pp. 140 ff.

immediate cause of the flare-up arose from Yugoslav interpretations of a seemingly innocuous reference to Trieste made by Signor Pella in his policy speeches of 19 and 24 August, and from Italian reactions to the Yugoslav attitude which it was feared might portend a formal annexation of Zone B. It may be doubted whether Signor De Gasperi would have acted so precipitately as did Signor Pella in at once ordering partial mobilisation along the frontier; and it also seems likely that Yugoslavia judged the moment suitable to press her claims now that the experienced guiding hand of De Gasperi was removed. Be that as it may, Signor Pella, who was acting as Foreign Minister as well as Prime Minister, adopted a strong line throughout the crisis, thereby earning the lasting approval of the Right and winning popularity throughout the country. It was not till the end of the year, when the danger had receded, that any question arose as to the position of his 'caretaker' Government.

Then, however, the searchings for a more permanent combination began afresh. The Pella Ministry, hastily formed as a temporary expedient, had never been regarded as a purely 'party' Government and had been created without consultation with the Christian Democrat party itself. Though Signor De Gasperi, who since September had become the party's Secretary, on several occasions affirmed its support for the Pella Government, the Christian Democrat Left wing was becoming increasingly disturbed at the Government's growing dependence on Monarchist support in Parliament. The Monarchists had, in fact, shown an unexpected responsibility and sense of moderation during Signor Pella's régime; but they were now beginning to ask for more than he could give them. The widespread support which he had received from all the conservative forces in the country, intensified as a result of the Trieste crisis, had been based originally on the hope that he would gradually veer further to the Right, relax his financial policy, and impose limitations on social reforms. But here they reckoned without both Pella and his party. Signor Pella could not be expected as Prime Minister to undo all he had done for the past six years as Treasury and Budget Minister in defending the lira and the situation of the middle and working classes. Neither could he have hoped to carry his party with him in such a policy: the proof was to be seen in the strength of its progressive Left wing and in such incidents as the support afforded in Catholic and Christian Democrat circles to the workers during the Pignone factory dispute of November 1953.[1] Signor Pella himself felt unable to carry on his Government without the wholehearted support of the party, which in view of its internal uncertainties he seemed unlikely to obtain. It was at first thought that the growing demand for change might be met by a mere Cabinet reshuffle; but this proved impossible and on 5 January 1954 Signor Pella tendered his resignation.

The pendulum then swung in the other direction when Signor Amintore Fanfani, leader of the Iniziativa Democratica trend within the Christian Democrat party, was asked to form a Government. But the single-party Ministry which he put forward, and which included representatives from all the different trends in his party, was rejected on 30 January, only the small Republican party joining the Christian Democrats to vote in its favour, while the Liberals abstained and all the rest opposed. In the refusal of the Social Democrats and Liberals to support the Fanfani Government can be seen the innate unwillingness of these secular parties to ally themselves with a Government of pronouncedly Catholic tinge. Fanfani was known on his past record as Minister of Labour and of Agriculture to be a man of tremendous energy which would be devoted to bringing about improvements in the social sphere. But though less extreme in his views than his former colleague Dossetti, he nevertheless came from the same school of Catholic integralism which, at least in theory, would permit of no conciliation with Liberalism or social democracy. Such considerations probably had at least as much validity as the more technical ones concerning future electoral methods which were advanced by the PSDI to account for their opposition.

This setback served to convince the Christian Democrats that it was useless to attempt to govern alone. During the past six months a good deal of soul-searching had been going on in their ranks, and clearer views were beginning to emerge.

[1] When the Pignone factories in Florence were closed down as a result of reorganisation workers occupied and continued to run the factory; they received support for their action from the town's Christian Democrat Mayor, La Pira, as well as from other Christian Democrats and clergy.

At the beginning of the year the party's Central Directorate had issued a four-point list of the requirements of a future Government:[1] (i) it must carry out the reforms and social measures already initiated or decided on; (ii) priority must be given to a policy for increasing employment and production; (iii) the Government must defend the authority and prestige of the Republic and must guarantee liberty and the consolidation of democratic institutions; and (iv) it must safeguard Italian interests within the framework of the Atlantic Alliance and of European co-operation. While the first two of these points verged on the obvious, the last two defined the Government's limits both to the Right, with the implicit restrictions on the Monarchists through the reference to the Republic, and to the Left with the reaffirmation of the Atlantic policy. By a process of elimination the Christian Democrats had themselves come back from their tour of political experiments to their leader's original point of departure—the four-party coalition.

The other Centre parties were by now also less intransigent, and the changes of the past few months in the Christian Democrat party's outlook made them more ready to collaborate with it. After both Signor De Gasperi and Signor Piccioni had been asked to attempt once more to form a four-party coalition and had refused, the choice finally fell on Signor Mario Scelba, a Sicilian, who belonged to the party's centre trend and as Minister of the Interior in all the De Gasperi Governments from 1947 to 1953 had shown great firmness in maintaining law and order and in the struggle against Communism.

The Government which he announced on 10 February 1954 was composed of Christian Democrats, Social Democrats, and Liberals, with the promised support in Parliament of the Republican party. Signor Scelba himself continued to be Minister of the Interior, and the Social Democrat leader Signor Saragat became Deputy Prime Minister. The Cabinet, shorn of some of the more controversial Christian Democrat figures of the past, was strengthened on the side of social reform by the inclusion of two prominent Social Democrats, Roberto Tremelloni (Finance) and Ezio Vigorelli (Labour), who had already been closely associated with moves for social

[1] *Il Popolo*, 8 January 1954.

improvement through their recent chairmanships, respectively, of the Parliamentary Inquiries on Unemployment and on Poverty. Another important innovation, especially welcomed by the secular democratic parties, was the passing of the Ministry of Education from Christian Democrat hands into those of a Liberal, Professor Gaetano Martino.[1]

Signor Scelba's programme laid great stress on the Government's intention to tackle speedily some of the most urgent social problems such as unemployment, housing, social insurance, and school building, while continuing the land reform policy and intensifying measures for Southern development. In foreign affairs, the Government pledged itself to secure speedy ratification of the EDC treaty.

This programme met with general approval, and the Scelba Government received votes of confidence in the Senate on 26 February and in the Chamber on 8 March. The margins were narrow, for in both cases only the Centre parties voted in favour while all the other parties opposed. But support for the Government was probably a good deal more widespread in the country than in Parliament itself. People were tired of experiments and asked only for good administration, and there was a general feeling that the Scelba Government, with its more representative composition and its emphasis on social reform, might have a reasonable chance of lasting.

[1] See below, pp. 108, 240.

CHAPTER XI

THE SCELBA COALITION

THOUGH the Scelba régime opened in an atmosphere of greater optimism than its predecessors, storms blew up in the first weeks of its existence. The Left parties doubtless realized that this revival of the Centre coalition in what promised to be a more lasting form represented a greater threat to their position than any other combination hitherto attempted. They therefore intensified their opposition tactics, and on 10 February 1954, the very day on which the new Government was announced, the CGIL proclaimed strikes of industrial and transport workers in Liguria and Lombardy which were to be the prelude to a nation-wide campaign for higher wages.

Two other episodes played into the hands of the Left in its efforts to discredit the new Government from the outset. The first, which had only momentary repercussions, was the death in prison near Palermo on 9 February of the Sicilian bandit Gaspare Pisciotta, lieutenant of the notorious bandit Giuliano who had been captured and killed in somewhat mysterious circumstances in 1950 (Pisciotta himself claimed to have killed Giuliano, whereas the official version was that Giuliano had been captured and shot by the Carabinieri). This alone was enough for the Communists to recall that Signor Scelba, himself a Sicilian, had been Minister of the Interior at the time of Giuliano's death, the facts concerning which had never been fully explained. This damp squib would, however, probably have fizzled out in any case: the story was four years old and inextricably wrapped up in the convolutions of Sicilian bandit intrigues. Much more serious was the emergence, early in March, of what was to prove the biggest Roman scandal for many a year—the Montesi affair.

This scandal concerned the unexplained death in April 1953 of a young Roman girl, Wilma Montesi, who had been found apparently drowned on the beach near Ostia. At the time a simple verdict of death by drowning had been given, but subsequent rumours and investigations by the press cast doubts on it. Instead, foul play was suggested, and it was rumoured that no less a person than the Foreign Minister's son, Piero Piccioni, had been implicated in the affair, aided and abetted by a well-known speculator and drug-trafficker by the name of Marchese Ugo Montagna (there was some doubt as to whether he was entitled to call himself 'Marchese', but he seems to have been given the title during the Fascist period). These rumours had been brought to the notice of the authorities, and inquiries had been going on throughout the winter.

Now, however, the affair burst into the full blaze of publicity, and Left-wing propaganda did not hesitate to suggest that various other prominent Christian Democrats had also been familiar with the Montagna circle. Most of these random accusations could be easily refuted, and there was never any suggestion that the Foreign Minister, Signor Attilio Piccioni, was himself in any way personally involved. When he offered his resignation at this time it was rejected by his colleagues. But to the public mind, and to the Left in particular, the whole circumstances of the case seemed to point to inadequate investigation by the police in the first instance, coupled with laxity in high places and a general desire to hush up the affair. The chief of police was at once dismissed, and the Government initiated an inquiry, conducted by the Liberal Minister Raffaele De Caro, into the more than dubious affairs of Marchese Montagna. Investigations dragged on throughout the summer, and culminated in September in the arrest of Piero Piccioni and Montagna. Signor Attilio Piccioni resigned his post as Foreign Minister just before his son's arrest, and his place was taken by the Liberal Professor Gaetano Martino, since February Minister of Education—thus bringing to an end, incidentally, the lay parties' shortlived rejoicings at finding the conduct of education in secular hands, for his successor was once more a Christian Democrat. Piero Piccioni and Montagna were provisionally released in November, and though the case was still *sub judice* its repercussions, which had been likened to those of the Dreyfus case, had begun to die down by the end of the year.

It said much for the Government's steadfastness that it

managed to withstand the attacks to which it was subjected as a result of this scandal. Foreign affairs too provided difficulties. Uncertainty regarding the Trieste situation overshadowed all the early months of the Scelba régime, for matters had now reached the stage of long-drawn-out negotiations in London.[1] The speedy ratification of EDC to which the Government was pledged appeared hazardous in view of the Centre's small majority, and Signor Scelba sought to obtain more support for it before putting the question to the test in Parliament. That support could only come from the Monarchists, but they seemed determined to make their co-operation conditional on the implementation of the much disputed United States–United Kingdom undertaking of 8 October 1953 to hand over Zone A of the Trieste Free Territory to Italian administration.[2] Early in June, however, a few Deputies and Senators split away from the Partito Nazionale Monarchico to form, under the ex-PNM leader Achille Lauro, a new party, the Partito Monarchico Popolare, which appeared ready to support EDC. But before the ratification debate could take place the question was solved for Italy in summary fashion by France's rejection of the treaty, and in the improved atmosphere which developed after the Trieste settlement and the London and Paris conferences the Scelba Government succeeded in obtaining the biggest majority of its career when the Chamber on 23 December voted in favour of the Paris Agreements,[3] with the Communists and Socialists alone opposing.

Despite all these difficulties the Government made a beginning in carrying out its promises concerning social reforms. By the end of 1954 legislation had been approved for the extension of health assistance to pensioners and of insurance to tenant farmers, for pensions to the blind, for special measures in Calabria (with an allocation of 204,000 million lire to carry them out), and for vocational training for the unemployed and especially for young people, while further long-term housing and school-building schemes were set on foot.[4] The law on the taxation of companies[5] marked a further step in carrying out the taxation reforms initiated in 1951; while Signor Vanoni's ten-year-plan, announced early in January 1955,[6] promised

[1] See below, pp. 146–7. [2] See below, p. 141. [3] See below, pp. 125–6.
[4] See below, pp. 215, 241. [5] See below, p. 185. [6] See below, p. 188.

a means of seriously tackling the unemployed problem on a long-term basis. After prolonged discussion and emendation a Bill giving the Government powers to review and reorganise the whole situation of the civil service was finally approved in December. It was hoped that this measure might eventually lead to greater administrative efficiency and to a pruning of the swollen ranks of the bureaucracy, now numbering over 1,100,000, or 42 per cent more than before the war. But pending this hypothetical if much needed reform it was decided that something must be done at once to raise the low salaries of existing civil servants, and the Bill provided for pay increases which it was estimated would cost the Treasury an additional 125,000 million lire a year, to be met by fresh taxation on certain commodities.

Both in pressing the civil servants' claims and also in the industrial wages dispute, which dragged on through the early months of 1954, an important part had been played by the main non-Communist (and predominantly Catholic) trade union, the CISL. In the early stages of the dispute on industrial wages the Communist union, the CGIL, had had the support of the non-Communist UIL in pushing extreme claims. But this temporary alliance soon broke down, and an agreement providing for increases of pay was reached on 12 June between the employers' Confederation and all the non-Communist trade unions. This agreement marked a considerable success for the non-Communist unions, as the violence of CGIL criticism of it then and later demonstrated. The CISL's position, after a stationary period, was in fact now definitely improving. Its representatives were playing a greater part in Christian Democrat counsels, and it was giving valuable support to the Government's intensified social policy. It was also gaining more ground among the workers, as could be seen from its successes in factory committee elections in the latter part of 1954, a trend which continued in 1955.[1] Speaking at the CISL National Congress in April 1955, the Secretary Signor Pastore estimated CISL membership at over 2 million, as against the CGIL's 4 million.

[1] At the end of 1954 it was claimed that in factory committee elections in 5,183 concerns (some 80 per cent of those holding regular elections) the CISL had obtained a majority in 1997 (31·3 per cent) and the CGIL in 3,783 (59·4 per cent). Similar percentages in 1952 were: CISL 24·1, CGIL 67·5 (see, e.g., *Il*

The new sense of urgency and awareness on the side of social action was reflected not only in Government policy but in the attitude of the Christian Democrat party itself. How far-reaching was the reassessment which had taken place in Christian Democrat ranks since June 1953 became apparent at the party's Congress, held in Naples a year later (26–29 June 1954). On that occasion Signor De Gasperi, as the party's Secretary, in a sweeping review of policy and prospects stressed the need for enlightened social action ('It is impossible to operate with the paternalism of a Bossuet under a democratic régime in the twentieth century') and for unity, both within the party and the coalition, in carrying it out. In the debate which followed several speakers showed an attention to practical needs which sounded a new note in Christian Democrat discussions. Signor Fanfani, paying tribute to Signor De Gasperi's leadership, emphasised that the soundest way to fight Communism was to inspire popular confidence in the State and the Government; the party and the trade unions should be the link with the people, and 'the people must be brought in or democracy will wither'. The CISL leader Signor Pastore pressed for further action in continuance of the fiscal and agrarian reforms and for a speedy settlement of the leasehold land tenure contracts question. Signor Colombo, a Southern deputy of the Iniziativa Democratica trend, contended that the Communist advance in the South would have been much more effective had it not been for the structural reforms already embarked on by the State: the Christian Democrat party now needed to establish a clear distinction between itself and the Right if it was to secure the floating vote of the 'proletariat humiliated by inadequate social conditions'.

The Congress's final resolutions fully endorsed the policy of intensified social action. Moreover the voting for the party's National Council showed a very definite swing towards the Left: of the 63 Councillors elected, 51 were of the Iniziativa Democratica trend, while 8 were from the trade union ('Forze Sociali') group. Hopes were expressed on all sides that Signor De Gasperi would continue as party Secretary, but he pre-

Globo, 1 January 1955). In elections at the Fiat motor works in March 1955 the CGIL polled only 36·7 per cent of the votes, as compared with 63 per cent in 1954 (*Messaggero*, 30 March 1955).

ferred to withdraw and the Iniziativa Democratica leader Signor Fanfani was elected in his stead, Signor De Gasperi becoming the party's President.

He was to hold this office for only a few weeks. On 19 August the whole country was shocked by the news that this greatest of its post-war statesmen had died of a heart attack at his Trentino country home of Valsugana. Signor De Gasperi was then 73 and though no longer Prime Minister during the past year he had not spared himself. To the last his thoughts were for his country, for the role Christian Democracy had to play in its life, and for his cherished ideal of European unity—it so happened that he died on the opening day of the abortive Brussels Conference and only a few hours before the end was anxiously discussing with Signor Piccioni the policy that Italy should pursue there.

The feeling of loss was tremendous, and tributes came from all over Italy, from the humblest peasants to the political leaders who in life had been his stoutest opponents. There was a general realisation of the benefits Italy had derived during the difficult post-war years from the guidance of a man so richly endowed with the gifts of idealism and political wisdom, who by his example had shown the younger generation how to put into practice the parliamentary method. In the Christian Democrat party itself the sense of personal bereavement was quickly followed by a desire, expressed in the commemorative speeches of his successors Scelba and Fanfani, to redouble the efforts to carry on in the path he had traced. Signor De Gasperi's last letter to Fanfani, written on 9 August when he was already ill and expressing some of his own most abiding ideals as to the party's role, was widely publicised and soon came to be regarded as a 'last testament'.[1] A special fund

[1] '. . . I have lately been rereading that instructive tome, Vistalli's life of Toniolo [the well-known Catholic sociologist and a founder of Christian Democracy in the last century]. What food for thought it provides on the subject of missed opportunities! Why was Toniolo's work of so little effect *nationally* speaking? Because the times and the men never permitted him to escape from the Guelph-Ghibelline alternative, and so on the political plane he never emerged from that traditional confined framework, though on the social plane he did. Later on, our own great effort was directed towards escaping from that stranglehold. Often we did not succeed, but at a certain point Christian Democracy did become a movement, an Italian party, over and above the historic conflict. Let us bear this always in mind: we must not let ourselves become entangled in the toils of that traditional dilemma.' (*Il Popolo*, 21 August 1954.)

for the 'depressed areas' in the South and elsewhere, initiated after the party Congress, received a tremendous impetus when it was dedicated to his memory.

Signor De Gasperi did not live to witness the clarification which took place that autumn concerning two of the main problems which had beset his latter years, Trieste and European defence.[1] The consequent easing of tension left the Government freer to tackle domestic matters, and foremost among them the ever-present fight against the Communists. Signor Scelba when he entered office had pledged himself to fresh measures to check their advance, but in fact little had so far been done beyond the recovery by the State of the many former Fascist premises which the Communists, often as partisans, had occupied at the end of the war and had never returned to the Government. Now, early in December, Signor Scelba announced a series of administrative measures designed to 'curb the Communist threat to Italy's democratic institutions'. Their aim was twofold: to prevent the penetration of central and local administrations by persons regarded as security risks; and to restrict the activities of Communist-controlled companies which, through a vast network of business connections, had not only succeeded in obtaining contracts at home but had acquired a near-monopoly of trade with Eastern Europe; and a large part of the profits were believed to have gone to swell the Communist Party funds. All concessions hitherto granted were now to be re-examined, and the list of approved firms entitled to handle public contracts was to be revised, while steps were to be taken to ensure that the most responsible public posts would be entrusted only to persons whose fidelity to the democratic State was beyond doubt.

These measures were generally welcomed as both moderate and shrewd. Their purely administrative character, involving no special legislation, was a strong recommendation. Moreover the psychological effect of such measures, if firmly carried out, seemed likely, by re-establishing confidence in the Government's will to act firmly against the Communists, to be at least as far-reaching as the practical results. The measures were, of course, received with a storm of protest from the Left; and they were also strongly criticised by such staunch up-

[1] See below, pp. 125, 147.

holders of individual liberty and constitutional practice as Avv. Calamandrei and Professor Salvemini.[1]

At the Communist Party's fourth National Conference, held in January 1955, further protests were registered against the 'anti-democratic campaign' which Signor Togliatti described as 'reminiscent of some of the most repugnant aspects of Fascism'. Yet despite the tone of righteous indignation, the emphasis on past successes, and the façade of a united front which yet allowed of scope for internal criticism, the picture that emerged both from the Conference itself and from a backward glance at the Communists' progress over the past year was not over-impressive. Their opportunities after the 1953 Election had seemed great, and the Government's slender majority had afforded them grounds for hopes of fresh advances. But instead the Government coalition remained firm and its policy showed a new decision and awareness of conditions, while it derived further strength from the settlement of the Trieste question and from the brighter prospects for collaboration in Western European Union. In the parliamentary debates on both these matters of foreign affairs Communist leadership showed itself uncertain and indecisive. In domestic affairs, the Centre parties achieved a success in the Val d'Aosta regional elections in November, where the Left vote fell considerably. The strike campaign of 1954 was relatively a failure, and the successful negotiation of the wages agreement by the non-Communist trade unions was a serious setback which the Communist leaders themselves recognised —in their plans for the future they laid stress on the need to intensify trade union action, to make friendly overtures to Catholic workers, and in particular to develop trade unionism in the South, where it had always been weakest. Moreover, after posing as the upholders of public morality in their strictures on the Government's conduct of the Montesi affair, the Communists later in the year found themselves landed with scandals in their own ranks concerning both local tax collections and the private life of the Communist president of the Rome Provincial Administration, Avv. Sotgiu.

Nevertheless the programme of action outlined at the Conference by Signor Togliatti suggested no departure from the

[1] See *Il Ponte*, December 1954.

non-revolutionary tactics hitherto pursued. The line was still to broaden the front as widely as possible, to bring in marginal sympathisers on topics with a wide human appeal such as the Partisans of Peace and the threat of atomic war, to stand as the champions of the workers in all disputes on wages, contracts, land tenure and so forth, and, while carefully remaining within the law and the Constitution, to attack not by force but by erosion. It was the continuance of these tactics which led to disputes among the party leadership which came to a head during the conference and resulted in the removal of Pietro Secchia, reputedly the leader of the 'tough' and revolutionary faction, from the post of Party Vice-Secretary to that of Regional Secretary for Lombardy.

Yet even this seeming 'demotion' of one of the Old Guard was accomplished undramatically and was made to appear as a mere transfer to a key post. In the Italian 'cold war' of 1955 peaceful methods were still to be the order of the day, and the struggle for supremacy was to go on by means of tactics that never quite overstepped the bounds of constitutional practice. The Government response, confined within an even stricter observance of these same limits, could only lie in firmness and vigilance, and in the patient and unspectacular building up of a democratic State in which individual freedom, prosperity, and equality of opportunity would themselves give the lie to Communist contentions.

The immediate need was for a stable administration to carry on this policy. Unfortunately, however, the Scelba Government did not live up to the promise of its initial period. Early in 1955 cracks began to appear in the coalition façade. Disagreements arose between the parties concerning the best way of achieving a settlement of the long-disputed farm tenancy lease question, concerning which the Liberal party, in particular, took an extreme line in objecting to the Segni proposals of 1950;[1] and in March the small Republican party, hitherto outside the Government but supporting it, rejected the Government's proposed compromise on the farm tenancy question and decided to withdraw its support from the coalition. There were other subjects awaiting settlement on which the Centre parties held differing views, such as the reform of

[1] See below, p. 168.

IRI, the extension to the whole country of regional administration and of land reform, and the question of mining and mineral rights. Moreover this disunity was not confined to inter-party disputes, but extended also to the ranks of the coalition's major partner, the Christian Democrats.

The divergent trends within this large and heterogeneous party had often in the past created difficulties for Signor De Gasperi: but now he was no longer there to cope with them—and, incidentally, many thoughtful Italians, not necessarily of his own way of thinking, were beginning to realise more fully what the absence of his skilful guidance meant. The various schools of thought within the party might sink their differences temporarily when faced with a setback such as the 1953 Election, or when the defeat of attempts to form a single-party Government forcibly brought home to them the need for allies and for compromise. But while Christian Democrats of the centre still believed in the practical necessity of the four-party coalition (even if Catholic-secular collaboration might not appear to some of them as the urgent article of faith that it had represented for Signor De Gasperi), the more extreme elements at either end of the party gamut soon reverted to their desire to experiment with some other form of Government. The Right wing of the party, centring round such men as Giuseppe Pella, the former party Secretary Guido Gonella, and the industrialist Giuseppe Togni, had been deliberately excluded from the composition of Signor Scelba's Government. Objections to the inclusion of representatives from this trend had indeed been one of the reasons for the failure of his predecessor, Signor Fanfani, to obtain support for his Government. These Right-wingers still hankered after a single-party Christian Democrat Government, based on support from the Liberals and Monarchists, such as the country had experienced for a brief period under Signor Pella; some hoped for a return of Signor Pella himself.

At the other end of the scale, some few Christian Democrats of the Left, notably the President of the Chamber Signor Gronchi, had not yet abandoned their hopes of an alliance with Signor Nenni's Socialists, and their longings in this direction received fresh impetus from the Socialist Party's Congress held in Turin (31 March–3 April 1955), at which Signor Nenni renewed his offers of collaboration. Indeed, on this occasion he went further than ever before in advocating collaboration between the Catholic and Socialist masses on a basis of working-class solidarity; such collaboration, he said, could begin on the economic plane, where views were in many respects similar (he appeared to regard the Vanoni Plan as a bridge in this direction). As to the political side, Signor Nenni claimed that his party's 'Unity of Action' pact with the Communists had never caused the Socialists to lose their autonomy: 'it does not stand in the way of better relations between Socialists and Christian Democrats, and such an improvement does not necessarily imply the establishment of similar relations between Communists and Christian Democrats'.[1] As to foreign policy, the leading Socialist Riccardo Lombardi went so far as to say that he did not think it was possible to overthrow existing alliances, though he added that WEU and the Atlantic Pact must be 'rendered innocuous'.

All this was certainly an advance on any of the Socialist party's earlier feelers towards collaboration. But there were two major drawbacks: first, Signor Nenni at no point specifically committed himself to renunciation of the Communist–Socialist pact; and secondly, as was shown during the Congress's discussions, his views were plainly in advance of those of most of his party (Lombardi was an outstanding exception). The majority of Christian Democrats, Signor Fanfani among them, felt, at least, that the time was not yet ripe and that more substantial guarantees would be needed to warrant acceptance of these offers. Yet there was a feeling that Signor Nenni's latest moves might herald the possibility of an eventual change, even if it was still far off.

This impression that a new element had been introduced into the situation combined with the existing sources of disagreement to produce a demand for 'clarification' both from the smaller Centre parties and from the dissatisfied elements among the Christian Democrats. These latter elements joined forces to harass Signor Scelba, combining to form a heterogeneous body of Right- and Left-wing 'have-nots' which became known as the *Concentrazione*. The impending 'clarification'—taken variously to imply a new programme, a Cabinet

[1] *Avanti!*, 1 April 1955.

reshuffle, or an outright change of Government—haunted all political discussion during the early months of 1955. But various obstacles caused its repeated postponement: first, in March, Signor Scelba and Signor Martino visited the United States; then came the Presidential election at the end of April; and finally the Sicilian Regional elections on 5 June. Each of these fixtures was made a reason for delay; in the meantime the factions squabbled and the country's administration virtually came to a standstill.

The unsettled state of the parties was thrown into relief at the election of the Republic's new President on 28–9 April. Signor Einaudi, already eighty-one, had been unwilling to stand again, and it was difficult to find an alternative candidate who both possessed the wisdom of an elder statesman which he had so conspicuously shown and who also stood above party strife. The Presidential appointment is, of course, in theory a non-party affair; but inevitably party politics on this occasion came into the picture. The Christian Democrats, in particular, displayed their internal divisions before the outside world through their inability to agree till the last moment on their official candidate. The result was a remarkable one from their point of view: one of their own members, Signor Giovanni Gronchi, was elected, but primarily as the choice of the Left and the *Concentrazione*, and only in the final ballot with the official support of the Christian Democrats, whose last-minute candidate Senator Merzagora had withdrawn in the face of Gronchi's lead, obtained through the vote not only of the Communists and Socialists but also of a considerable proportion of Christian Democrats who had ignored the party line.

The Sicilian Regional elections on 5 June did something to restore the Christian Democrats' ruffled equanimity, producing as they did perceptible gains for their party which were in no small part due to Signor Fanfani's energetic and efficient organization of the campaign. But the elections brought little satisfaction to the smaller Centre parties, who, as in 1953, found themselves heavily outvoted, and who thus felt their bargaining hands weakened in the 'clarification' that could now no longer be avoided.

Nevertheless, uneasy as the Centre coalition had often proved, there was still a wide body of opinion which realised that any alternative form of Government might run into even greater difficulties. It was in this belief that Signor Scelba in mid-June attempted to give new life to his Ministry by means of a Cabinet reshuffle (which should bring back the Republicans to the fold) and a new programme, based on a combination of the Christian Democrats' minimum agreed demands and those of the other parties. He very nearly succeeded; but at the last moment the Republicans again backed out owing to disagreement on the Cabinet post to be allotted to them, and this provided an excuse for the Christian Democrat *Concentrazione* faction to contend that Signor Scelba had failed to reconstruct the coalition as he had promised. He therefore tendered his Government's resignation to President Gronchi on 22 June without awaiting the verdict of Parliament on his proposals.

Thus the Scelba régime, full of promise in its early stages, came to an ignominious end, largely owing to rifts and personal rivalries within its major party. Nor were these divisions likely to be healed easily. We have to close this survey of Italy's internal political situation with a question-mark: would Signor Scelba's immediate successor Signor Antonio Segni, or some other Christian Democrat, be able to play the much-needed unifying role both within his own party and in the wider coalition which still, despite its difficulties, seemed to offer the best hope for the country's stable government?

Part III
Italy and the World

CHAPTER XII
FOREIGN RELATIONS

A WESTERN ORIENTATION

ITALY'S domestic policy after 1947 is inextricably bound up with foreign policy, and with the course of events in the world at large. Till after the ratification of the peace treaty she was not in a position to take the initiative in her relations with other countries. But from 1948 onwards a change from a passive to an active foreign policy, as Count Sforza expressed it, developed steadily, step by step with the gradual liquidation of the major restrictions and problems arising out of the peace treaty. During the following years Italy to an increasing extent took her place once more as an equal among the other nations; and the period is characterised by the consolidation of that Western orientation which she had already chosen in June 1947 when she adhered to the Marshall Plan. It is also closely identified with the views of the two main arbiters of Italian post-war foreign policy, Count Sforza and Signor De Gasperi. Both were ardent believers in European federation—Count Sforza, indeed, had been an advocate of it while still in exile in America. It was the dominating theme of his term of office as Foreign Minister from February 1947 till July 1951, and when on his retirement Signor De Gasperi became his own Foreign Minister he carried on the same policy of Italian support for, and inclusion in, all plans tending towards European integration.

This policy from the first encountered strong opposition from some quarters within Italy—primarily, of course, from the Left, but also from other circles where motives were less clear-cut. There was, as has already been said, a strong leaning towards neutralism among people who, though by no means in sympathy with Communism, nevertheless feared that a too emphatic pro-Western policy might lead Italy into military commitments which she could ill afford to shoulder. This kind of opinion was not confined to any particular stratum or political group: it might extend from the thoughtful Left-wing Social Democrat who could support his view with reasoned arguments, to the inarticulate Southern peasant whose signature went to swell the 15 million names said to have been collected in favour of the Soviet Peace Pledge in 1950. The Italians are in any case a people averse from war, and their horror of it had been intensified by their recent experience of it on their own soil: with many of them, opposition to a foreign policy which might carry with it explicit military commitments was nothing more than a simple reaction against the possibility that such an experience might have to be faced again.

As time went on, however, another factor came into the picture: a chariness of being too closely bound to the United States. Italy realised her deep indebtedness to America for the aid which had virtually set her on her feet again; but as the war receded and conditions improved, many people began to wonder if the Government was not overdoing its enthusiastic acceptance of American suggestions for the country's improvement which also appeared to carry with it the acceptance of heavy defence burdens, of supervision and criticism as to the spending of American aid, and of general 'interference' in the country's own affairs. This presentation of the situation, suitably distorted and exaggerated, was of course widely exploited by Left-wing propaganda. But by the time of the 1953 Election it was being adopted also, from a slightly different angle, by the Right as well: during the election campaign Monarchists would argue that if Italy still had a King she would be more likely to be 'respected' by other countries, while the out-and-out neo-Fascist nationalist would proclaim that the country's independence was being destroyed by subservience to a foreign Power—echoing, in these diatribes, arguments practically indistinguishable from those of the Communists at the other end of the political scale.

It was against this background, therefore, that Italy embarked on the uphill task of her reintegration into the Western

European framework. The first steps were taken with her inclusion in OEEC, the central organisation for the operation of the Marshall Plan, which was established by a convention signed by the sixteen participating nations, including Italy, on 16 April 1948; while the bilateral ERP agreement between Italy and the United States was signed on 28 June, her allocation for the first fifteen months (April 1948 to June 1949) being fixed at $601 million. It is perhaps important to stress Italy's inclusion in OEEC, the first post-war international organisation in which she played a part: for owing to her continued exclusion from the United Nations she had hitherto lacked the opportunity for those international contacts which were so important after her long period of isolation. In OEEC her leading economists found a meeting-ground for discussions with their colleagues from other countries.

Earlier in 1948 an attempt had been made to establish closer economic co-operation with France by means of a Franco-Italian Customs Union, concluded on 28 March. Much was anticipated from this experiment, which it was hoped might eventually be expanded to include also the Benelux countries; but it foundered owing to technical difficulties and the fierce opposition of the French wine growers, and the treaty was never ratified.

On 24 August 1948 Count Sforza addressed a Memorandum to the French Government in which he put forward the idea that OEEC might be made the basis for some form of European Union; in this the Western Union Powers already united in the Brussels Pact of March 1948 (Britain, France, and the Benelux countries) might take the initiative. An Italian Memorandum on similar lines also went to all the OEEC countries on 27 October. It is interesting to note that this proposal of Count Sforza's for utilising an existing combination, originally formed for economic ends, as the basis for building up a European political organisation foreshadowed what was eventually to come to pass in 1952, when the European Coal and Steel Organisation was charged with the drafting of a Constitution for the European Political Community.

The spring of 1949 witnessed two important steps in Italy's re-entry into international political life. On 4 April in Washington Count Sforza on behalf of Italy signed the North Atlantic

Treaty; and on 5 May in London he signed the Statute of the Council of Europe. Both these treaties encountered strong opposition from the Left, though dislike of the NATO commitment was naturally much more vocal and widespread. In July, when both treaties were ratified, Signor Togliatti during the North Atlantic Treaty debate accused the Government of being unable to recognise Italy's true interests, while the Communist Deputies walked out of the Chamber when the voting on ratification of the Council of Europe Statute took place. In the latter debate the Communists had elected to take their stand on the ground that they were not to be included in the Italian delegation to the Council, which brought forth the repartee from the Social Democrat Deputy Calosso: 'If a Council of Firemen were being appointed, would the incendiaries have the right to serve on it?'

Italy's commitments under NATO necessarily involved greatly increased defence expenditure in view of the restrictions hitherto placed on her rearmament. It will be recalled that under the peace treaty her army was limited to 250,000 men, and her navy and air force to 25,000 each. But in the immediate post-war years Italy's armed forces were in fact much below these limits. Compulsory military service remained in force, but recruits were selected and limited by a wide use of exemptions, and the training period, in theory still eighteen months, had in practice been reduced to eleven months. Moreover equipment in all three services was insufficient, out of date, and inadequate for training purposes. A good deal of reconstruction went on between 1947 and 1949, particular attention being paid to training establishments. But when Italy joined NATO it was obvious that she had a long way to go before she could produce the twelve divisions which were the target allotted for her army by 1952. In the intervening years her material equipment was greatly expanded under the Military Aid Programme. Naval and air bases were reconstructed and re-equipped—the latter a particularly heavy undertaking, given the extent of wartime destruction. By mid-1953 Italy had a total of 185,000 men under arms (not including Carabinieri or Military Police) with up-to-date equipment; these included 10 infantry divisions, 3 Alpine brigades, and 2 armoured divisions. Similar advances had been made in the recruitment and equipment of the navy and air force. Naples became the headquarters of the NATO South European Command, of which an Italian General was appointed Commander.

Expenditure on defence during this period of reorganisation was naturally very heavy. Special additional military credits of 250,000 million lire for three years were voted in 1952, and in 1952–3 the total Budget allocation for defence was 618,000 million lire, or 23 per cent of the year's total expenditure. From 1952 onwards 'offshore' orders for military equipment for the NATO forces were placed with Italian industry, a good deal of this equipment being used for the Italian armed forces themselves in addition to the arms Italy received through the Mutual Security Agency.

By 1951 it had come to be recognised that Italy was in an anomalous position in relation to her obligations as a member of NATO owing to the continued restrictions of the peace treaty. Early in that year Count Sforza therefore raised the question of treaty revision, asking for public recognition that the treaty was now 'out of date on a moral plane'. After the Ottawa meeting of the North Atlantic Council in September, which was followed by discussions in Washington between Signor De Gasperi, President Truman, and Mr Acheson, a joint Declaration was issued on 26 September by the United States, British, and French Governments expressing their readiness to consider the removal of the peace treaty restrictions and to attempt to secure Italy's admission to the United Nations,[1] and by the end of the year eleven of the signatory Powers (though not the USSR) had adhered to Italy's request for revision, made early in December. But despite an overwhelming vote of 54 to 5 in the General Assembly on 7 December in favour of Italy's admission to the United Nations, the Soviet Union still insisted on making her admission conditional on that of twelve other countries, including the satellites. Thus, though now a member of the Trusteeship Council in virtue of her mandate over Somaliland,[2] she still remained excluded from the United Nations.

In April 1951 Italy joined in the Schuman Plan for a Euro-

[1] This declaration was reaffirmed at the NATO Council on 11 May 1955.
[2] See above, p. 37.

pean Coal and Steel Community, and in the autumn of 1952 Signor De Gasperi, now himself Italy's Foreign Minister since Count Sforza's retirement, played an important part in putting forward, with France, proposals for the setting up of a European political community for which the ECSC was to prepare a draft constitution.[1]

By this time the six countries adhering to the Schuman Plan—France, Italy, Western Germany, and the Benelux countries—had become recognised as a sort of 'Little Europe', and their association for defence purposes as well, originally proposed under M. Pleven's plan for a European army, followed with the creation of the European Defence Community on 27 May 1952. The EDC treaty encountered fierce opposition in Italy both from the Left and from others who saw in it a military commitment to the West even more specific than NATO and the definitive crystallisation of the breach between West and East. It and the 'Atlantic' policy in general became major targets for recrimination during the 1953 election campaign, and after the Election the question of Italy's ratification of the EDC treaty proved one of the rocks on which various attempts to form a Government foundered.[2] By the spring of 1954, when the question of ratification had become immediate (since Italy and France were then the only countries of the 'six' who had not yet ratified), it had become linked with the problem of finding a solution for the Trieste question.

The debate on ratification of EDC had not yet taken place when on 30 August 1954 the French Chamber rejected the treaty. Italy warmly welcomed the subsequent broposals made at the London and Paris Conferences of September-October 1954 for the creation of a Western European Union, and a special clause was included in the Paris Agreements providing for Italy's accession to the Brussels Treaty of 1948 (of which she had not been a signatory) out of which these agreements developed. In the meantime the Trieste question had at last been settled in October,[3] and this undoubtedly helped to pave the way for approval of the Paris Agreements, which were ratified in the Italian Chamber on 23 December 1954 by 335

[1] In May 1954 Signor De Gasperi was elected President of the ECSC, and after his death Signor Pella succeeded him in this post.

[2] See above, Ch. X. [3] See below, p. 147.

votes to 215—the largest majority hitherto obtained by Signor Scelba's Government—and in the Senate (by 139 votes to 82) on 11 March 1955.

The signature of the Austrian State Treaty on 15 May 1955 raised new problems for Italy; for with the prospect of the evacuation of Allied troops from Austria and of that country's neutralisation the North-Eastern Alps and the Brenner became one of the great strategic frontiers of Europe, thus placing Italy in the front line of Western European defence. Left-wing politicians lost no time in protesting against the possible transfer of American and British troops from Austria to Italy and reviving ideas of Italian neutrality in these changed circumstances, but the Foreign Minister, Signor Martino, emphasised that any such transfer would be purely the concern of NATO: Italy herself, he said, was 'neither big enough nor small enough to consider the idea of neutrality'.[1]

THE WESTERN POWERS

Among Italy's relations with the individual countries of Western Europe, those with France were naturally the closest. It is true that during the peace treaty negotiations France sponsored frontier settlements unfavourable to Italy, both in advancing her own claims for Briga and Tenda, and in proposing the so-called 'French line' which was the one eventually adopted in Venezia Giulia.[2] But subsequently France gave her support to Italy throughout the discussions on the fate of the colonies and also in the tripartite Declaration of 20 March 1948 on Trieste. Post-war Italy and France were in many respects faced with similar problems. Both had emerged from a war fought on their own territories, when each country was divided within itself. They had common problems arising out of the Resistance period and the subsequent development of strong Communist parties; on the other hand, shared experience and close association during the Resistance also counted for something. Moreover, ties of personal association with France existed for several of the anti-Fascist leaders now prominent in Italian politics who had been in exile there. In addition, since the war strong Catholic parties had taken the lead in both countries, and their leaders, Signor De Gasperi

[1] *Il Popolo*, 22 May 1955. [2] See above, p. 35.

and M. Schuman, both of them, incidentally, from frontier regions, were in personal sympathy and held similar views as to European integration, concerning which, as has been seen, French initiatives received the strongest support from Italy. This close collaboration in the promotion of European union, established during Count Sforza's meeting with M. Schuman at Cannes in December 1948,[1] was strengthened during the Franco-Italian conversations which took place at Santa Margherita from 12 to 14 February 1951, just before the Paris conference on the Pleven plan for a European army. At Santa Margherita Signor De Gasperi and Count Sforza for Italy, and M. Schuman and M. Pleven for France, confirmed their agreement on a wide range of questions of common interest, including problems arising out of the Atlantic Treaty and the various aspects of European integration, among the most important of which was the inclusion in Europe of a democratic Germany.

Franco-Italian understanding was, in fact, the more important at this particular juncture because of this question of Germany's inclusion in Western European plans, which was coming increasingly to the fore and in relation to which Italy felt that she could play a balancing role. Italy's own relations with Germany had gradually become more cordial. Full diplomatic relations between the two countries were resumed in May 1951, and in the following month Dr Adenauer visited Rome, while in Bonn in September 1952 Signor De Gasperi was awarded the Charlemagne prize for his work for European unity. Here again, as in France, the similarity of outlook and position of these two leaders of important Catholic parties did much to pave the way towards collaboration (incidentally, some acid comparisons were made in Italy concerning the success of Dr Adenauer's party in the German elections of September 1953, following so soon after the Italian Christian Democrats' own severe losses in June). Moreover, Italy benefited greatly by the revival of trade with Germany, formally one of her main trading partners.

Relations between Italy and Britain have been going through a difficult period since the war. The ties of personal association with anti-Fascists were less strong in Britain than in France,

[1] See Carlo Sforza, *Cinque Anni a Palazzo Chigi* (Rome, Atlante, 1952), Ch. 4.

and in the United Kingdom there was no local equivalent of a Christian Democrat party to form a bridge, while the attempts of the British Labour Party to establish a link with Italian Socialism, so divided within itself, did not always lead to particularly happy results. Moreover, the effects of Fascist anti-British propaganda died hard; and there was a feeling that wartime promises as to Italy's future had not been fulfilled despite Italy's own efforts and the part played by the Resistance. This feeling was reawakened in June 1950 when Field-Marshal Alexander's report on the earlier stages of the Italian campaign was published and was found to contain criticisms of the Italian attitude at the time of the Armistice and to cast doubts on the value of the Resistance movement. This misunderstanding was cleared up later when the second volume of the report appeared, dealing much more fully and appreciatively with the part played by Italian Resistance; but the affair left a bitter taste.

Other sources of strain arose out of the peace treaty, especially the colonial question, where many Italians felt that greater support for their claims might have been forthcoming from Britain. There was, too, the inevitable friction arising out of Britain's prolonged occupation of the Italian colonies and the many problems of Italian nationals and property there. These matters were in fact no exclusive concern of Britain, but of all the treaty Powers, and latterly of the United Nations; moreover it was in the U.N. General Assembly that the solution for the colonial question proposed in 1949 by Mr Bevin in agreement with Count Sforza[1] (which would have been more favourable to Italy than the eventual settlement) was defeated. But Italian opinion, wounded at the loss of the colonies, cast Britain for the role of scapegoat; and the same thing happened later on over the Trieste question.[2] Italy, too, in common with other Continental countries, was disappointed at British reserve towards plans for European unity. Economic problems also played their part: British import restrictions during 1952–3 hit Italian exporters hard, and in conjunction with the similar restrictions imposed by other countries made it difficult for Italy to carry out the policy of liberalisation of trade by which the Government set great store.[3] The imaginative plan,

[1] See above, p. 37. [2] See below, Ch. XIII. [3] See below, pp. 177, 180.

launched in 1951, to bring over contingents of Italian miners to work in the British coal mines, which was welcomed on both sides as a means of simultaneously reducing Italian unemployment and increasing manpower in the British mines, foundered owing largely to the short-sighted obstruction of the trade unions in Britain. Here the Italian authorities, and the Italian press correspondents in Britain, showed a sympathetic understanding of the difficulties; but to the Italian public this was just another rebuff.

On the other hand, the visit which Signor De Gasperi and Count Sforza paid to Britain in March 1951, soon after the Santa Margherita meeting with the French leaders, did much to clear up past misunderstandings. Signor De Gasperi visited Britain again, at a most difficult juncture in Italian domestic affairs just after the Election of June 1953, to receive an honorary degree at Oxford. On that occasion the Public Orator said, 'To him, if to anyone, may be assigned the credit for Italy's resumption, after her trials, of the old and honourable place she used to hold in the world.' The visit to Britain of Signor Scelba and his Foreign Minister, Professor Martino, which took place in February 1955 in the greatly improved atmosphere that followed the settlement of the Trieste dispute, was generally regarded as marking the beginning of a new and more cordial era in Anglo-Italian relationships.

The emergence of the United States as the paramount external influence in Italy came about there—as in Greece also—largely owing to Britain's physical inability to maintain the position which, by tacit agreement between Mr Churchill and President Roosevelt, she had held in relation to both those countries during the war. Earlier in this chapter mention has been made of some Italian reactions to American predominance. They represent, of course, only one side of a highly complex picture; for American policies towards Italy have by now become closely interwoven into the country's life, especially on the economic side. This was inevitable in view of two factors: first, Italy's economic situation after the war, which dictated her dependence on American aid for a long period; and secondly, American perception of the especial need to fight Communism in Italy, given her geographical situation and the strength of the Communist Party there.

Close ties between Italy and the United States are, of course, no mere post-war phenomenon. The vast numbers of Italians who migrated to the United States in the decades before the first world war had forged a living link between the two countries, and though subsequently American immigration restrictions reduced the flood of Italian immigrants to a mere trickle, America still represents the promised land to many a Calabrian peasant. Countless Italian families have relatives in the States whose remittances home still represent a considerable invisible item in Italy's balance of payments. Not all emigrants made their fortunes and fulfilled their dream of returning home to buy a plot of land and settle down there; but enough of them did—or at any rate irrupted on visits to their families from another, easier world—to lend substance to the legend of America as the source of all prosperity.

Thus to Italians there was nothing unnatural in American post-war generosity and their acceptance of it. They accepted, too, and with enthusiasm, many of the outward and visible signs of the American way of life—the glossy super-cars, the neon signs, the films (much more widely popular than their own), the countless gadgets and the technological 'know-how', even down to the Coca-Cola. Not, of course, that the vast majority of Italians could afford most of these emblems of prosperity for themselves; but they admired them, and still more they admired the success for which they stood. The age of mechanical progress has made itself felt in Italy no less than elsewhere, and her youth is attracted and fascinated by the new possibilities it seems to open up—the more so because, in the backward regions, at least, the possibilities of transition to a different life suddenly appear, if quite illusorily, to be within grasp.

So there was a general temper of readiness to accept things American; and if that temper cooled somewhat when the relative disadvantages and corresponding obligations for Italy became more apparent, that is not to say that many Italians—and the majority in official or business circles—did not realise the incalculable importance of the part played by American intervention in furthering the country's economic reconstruction. But in certain specific spheres Italy continued to hope for alleviations which the United States found difficulty in granting. These chiefly concerned migration and trade. The permitted quota for Italian immigrants was even further reduced under the McCarran Act of 1952,[1] while United States tariff barriers restricted the importation by America of some characteristic Italian exports, thus hampering the operation of Italy's own trade liberalisation policy and making it more difficult for her to pay her own way.

On the American side, there was—notably in 1949[2]—some criticism of the way in which Italy was spending Marshall aid funds—or rather not spending, for the criticism was directed towards Italy's inclination to use too much of the funds to swell her foreign exchange reserves instead of investing it in capital equipment. This was remedied later on as Italian plans for long-term productive investment, notably in the South, got under way. More serious was American disappointment at the failure to arrest the growth of Communism which became apparent with the results of the 1953 Election. Apart from the original impulse of generosity which had given rise to the various schemes for aid to Europe—especially strong in Italy's case, given the number of United States citizens of Italian origin—the whole basis of United States policy had rested on the supposition that Italy must be kept within the Western orbit and that Communism must be held in check there. It now seemed to some American critics that United States aid might perhaps have been squandered in vain, and they tended to blame the Italian Government for not implementing more rapidly the plans for improving social and economic conditions with which it was hoped to counter the Communist advance. Italians, in their turn, resented this view, which they thought an over-simplification of their admittedly difficult but not yet desperate situation. They were also by this time (1953–4) suspicious of the growing American (and British) sympathy towards Yugoslavia and its possible effects on a solution of the Trieste dispute.[3]

THE USSR AND EASTERN EUROPE

With the fourth great Power signatory of the peace treaty, the USSR, Italy's relations inevitably became increasingly difficult as Soviet post-war policy developed. Apart from the

[1] See below, p. 228. [2] See below, p. 176. [3] See below, p. 139.

problems arising out of the Italian Communist Party's policy and its subservience to Cominform and Moscow dictates, Italy, as we have seen, met with much less sympathy from Russia than from the Western Powers in the interpretation of the peace treaty,[1] while her continued exclusion from membership of the United Nations was solely due to Soviet intransigence. Another cause of dispute was the question of Italian prisoners of war in Russia, thousands of whom still remained unaccounted for ten years after the war ended: thirty-four prisoners repatriated early in 1954 were declared by Moscow to have been the only remaining Italian prisoners then known of by the Soviet authorities.[2] Despite these sources of friction, however, no definite ban has been placed on cultural exchanges between Italy and the USSR, and exchanges of visits between Soviet and Italian 'intellectuals' and others, organised by the Society for Cultural Relations between Italy and the USSR, are fairly frequent. On the economic side, too, a trade treaty concluded in December 1948 at the same time as the reparations agreement has since been renewed, and visits are exchanged between Italian and Soviet trade delegations and business men.

The decline of contact with the Balkan countries, with whom before the war Italy was in close touch both politically and economically, had some effect on the pattern of Italian trade, and more especially, of course, on that of Trieste.[3] The limited amount of trade still maintained tended to be monopolised by Communist concerns, a position which Signor Scelba strove to break by the measures he introduced in December 1954.[4] The Foreign Minister, Signor Martino, seized that occasion to protest to the Czechoslovak Government concerning the systematically defamatory broadcasts in Italian which for some time had been emanating from a Prague radio station, some of which were said to have been recorded in Italy. Czechoslovakia, as the nearest Cominform country, had become both a training ground for some Italian

[1] See above, pp. 30 ff.

[2] At the UN Committee on Prisoners of War on 10 September 1954 the Italian delegate denied Soviet claims that the 21,000 Italians repatriated since the war ended represented all the Italian prisoners taken by the Russians. He stated his Government's belief that there were still 60,000 Italians detained in Russia.

[3] See below, p. 152. [4] See above, p. 113.

Communists and an asylum for those that fell foul of the Italian authorities.[1]

Italy's special pre-war relationship with the most obscure of the satellite countries, Albania, was officially terminated by the peace treaty in which she renounced all claim to Albania and undertook to pay her $25 million in reparations. Thereafter there was virtually no official contact between the two countries till 1950, when diplomatic relations were reopened; but refugees from Albania found a home for their National Committee in Rome. An Italo-Albanian commercial agreement was signed in December 1954, the first of its kind to be concluded by satellite Albania outside the Soviet sphere.

THE MEDITERRANEAN AND THE MIDDLE EAST

The conclusion of the Balkan Pact, the treaty of friendship and collaboration between Greece, Turkey, and Yugoslavia signed on 28 February 1953, caused some anxiety in Italy. Earlier, Italy had herself concluded treaties of friendship with Greece (in November 1949) and with Turkey (in March 1950) which at one time seemed to be a possible prelude to a Mediterranean Pact. But in the meantime Greece and Turkey had become members of NATO, while Italy's relations with Yugoslavia had worsened to such an extent that there could be no question of her joining in a localised agreement which included that country until the Trieste question was settled. Italy, therefore, while maintaining friendly relations with Greece and Turkey, held aloof from the Balkan Pact (which at that time was a non-military alliance). In 1953 visits were exchanged between Signor De Gasperi and Marshal Papagos, while in November 1953 Signor Pella found time to visit Turkey during the most difficult days of the Trieste dispute. When in August 1954 the Balkan Pact was transformed by the Treaty of Bled into a formal alliance, including clauses providing for mutual aid in the event of aggression, there was fresh talk of the possibility of Italy's adherence to it. The settlement of the Trieste question three months later seemed to

[1] For example, the Communist Deputy Francesco Moranino, a former partisan, escaped to Prague in 1952 to avoid arrest on a charge of murder committed during the Resistance period, carried on training activities there, and only returned to Italy when his re-election as Deputy in June 1953 caused him to revive his claim to parliamentary immunity. He subsequently went back to Prague.

have removed the major obstacle; but both Italy and the Balkan partners appeared cautious about taking the next step.

Italo-Yugoslav relations underwent a rapid improvement as soon as the Trieste question was settled. The various details attendant on the settlement were discussed with a minimum of friction, and trade talks, virtually at a standstill for years, were reopened with the visit to Belgrade of three separate Italian economic delegations in December 1954, while a number of economic agreements were signed on 31 March 1955. Yugoslavia afforded promising openings for Italian investment, capital goods, and technicians, and she could offer Italy timber and raw materials.

Italy resumed diplomatic relations with Spain in January 1951, after the United Nations and the United States had made it clear that the boycott on Spain was to be lifted. But she was the last country to do so. Although since then relations have been eminently correct, a distaste for the Franco régime is not confined to extreme Left-wing circles alone; such men as, for instance, the Republican party leader Randolfo Pacciardi, Defence Minister till June 1953, who fought against Franco in the Spanish civil war, would deprecate close ties with Spain. Economic relations are on a better footing, and Italian industry, especially the automobile industry, has developed considerable interests in Spain.

Relations with the Arab States improved perceptibly after the question of the colonies was settled. These States, which had *en bloc* opposed the Bevin–Sforza proposals in the spring of 1949, welcomed the subsequent change in Italy's policy when, after those proposals were rejected, she gave her support to the creation of an independent Libya.[1] Since then Italy has done much to cultivate good relations with the Arab States. A Centre for Italo-Arabic Relations was set up in Rome in 1952, and in March 1953 the newly-inaugurated Centre for Mediterranean Co-operation in Palermo held its first Congress, while in September 1953 an Italo-Arab economic conference met in Bari during the annual Levant Fair there and discussed the development of Italian trade with Middle Eastern countries. Signor Pacciardi, then Defence Minister, visited Egypt

[1] See above, p. 37.

in February 1953 at General Nagib's invitation, when economic collaboration in technical spheres was discussed.

A spectacular episode in Italy's Middle Eastern relations was the attempt made during 1952 by Italian tankers (the first and most famous was the *Miriella*) to run cargoes of oil to Italy from Persia. Several cargoes got through successfully, but once arrived in Venice import licences were not granted, so the oil remained in bond pending litigation to establish the title. Eventually, on 16 September 1954, a Rome court gave judgment against the Anglo-Iranian Oil Company in the company's action against the Supor Oil Company of Genoa, to which the *Miriella* belonged. Earlier on in the Persian oil dispute Persia had attempted to obtain the aid of Italian technicians. In 1952 a contract for crude oil was said to have been signed between an Italian company, the Ente Petrolifero Medio-Oriente, and the Persian Government, and the first cargo of oil to leave Abadan since nationalisation did so in the *Rose Mary*, a vessel under Swiss charter but in which Italian interests appeared to be concerned and which was bound for Italy.

LATIN AMERICA

Italy's relations with the Latin American countries chiefly concern trade and emigration, and will be dealt with elsewhere under those headings.[1] It may be mentioned, however, that both Argentina and Brazil provided a refuge for exiled Fascists; some members of Mussolini's family settled in Argentina after the war, while Count Grandi went to Brazil and embarked on considerable business activities there.

[1] See below, pp. 181, 226 ff.

CHAPTER XIII

THE TRIESTE QUESTION: (1) EFFORTS TO REACH A SETTLEMENT

UNTIL its fate was decided in October 1954 Trieste presented a perennial problem in Italy's post-war foreign affairs. Failure to find a solution vitiated her relations with her near neighbour Yugoslavia, while it also at times threatened to cause serious tension with the Western Powers.

THE STILLBORN FREE TERRITORY

The genesis of the problem has been outlined earlier,[1] when it was shown how the autonomous Free Territory of Trieste was set up under the peace treaty in an attempt to solve the question of rival Italian and Yugoslav claims in Venezia Giulia.[2] But in fact the Free Territory plan never advanced beyond the blueprint stage, since the four great Powers who signed the Italian peace treaty could not agree on the appointment of a Governor. During the winter of 1947–8 various candidates were suggested by the Western Powers on the one hand and by Russia on the other, but each side rejected the other's proposals. A sub-committee of the UN Security Council was no more successful; and the Italian and Yugoslav Govern-

[1] See above, pp. 33–6.

[2] Within the Trieste Free Territory (area 285 sq. miles) Zone A (British/US occupation) covered 86 sq. miles and Zone B (Yugoslav occupation) 199 sq. miles. Population estimates of 1952 for Zone A were:

Communes	*Italian*	*Slovene*	*Total*
Trieste	230,000	50,000	280,000
Other communes	9,200	13,000	22,200
	239,200	63,000	302,200

The population of Zone B was at that time estimated at 73,500 (based on 1940 statistics). No precise statistics were available as to the division of Zone B's population between Slovenes and Italians. This had in the past been estimated at roughly half and half, but by 1954 the number of Slovenes presumably exceeded that of Italians, given infiltration from Yugoslavia and the exodus of refugees to Italy, which was heavy in the earlier years after 1947 and was renewed during the tension in the autumn of 1953 (between 8 October 1953 and March 1954 over 3,000 Italians were said to have left Zone B—see *Italian Affairs*, March 1954, p. 53).

ments also failed to reach agreement when the Security Council asked them to consult together and recommend a nominee for the post.

It was partly because of this deadlock, but also because of Yugoslav attempts in the meantime to assimilate Zone B, that the three Western Powers on 20 March 1948 issued their Declaration recommending the return of the whole Free Territory to Italy.[1] This proposal was emphatically rejected by both the Yugoslav and the Soviet Governments; but the Declaration was taken as the basis for all subsequent Italian policy concerning Trieste, and it was reconfirmed by the Western Powers (e.g. in 1951, by France at Santa Margherita, and by Britain during Signor De Gasperi's and Count Sforza's visit to London), if with waning conviction as the situation became more complicated. Only three months after the Declaration, indeed, an event occurred which was to put a different complexion on the whole Trieste question: on 28 June 1948 Yugoslavia left the Cominform. This meant, on the one hand, that Yugoslavia could no longer rely on tacit or overt support for her claims but must play a lone hand, while on the other hand in Western eyes she acquired increasing significance because of the part she might play in the gradually developing schemes of Western defence.

For four years after the tripartite Declaration no major event occurred concerning the Free Territory (as it was now inaccurately termed). In Zone A, under agreements between Allied Military Government and the Italian Government, currency, finance, and foreign exchange were supplied to the Zone by Italy, who also made up the annual Budget deficit. With this help and with aid through ERP and MSA[2] it was possible to complete the reconstruction of Trieste's severely damaged port and to embark on the building of a new industrial port, as well as starting several important new industries. But the port's prosperity, which had already suffered one major reversal after the first world war with the break-up of

[1] See above, p. 56. The Declaration stated that 'abundant evidence' existed to show that 'the Yugoslav zone has been completely transformed in character and has been virtually incorporated into Yugoslavia'.

[2] ERP and MSA allotments to Zone A from April 1948 to July 1953 totalled \$31·8 million. (*Monthly Report on the European and Far East Programmes to the Public Advisory Board*, Foreign Operations Administration, Washington, 18 September 1953).

its natural economic hinterland the Hapsburg Empire, was again severely affected by the political changes which followed the second world war. Trade over Trieste from Hungary and Czechoslovakia dropped to a very low level, compensated for only by the great increase in traffic to Austria from 1948 onwards arising out of ERP shipments for that country. These circumstances tended to accentuate Trieste's dependence on Italy, with whose economy the city and its surroundings were linked in a variety of ways: there were no Customs barriers between the two, and Zone A was to a great extent dependent on Italy for supplies of nearly all foodstuffs, as well as of raw materials for its industries. Thus it is not surprising that throughout these years the then Zone Commander, General T. S. Airey, in his Reports to the Security Council[1] repeatedly stressed the view that the well-being of the area could best be achieved by its return to Italy. Local elections in 1949 and 1952 showed a considerable majority for the pro-Italian parties in favour of such a return.

In Zone B, on the other hand, the gradual assimilation of the area to Yugoslavia continued. The dinar was introduced as currency there, Customs barriers between the Zone and Yugoslavia were abolished, frontier restrictions were periodically imposed on free passage between Zones A and B, and at intervals the persecution or arrest of Italian citizens, including priests and school teachers, was reported. Local elections in 1950 and 1953 showed, as was to be expected, a practically unanimous Popular Front majority.

During these years the Western Powers apparently hoped that some solution might be found through bilateral negotiations between Italy and Yugoslavia, and such negotiations were in fact attempted on various occasions during 1951 and the first half of 1952;[2] but the differences of opinion were too great to be bridged. Despite some appearances of normality and even of a precarious prosperity in Trieste, the whole arrangement, designed to be only temporary, was wearing thin. On 20 March 1952, the fourth anniversary of the tripartite Declaration, demonstrations took place in Trieste in protest

[1] *Reports of the Administration of the British/United States Zone of the Free Territory of Trieste*. Quarterly from December 1947 to December 1949, then annually.

[2] See, e.g., Count Sforza's *Cinque Anni a Palazzo Chigi*, pp. 417 ff.

against the delay in carrying out its recommendations, and led to clashes with the police during which some thirty persons were injured. Rioting and anti-British demonstrations followed, a twelve-hour strike was proclaimed, and the Italian diplomatic representative in Trieste handed a Note of protest against the severity of the police action to General Winterton, who had succeeded General Airey as Zone Commander in 1951.

This episode seemed later, by comparison with the much more serious disturbances of November 1953, to have been something of a storm in a teacup. But it was taken sufficiently seriously at the time to warrant a conference in London between British, United States, and Italian representatives, at which the decision was reached to arrange for increased Italian participation in local administration, including the appointment of Italian officials as Political Adviser to the Zone Commander and as Senior Director of Administration.[1] It was expressly stated that this arrangement should not prejudice an ultimate settlement concerning the Free Territory as a whole.

Once more an appearance of normality descended. The new provisions came into force on 1 September, despite protests from Yugoslavia and the USSR. When the next anniversary of the tripartite Declaration came round the coming Italian General Election was already the centre of attention, and 20 March 1953 passed off without major incident. But behind the scenes there was an increasing feeling that the continued uncertainty about Trieste must be ended. Italy's anxiety at the leniency now displayed by the Western Powers towards Yugoslavia was not allayed by the exchange of visits between Mr Eden and Marshal Tito in September 1952 and March 1953. Moreover Yugoslavia had since the end of 1951 been receiving aid through MSA, and Italy could not fail to realise her rival's significant role in Western defence schemes and the consequent unwillingness of the West to antagonise her. The Western Powers, too, were well aware of the gap in such schemes which must remain unbridged until the Trieste problem was settled.

[1] See Communiqué issued at the end of the London Conference, 9 May 1952 (Cmd. 8544).

The Yugoslav position at this time is more difficult to assess. Marshal Tito would have welcomed a diplomatic success concerning the Trieste question in order to counter domestic difficulties and, in particular, to steal the thunder of the extreme Left elements in Yugoslavia who viewed askance the country's increasing rapprochement with the West. But equally, and for the same reasons, he could not afford to urge a settlement which might turn out unfavourably for him. In any case, with the Italian Election in the offing this was not the time to press for an immediate settlement. Yugoslavia therefore confined herself to renewing the proposal she had already made on 25 February 1952, for a continuance of the Free Territory but under joint Italo-Yugoslav condominium. Italy had rejected this proposal and instead advocated a solution on ethnic lines, as first put forward by Count Sforza on 8 April 1950.

THE RENEWAL OF TENSION, AUGUST-SEPTEMBER 1953

The Election of 7 June 1953 brought a change in the balance of political forces in Italy, with losses for the Christian Democrats and other Centre parties and an increase of strength for both Left and Right.[1] Signor De Gasperi was unable to form a Government, and Signor Giuseppe Pella became Prime Minister. In his policy speech on 24 August he referred to Trieste, saying that his attitude was the same as Signor De Gasperi's and adding that 'the defence of the nation's interests on the part of Italy and respect on the part of others for the undertakings entered into—the first and foremost of which is the tripartite Declaration of 1948—form an indivisible whole'.

There was thus nothing new or spectacular in the Trieste policy announced by Signor Pella, for reference to the tripartite Declaration of 1948 had been common form in all Italian pronouncements on the question for the past five years. Nevertheless on 28 August the official Yugoslav news agency Yugopress issued a statement saying that because of Italy's failure to respond to Yugoslavia's 'conciliatory attitude' over Trieste, the Government would have to re-examine the whole question. It added that this reconsideration was expected to yield results which were 'inevitable' in the situation created by 'the process of cold annexation of Trieste practised by Italy'.

[1] See above, pp. 88 ff.

This somewhat obscure statement was interpreted in Rome as a threat by Yugoslavia formally to annex Zone B. Such an intention was disclaimed by Yugoslavia on 30 August, but Signor Pella had in the meantime, on 29 August, summoned his Defence Minister and the Chief of the Italian General Staff, and had also held conversations with the envoys of the three Western Powers in Rome. An Italian cruiser and two destroyers arrived in Venice harbour on 30 August, and Italian frontier troops moved up closer to the frontier. Several sharp Notes were exchanged between 1 and 5 September, Yugoslavia protesting against 'armed demonstrations' and Italy replying that she had been obliged by Yugoslavia's 'threatening attitude' to take 'protective and precautionary measures'.

In a speech on 6 September Marshal Tito denied that Yugoslavia intended to annex Zone B ('there would be no point, as Yugoslavia is already there'), again rejected the tripartite Declaration of 1948, and said that the only acceptable solution now would be the internationalisation of Trieste city and the incorporation of the whole hinterland with Yugoslavia. Signor Pella replied on 13 September with a counter-proposal of a plebiscite for the whole Free Territory, to be organised by a five-Power conference of the three Western Powers, Italy, and Yugoslavia. But on the same day President Tito had already expressed his opposition to a plebiscite because of the 'denationalisation' of the Slovene population which had been carried out in Zone A; and on 29 September he formally rejected the proposal. On 6 October Signor Pella countered Yugoslav objections by suggesting that the plebiscite should be limited to persons born in the Free Territory area before 1918.

THE UNITED KINGDOM–UNITED STATES DECLARATION OF 8 OCTOBER 1953

Thus in early October matters had reached the stage of discussions between the Western Powers about the possibility of summoning a five-Power conference to consider these various proposals. But the whole complexion of the dispute was to be changed when on 8 October the British and United States Governments announced that, 'viewing with concern the recent deterioration of Italo-Yugoslav relations', they had decided to terminate Allied Military Government in Zone A and relinquish its administration to Italy.

The effect of this announcement was electric. In Italy it was received with jubilation, offering as it did the prospect of that parity in subsequent negotiations with Yugoslavia which Italy had so long desired, and which had been advocated as a first step in some quarters since early in 1952. Moreover, owing to the ambiguous wording of the Declaration, Signor Pella did not hesitate to draw the inference that the handing over of Zone A would not prejudice the eventual solution regarding Zone B—in other words, that the tripartite Declaration (of which no mention was made in the announcement of 8 October) was still valid.

Yugoslavia, on the other hand, at once protested strongly against the decision itself and against the failure to notify her beforehand (apparently neither Italy nor Yugoslavia had received prior notification). President Tito in speeches of 10 and 11 October declared that Yugoslavia would regard the entry of Italian troops into Zone A as an act of aggression, to be countered, if it took place, by a similar move on the part of Yugoslav troops (which had in the meantime already moved into Zone B). Anti-British and anti-American demonstrations took place in Yugoslavia, and on 12 October the Yugoslav Government insisted that any conference to be held should take place before the handing over of Zone A to Italy.

Thus the Declaration of 8 October, far from providing even the first step towards a solution, appeared only to have increased the tension. The attitudes of the two contestants hardened around the question of its implementation, Signor Pella insisting on its fulfilment as a prior condition for Italy's entry into any conference, and even suggesting that failure to carry out its promises might lead to the resignation of his Government, thus jeopardising the prospects of ratification of the EDC treaty; while President Tito was equally firm that Yugoslavia could enter no conference unless the decision of 8 October was abrogated.

The rest of October passed in negotiations among the Western Powers towards finding a way out of this new impasse. In the meantime the evacuation of some British and American troops from Zone A had begun, but no final evacuation date had been fixed, and the Allied Commander in Trieste, General Sir John Winterton, remained with other senior officials.

Into this atmosphere of mounting hysteria came one of those anniversaries which even in normal circumstances provide the occasion for a display of national sentiment. On 3 November 1918 the first Italian troops had landed at Trieste, till then for centuries under Austrian rule; 4 November is the anniversary of the end of the 1914–18 war in Italy, celebrated according to long-standing custom with a ceremony at Redipuglia, near the eastern frontier, in memory of the Italian dead. This year the circumstances were far from normal, and various precautions were taken lest an outburst of patriotic fervour should lead to trouble. The Redipuglia ceremony itself passed off without incident, if in an atmosphere charged with emotion. Signor Pella attended it but made no speech; several thousand Triestini crossed the border to be present, and Italians came from all parts of the country. After the ceremony the Allied Military Government authorities turned back from the frontier many coach-loads of Italians (some 3,000 persons in all) who attempted to visit Trieste; but some managed to get through.

In Trieste itself crowds paraded in the streets, and when it was learnt that an attempt to hoist the Italian flag on the Town Hall had been frustrated by the Allied Military Government authorities, rioting broke out and the Venezia Giulia police[1] opened fire to disperse the crowds. On the following days (5–6 November) further demonstrations by students and others took place, directed especially against British (rather than American) troops and installations. The police several times had to fire to quell the riots, one of the most serious incidents occurring when demonstrators fighting outside the church of Sant' Antonio, near the waterfront, were pursued into it by the police. Total casualties numbered 6 killed (all Triestini) and 162 injured, including 79 police. The Italian press expressed great indignation at the severity of the police methods, demanding the replacement of General Winterton by an American, and anti-British demonstrations took place on 6 and 7 November in Rome and other cities of Italy.

[1] The Venezia Giulia Police Force was a specially created unit which was organised in 1945 to maintain law and order in Zone A under the Allied authorities. It consisted of about 6,000 officers and men locally recruited and operating under the supervision of Allied officers.

For some days after the riots it seemed as if the prospects of settlement had received a very severe setback, and any hope of solution appeared further off than ever. Mr Eden voiced the British Government's serious view of the disturbances and, while deploring the loss of life, said that the Government attributed the sole responsibility to extremist elements organised from outside Trieste. Both the British and United States Governments expressed their confidence in the Allied Commander and in his handling of the situation. The Italian Government, on the other hand, protested to Britain against the police action, and Signor Pella on 8 November demanded an inquiry, attributing the origin of the trouble to the failure of those responsible to appreciate the need for different methods in this transitional phase.

But tension gradually died down, and on 13 November the Western Powers put forward a proposal, on lines similar to a suggestion from Yugoslavia some days earlier, for a five-Power Conference limited to technical experts, to precede and pave the way for a full-dress conference. It was thought that such a preliminary conference could be attended by Italy and Yugoslavia without fulfilment of the prior conditions on which each had insisted, and thus without loss of prestige on either side. On 15 November President Tito expressed Yugoslavia's readiness to take part in a conference so long as it was not based on the decision of 8 October, and he further suggested that the question of Trieste city should be regarded as separate from that of its Zone A hinterland. Signor Pella, on his side, on 21 November notified the Western Powers of Italy's readiness to take part in a conference 'for the purpose of securing a definitive settlement of the Trieste Free Territory as a whole'. He had earlier (18 November) outlined four 'fundamental ideas' to which the Government intended to adhere in discussions on the Trieste situation. These were (i) efforts to find a solution must concern the whole Territory and not merely Zone A; (ii) the Italian proposal for a plebiscite should be placed on the agenda; (iii) the Allied decision to hand over Zone A must remain irrevocable; (iv) the conference must be adequately prepared to avoid the risk of failure. But on 25 November Yugoslavia rejected the proposals for a conference in their existing form, and on 29 November President

Tito in a speech reiterated his condition that there should be no intention of carrying out the decision of 8 October in its entirety.

Nevertheless on 5 December both Italy and Yugoslavia agreed to the simultaneous withdrawal of troops to their respective garrisons, and this operation was completed by 20 December. Thus 1953 ended in a calmer atmosphere, though with neither a conference nor any other prospect of settlement immediately in sight.

CHAPTER XIV

THE TRIESTE QUESTION: (2) THE MEMORANDUM OF UNDERSTANDING OF 5 OCTOBER 1954

THE NEGOTIATIONS

A NEW approach to the Trieste impasse had to be found, and early in 1954 the British and American Governments decided to undertake soundings, in consultation with Italian and Yugoslav representatives, to see if a common basis of agreement could be reached. These negotiations began in London on 21 January, and were conducted by Mr Llewellyn Thompson, United States Ambassador and High Commissioner in Vienna, and Mr Geoffrey Harrison, British Under-Secretary for Foreign Affairs, in consultation with the Italian and Yugoslav Ambassadors in London, Signor Manlio Brosio and Dr Vladimir Velebit.

Passions had cooled somewhat in both countries, and in Italy, as has been seen, the Pella Government was replaced in February by the more moderate four-party coalition under Signor Scelba. Nevertheless the London conversations proved extremely difficult, and in the event occupied eight months of painstaking daily negotiation, conducted in such secrecy that the general public throughout had no inkling of how the talks were progressing.[1] By the end of June it had become apparent that both sides wished to reach agreement and realised that each must make some concessions. But at the same time both were hampered by the need to take into account public opinion in their respective countries. Besides the strong views still held in some quarters within Italy, the Italian Government received statements from the pro-Italian parties in Trieste making plain their unwillingness to accept any plan for partition of the Free Territory, and on 31 March Professor Diego De Castro, the Italian political adviser to Allied Military Government in

[1] See account of the negotiations given by Mr Llewellyn Thompson to a correspondent of the *Corriere della Sera*, 15 October 1954.

Zone A and himself an Istrian from the Zone B area, had resigned his post in protest against the Italian Government's policy which he felt was tending towards partition. Some circles in Italy, particularly those of the Right, were, moreover, inclined to make Italy's ratification of the EDC Treaty dependent on a prior satisfactory solution of the Trieste question.[1]

In Yugoslavia, on the other hand, Marshal Tito was unwilling to make too brusque concessions, especially in view of Slovene intransigence. He had on 7 May proposed a new settlement, involving some alterations in Yugoslavia's favour in the Zone A–Zone B frontier, and suggesting that if Italy were to retain Trieste the West should provide help for Yugoslavia to construct a port near Kopar (Capodistria), in Zone B. He also mentioned Yugoslavia's readiness, once a settlement on Trieste should be reached, to support Italy's adhesion to the Balkan Alliance, to which Signor Piccioni replied by pointing out that any move towards expanding the Balkan Pact into a military alliance would require the consent of NATO. In general it may be said that the attempts made in various quarters to link the Trieste issue directly either with EDC ratification or with the Balkan Alliance question were not particularly effective in themselves; though these wider issues were of course constantly present, and after the signature of the Treaty of Bled on 9 August[2] the reasons for desiring a speedy settlement on Trieste became stronger than ever.

The final phase in the negotiations was reached in mid-September when Mr Robert Murphy, the United States Deputy Under-Secretary of State, visited both Belgrade and Rome. On 5 October (two days, incidentally, after the successful conclusion of the London Nine-Power Conference) the four negotiators at last met together and initialled in London a 'Memorandum of Understanding' and annexes providing for a settlement of the Trieste question.

THE SETTLEMENT

The Memorandum of Understanding[3] provided for the transfer of Zone A, after a minor frontier rectification, to

[1] See above, p. 125. [2] See above, p. 133.

[3] Text in Cmd. 9288. In order to stress its provisional character the word 'agreement' was expressly avoided.

Italian administration. The rectification concerned a small strip of territory some 9 sq. km. in area on the southern border of Zone A, with 4,000 inhabitants, the majority of them Slovenes, which was to be included in Zone B and come with it under Yugoslav administration.

Military administration was to end as soon as the boundary adjustments had been made, and British and United States troops were to be withdrawn forthwith from Zone A.

The Italian Government undertook to maintain the free port of Trieste in accordance with the provisions of Annex VIII of the peace treaty.[1]

No discrimination or prosecution was to be exercised by either Government in respect of past political activities of residents in connection with the solution of the Free Territory problem.

Local border traffic was to be facilitated (traffic between the two Zones had been practically at a standstill during the past year), and former residents who had left either area were to be permitted to return and to reacquire their property and enjoy the same rights as other residents.

A Special Statute (Annex II—Annex I being the maps showing the new frontier delimitation) stated the intention of both the Italian and the Yugoslav Governments to 'ensure human rights and fundamental freedom without discrimination of race, sex, language, and religion' in the areas coming under their administration. To this end, ethnic minorities in each territory were to have equal political and civil rights with nationals in every respect, including language, education, eligibility for public office and for social assistance, and equality of opportunity in all trades or professions. The ethnic character of minorities was to be safeguarded: minorities in either territory were to have their own press in their mother tongue, and their own schools and cultural institutions, with freedom to organise them. Incitement to national and racial hatred was forbidden and punishable. A Mixed Italo-Yugoslav Commission was to be set up to examine complaints.

In connection with paragraph 5 of the Memorandum of

[1] This provided for 'a customs free port' whose area was to include 'the territory and installations of the free zones of the port of Trieste within the limits of the 1939 boundaries'.

Understanding, regarding the Free Port, Signor Brosio pointed out in a letter to Dr Velebit that the measures concerning an international régime of the Free Port, outlined in Annex VIII of the peace treaty, were no longer applicable. The Italian Government therefore invited the Yugoslav Government to participate with other interested Governments in a conference to be called in the near future to decide on measures necessary to apply, in the present situation, Articles 1–20 of Annex VIII of the peace treaty, with a view to ensuring the widest possible use of the Free Port.[1]

A further exchange of letters between Signor Brosio and Dr Velebit provided for the opening of Italian consular offices in Kopar (Capodistria), in Zone B, and for the conversion into consular offices of the existing Yugoslav (ex-Military Government) offices in Trieste.

EFFECTS AND REACTIONS

Under this settlement the Free Territory still remained in existence in theory, and in certain administrative, political, and economic respects: it could not be abolished without an agreed alteration of the peace treaty involving all the signatories. Instead the new measures, by maintaining the differentiation between the two Zones and their respective national territories, ensured the provisional character of the settlement, excluding the direct annexation of either Zone by the country administering it. Though differing little in its practical application from the ill-fated Anglo-American Declaration of 8 October 1953, the settlement received a very different welcome in both Yugoslavia and Italy; for it was, above all, not the result of a pronouncement made from above, by the occupying Powers of Zone A alone, but the outcome of agreed negotiation among all the Powers directly concerned.

In framing these provisions it was constantly borne in mind that no radical change could be made in the peace treaty without the consent of the other major signatory, the USSR; and the maintenance of a 'provisional' character in the settle-

[1] Trieste, originally proclaimed a Free Port in 1719, retained that status till 1891, when the harbour alone was left outside the Customs limit. At present (as for many years before the war) there are two free zones (in which goods in bond can be warehoused free of Customs duties etc.), situated at either end of the harbour, and, between them, a Customs zone.

ment was in part dictated by this consideration. It will be recalled that throughout this dispute Russia had advocated strict adherence to the terms of the peace treaty, i.e. the establishment of an autonomous Free Territory of Trieste. It therefore came as something of a surprise when on 13 October Mr Vyshinsky, in a letter to the President of the Security Council, announced that, in view of the acceptance by Yugoslavia and Italy, and of the fact that the Memorandum would 'contribute towards a relaxation of tension', the USSR took cognisance of it.

Steps were at once taken to implement the settlement. Evacuation of the United Kingdom–United States forces from Zone A began on 8 October. Delimitation of the frontier strip between Zones A and B was completed by 24 October, and the next day the new frontier came into effect with the entry of Yugoslav troops into the ceded area. On 26 October Allied Military Government came to an end in Zone A. General Edmondo De Renzi entered Trieste with Italian troops and assumed all civil and military powers, while General Winterton and the last remaining United Kingdom and United States troops left by sea. On 29 October General De Renzi handed over authority to the Italian Government Commissioner, Signor Palamara, and military government in both zones came to an end.

The Trieste dispute has throughout been a question not only of genuine claims and grievances but of strong emotional reactions, some deeply felt, some whipped up for propaganda purposes; and it would be unrealistic to end this account without some reference to the feelings aroused by the settlement in the countries most immediately concerned.

On an official level it was warmly welcomed in both Italy and Yugoslavia. Italian statements of course deplored the handing over to Yugoslavia of yet more Italian nationals through the addition of a fresh strip of territory to Zone B, but on the whole the settlement was regarded in Government circles as the best that could be obtained, for it placed Italy on a footing of parity with Yugoslavia in that each now administered their respective zones. Moreover, though the Zone A–Zone B boundary line had moved slightly farther south, the new line was more favourable to Italy than the one originally proposed by Yugoslavia. That line, by taking in the whole promontory of Punto Sottile, would in fact have meant a serious threat to Zone A, for Punto Sottile overlooks Trieste harbour, and the extension of the twelve-mile limit of Yugoslav territorial waters from it would, given the prevailing north-easterly wind, the 'Bora', have made access to the harbour extremely difficult. Yugoslavia had to yield both on this point and on that of special facilities in or access to the port of Trieste; and President Tito, speaking on 25 October, said that the settlement had required 'great sacrifices' from Yugoslavia but they had been made in the interests of peace and international co-operation.

Right-wing circles in Italy blamed the Government for agreeing to a further abandonment of territory. Left-wing opinion, which had throughout conformed to the Moscow line of strict adherence to the peace treaty (i.e. the establishment of an autonomous Free Territory), at first loudly condemned the settlement, but changed its tune after Mr Vyshinsky on 13 October intimated the USSR's virtual approval of the settlement. Italian Communist Party leadership showed signs of uncertainty at this volte-face, which later produced further complications when the fiery leader of the Communist Party in Trieste, Vittorio Vidali, declared his unwillingness to submit his own hitherto autonomous party to the authority of the Italian Communist Party.

It was of course in the Trieste Territory itself that the settlement aroused the deepest feelings. In Trieste and Zone A, the ceremonial handing over of the city to Italian administration, with the advent of Italian troops and the reappearance of the tricolour after so many years, inevitably aroused the Triestini to great demonstrations. But beneath the initial rejoicings there were many different undercurrents. First and foremost, the plight of Italian nationals in Zone B and in the newly-ceded strip was deeply felt by the Triestini, many of whom had relatives in these regions. Trieste itself, too, is a highly complex entity. Fascism, coming so soon after its restoration to Italy in 1918, always set great store by this region and displayed a special interest in it (there was, moreover, the proximity of D'Annunzio's attempted nationalistic coup at Fiume); and the seeds then planted still bear fruit. Fascism is not dead in Trieste, and its exponents, while rejoicing at the city's return to Italy, were only too ready to ask for more.

Autonomist opinion, too, was steadily on the increase during the latter years of the Allied Military Government régime. The so-called 'Indipendentisti', or those in favour of an autonomous Free Territory, included people of many different shades of opinion and background as well as the orthodox Communists. In business circles fears were felt lest the return of Trieste to Italy should mean an increase of bureaucratic control, bringing with it a slowing down of business procedure, delays in obtaining import licences, and so forth—a contention borne out, some considered, by experience since 1953 when increased participation of Italian officials in Zone A administration was introduced.

The future of the port was in any case bound to cause anxiety. Its prosperity must depend ultimately on a revival of trade with the hinterland countries, since the war greatly restricted for political reasons. Some traffic for Czechoslovakia and Hungary still passed through Trieste—indeed goods to and from Czechoslovakia represented 6 per cent of Trieste's total rail traffic in 1953; the proportion of Hungarian trade was much smaller. But by far the greatest share was accounted for by transit trade for Austria, which at the height of ERP deliveries kept the port working to capacity, and which in 1953 still accounted for 68 per cent of Trieste's rail traffic. But even this traffic was threatened by growing competition from the North German ports: Trieste's share of Austrian transit trade fell from 63·7 per cent in 1952 to 55·3 per cent in 1953, while in the same years that of Bremen rose from 25·8 to 31·7 per cent. Another cause for alarm was the fact that Austria in 1953 began to make some use of Rijeka (Fiume)—only to the extent, it is true, of 1·4 per cent of her total trade, but the symptom was disturbing in view of the lower charges at Rijeka with which Trieste could not compete. In the new atmosphere of détente prevailing after the settlement considerable hopes were entertained for an increase in trade between Italy and Yugoslavia,[1] which in recent years had represented between 3 and 4 per cent of Trieste's rail traffic.

The Italian Government at the end of October raised a

[1] See above, p. 134.

30,000 million lire loan to assist Trieste's economic development through port and railway improvements, aid to industry and commerce, and house and school building, and to combat the increased unemployment inevitable after the withdrawal of Allied Military Government. The interested countries were also to confer early in 1955 as to the port's future and the facilities to be provided; in this connection some Triestini circles were advocating the abolition of the Customs zone and an extension of the free zone areas to the entire port. But by the end of June 1955 the proposed conference had not yet been held, and in the meantime Trieste citizens were becoming increasingly disturbed at the port's stagnation and at the Italian Government's apparent slowness to initiate measures for improving its situation.

Part IV

Economic and Social Problems

CHAPTER XV

INDUSTRY

We must now turn to consider in more detail some of the economic and social problems about which Italy's post-war Governments have been called upon to legislate. In an earlier chapter[1] those problems were broadly outlined and an indication was given of the basic features of the country's economy. From this it will be recalled that by the outbreak of the second world war industry and agriculture contributed in almost similar proportions (34 and 36 per cent respectively) to the national economy; but employment in industry, which provided work for 33 per cent of the working population, still fell far below that in agriculture (48 per cent).

The relative importance of the various branches of Italian industry may be roughly measured by the number of people employed, the motive power available, and the consumption of electric power and coal. The table on the opposite page shows the situation in 1938 in relation to these factors.

The principal industries were those for mechanical engineering, textiles, food production, and building. Apart from considerable advances in electrical power production and in the chemical industry, the relative positions remain much the same today.

FIRST STEPS TOWARDS RECOVERY

At the end of the war industrial revival in all branches was held up first and foremost by the shortage of coal and electric power. Italy's pre-war annual consumption of solid fuel averaged something over 15 million tons, of which only about a fifth was covered by domestic sources, the remainder (some

[1] See above, pp. 38 ff.

RELATIVE IMPORTANCE OF VARIOUS BRANCHES OF ITALIAN INDUSTRY
(*per cent*)

Class of Industry	*Labour Employed in 1938*	*H.P. available in 1938*	*Electric power in 1937*	*Coal in 1938*
Mines and quarries	3·1	3·3	1·5	0·7
Timber	2·3	2·3	0·8	0·1
Food	10·3	15·8	7·1	5·1
Metallurgical	2·4	14·4	25·4	18·2
Mechanical engineering	14·4	18·1	8·1	2·0
Stone, clay, and glass products	4·1	6·4	4·6	16·2
Building	11·0	2·6		0·5
Chemicals	2·3	7·5	27·5	5·6
Cokeries and gas works	0·2	0·9		35·4
Paper	1·2	3·6	4·3	1·6
Printing	1·3	0·7	0·3	0·1
Hides and leather	1·6	1·1	0·8	0·1
Textiles and clothing	14·5	13·8	12·4	8·2
Power stations	0·6	–	–	2·5
Rubber	0·6	1·2	3·5	0·4
Other industries	4·5	3·8		1·3
Total Industry	74·4	95·5	96·3	98·0
Total Handicrafts	25·6	4·5	3·7	2·0
GRAND TOTAL	100·0	100·0	100·0	100·0

(SOURCE: UNRRA, *Survey of Italy's Economy* (Rome, 1947), p. 68.)

12 million tons) being imported principally from Germany, followed at a distance by the United Kingdom and Poland. During the war Italy was entirely dependent on Germany for coal imports, with the result that in 1945 industrial activity came almost to a standstill because of the cessation of coal supplies. Though fortunately hydro-electrical installations in the industrial North suffered relatively little damage, overall power production in 1945—a year of serious drought—was nevertheless down to 12,830 million kwh, a drop of 35·41 per cent from the peak year 1941. The first need, therefore, was to restore the power stations to full working capacity and secure supplies of coal, as well as of industrial raw materials, since in most cases stocks were very low. This in the initial stages was extremely difficult owing to Italy's temporary inability to produce goods for export, her shortage of foreign exchange wherewith to pay for imports, and the condition of her merchant fleet, which at the end of the war was reduced to about

a tenth of its pre-war tonnage. The earliest stages of external aid under the UNRRA and other programmes were therefore directed towards remedying these deficiencies.

The supply of coal for Italy was organised in the first post-war months by FEA (the United States Foreign Economic Administration) and subsequently during 1946–7 largely by UNRRA. At first procurement difficulties and strikes in the United States held up shipments, but imports (which came from the United Kingdom, South Africa, Germany, and Poland as well as from the United States) between March 1946 and March 1947 totalled around 6 million tons and with Sardinian production (of something over a million tons) covered perhaps half the requirements of transport and industry. Subsequently, with the increasing normalisation of trade and with ERP aid Italy's coal imports rose steadily and totalled over 34 million tons during the period 1948–51, of which 23·5 per cent was supplied through ERP imports.[1]

The recovery of electricity production was remarkably rapid: from the lowest point of 12,830 million kwh in 1945 it rose to 17,500 million in 1946 and to 20,000 million in 1947. Even so it was far from sufficient to meet the increasing demand, and restrictions and power rationing had to be introduced which at times caused serious dislocation. Not until 1948 was it found possible to take co-ordinated measures to solve the power shortage. Then a big construction programme was initiated, based on the installation during 1948–53 of new hydro-electric plants to an aggregate capacity of 7,750 million kwh and also, with ECA financing, of a number of large thermic power plants, thereby correcting the hitherto complete dependence on hydro-electric power with its inevitable variabilities in times of drought. As a result of all this expansion, electric power production in 1953 had increased by more than 100 per cent over that of 1938.

The rapid recovery of electricity production was of great assistance in the revival of certain branches of industry, notably the important cotton and wool industries of the North in which hydro-electric plants provide the chief motive power. More difficult was the situation in the industries based on coal, such as the iron and steel industries, where in the early period

[1] *Lo Sviluppo dell'economia italiana* (Rome, Istituto Poligrafico dello Stato), p. 362.

of efforts towards revival many blast furnaces had to be extinguished for lack of coal. Shortage of raw materials was the other major problem. Some industries still had small stocks at the end of the war, but these were soon exhausted. As a temporary way out the textile industry during 1946 accepted work 'on commission'; raw cotton and wool were sent to Italy by foreign customers to be spun and woven for their account, the payment being made in raw materials for which Italy could not otherwise have paid. Food needs were at first so great that the larger proportion of foreign aid shipments, apart from coal and liquid fuel, had to be devoted to foodstuffs, and these in fact represented 65 per cent of UNRRA shipments in the first half of 1946. But as the food position gradually improved the proportion of shipments devoted to raw materials and capital equipment increased.

Another immediate problem was the reconversion of factories from wartime to peacetime production. Given the shortage of capital and the high rates of interest and bank charges, this could only be carried out with extensive State and foreign aid. State aid was provided through the Istituto per la Ricostruzione Industriale (IRI), an organization for State financing of industry which was founded to assist Italian industry during the crisis of the early 1930s and has remained in existence ever since.[1] IRI's participation in certain branches of industry is considerable, notably in the iron, steel, and shipbuilding industries. It was in these branches, and in the mechanical engineering industry, that reconversion and modernisation presented the greatest difficulties. Modernisation of plant and methods were essential in order to increase output and reduce production costs, which in Italy tend to be exceptionally high owing to the need to purchase raw materials from abroad and also to high labour costs. The latter are due in part to the surplus manpower situation, which for some time after the war made it necessary to suspend by law the dismissal of workers from factories that had expanded to meet wartime needs. Another reason for high labour costs is the exceptionally heavy incidence of social burdens (insurance, etc.) and other

[1] A basic reorganisation of IRI and of the methods of State intervention in industry has frequently been discussed and was to be debated in Parliament during 1955.

additional charges falling on the employer, which in Italy represent 69·25 per cent of the total wage bill (as compared with 39·62 per cent in France and only 8·6 per cent in Britain).[1]

PROGRESS IN THE PRIMARY AND MANUFACTURING INDUSTRIES

In the steel industry, in particular, it was important to bring down production costs, and hence the price of domestic steel, which also closely affected the engineering and shipbuilding industries. The pre-war steel output was around 2 million tons a year, and owing to loss of capacity through war damage it took about four years to restore output to that level. But at the same time a long-term plan was prepared and presented to the Paris Economic Conference of 1947, based on an estimated increase in demand for crude steel in the home market which would necessitate an annual output of at least 3½ million tons. In accordance with this plan, and in part with ECA financing, centralisation of plants was carried out and a great deal of up-to-date equipment installed, while greater specialisation was introduced in the individual factories. This led both to reduction of costs and increase in capacity and variety of output, including the domestic production of special types of steel hitherto imported; and output in 1952 reached the original estimate of 3½ million tons. A parallel development had in the meantime taken place in domestic steel consumption, which rose rapidly from 3 million tons in 1950 to 4·1 million tons in 1952. This reflected both the greater use of steel for constructional purposes and also the rapid expansion of certain branches of the mechanical engineering industries.

The engineering industries have presented perhaps the most difficult problem in Italy's industrial reconstruction. They make a large contribution to the national net industrial product, equalled only by that of the textile and garments industry (the 1953 percentage of each was 18·2). But while in some branches of engineering quite remarkable advances have been made since the war, others have lagged behind. Roughly speaking, the growing sectors are mainly in light engineering,

[1] See 'Les charges sociales dans les pays de l'OEEC', in *Etudes et Conjoncture* (Paris), March 1954. The difference in incidence of social charges is of course in part due to structural differences in methods of wage payments.

where steel costs are small: machine tools, motor-cycles and motor-scooters (the 'Vespas' now so familiar a sight—and sound—of the Italian scene), calculating machines, cash registers, typewriters, and so on; the automobile and electrical machinery industries have also made considerable advances. It is in heavy engineering that the greatest difficulties have been met, and particularly in some of the big shipyards and other concerns of the 'Finmeccanica' group controlled by IRI where basic structural reorganisation led in some instances to the closing down of factories and to consequent labour unrest. Some of the concerns which had hitherto not been working to capacity benefited from 1952 onwards from the placing of offshore orders for equipment under the United States military aid programme. Such orders between 1951–2 and 1953–4 amounted to a total of $455 million, of which orders to the value of $115 million had been executed and paid for by the end of 1954.[1]

It was in the iron and steel and engineering industries that fundamental reorganisation and modernisation of plant proved most necessary: and it was consequently these two sectors which, together with the electrical industry, received the lion's share of State and ECA financing, the latter used largely for the purchase of new equipment abroad. The textile industries, in many respects a main pillar of Italian economy, especially as to employment and exports, did not experience the same difficulties of post-war reconversion, and with modernised plant have, despite fluctuations and difficulties during the slump which followed the Korean boom period, reached production levels far higher than before the war. Oil-refining, once again assisted as to re-equipment by ECA financing, has made great advances since the war: by 1948 the industry was able to cover the needs of home consumption, and since then has produced considerable quantities for export. The chemical industries have also expanded greatly, especially in new lines such as oil and coal derivatives, including plastics, and fertilisers from natural gas.

[1] Earlier in 1954 it was feared in Italy that failure to ratify the EDC treaty might lead to a curtailment of orders. While these fears proved groundless, the US authorities did, in October 1954, withdraw orders from two firms which had disclosed a largely Communist vote in their factory committee elections. Such discrimination was thought in some quarters to be injudicious.

But the most spectacular development in post-war Italian industry is undoubtedly that of natural gas production, which from an insignificant pre-war figure had by 1953 increased to about 134 times the 1938 level, and over ten times the level of 1948. Major deposits of natural gas were discovered shortly after the end of the war in the Po Valley, in the course of prospecting for oil, which itself was found only in small quantities. Development was in the hands of the State-controlled Azienda Generale Italiana Petroli (AGIP) and was later supervised by the State-sponsored holding company Ente Nazionale Idrocarburi (ENI).[1] By 1952 natural gas supplied 5·3 per cent of the total fuel consumed, and in 1953 output reached a rate equivalent to 4½ million tons of coal a year, thus saving Italy over a third of her annual coal imports. The only limit to expansion in the early stages was the rate of pipeline installation, which is being carried out throughout North Italy: already considerable areas depend on natural gas for both industrial and domestic fuel. This dramatic new development may well go far towards revolutionising Italy's economy in the future by minimising one of her major weaknesses, her dependence on foreign sources of fuel.

To turn for a moment from the giant industrial enterprises to the more domestic crafts: no survey of Italy's industry could be complete without a brief reference to the handicraft industries for which she is traditionally renowned and which in the past played an important part in her economic life. Handicrafts, or *artigianato*—the production of leatherware, glassware, metalware, jewellery, hand-embroidered garments, and all the beautiful trifles that delight the foreign tourist—has naturally suffered with the development of industry on mass-production lines.[2] But the Italian is a craftsman at heart; he

[1] The exploitation of methane resources, as also of oil (see above, p. 40, n. 2) was the subject of considerable controversy between the supporters of State monopoly and the advocates of free competition. State monopoly of the resources in the Po Valley was ensured in 1953 by a law granting exclusive rights to the ENI, in which AGIP was incorporated. The rest of the country was left open to free enterprise, but since the existing law of 1927 provides that all resources discovered below ground surface are State property, a Bill had to be introduced to regulate concessions and royalties.

[2] In 1953 *artigianato*, and small domestic concerns employing fewer than five workers, together accounted for 13·7 per cent of the total employed population. But among the small concerns are included a host of minor repair businesses, hairdressers' shops, etc. which in mid-twentieth century are taking the place of some of the old skills. The extent of *artigianato* today is difficult to assess numerically.

suspects the mass-produced article, and will expend infinite patience on creating a thing of beauty. The traditional home crafts continue to flourish in out-of-the-way corners of Italy, and many towns and villages are still renowned for their characteristic wares, ranging from Venetian glass and Florentine leatherware to the embroideries of Calabria and the papier-maché saints and Holy Families of Matera and Lecce. But the handicraft industry today is in a difficult situation, in danger of being passed over in the tide of development and organised assistance for its stronger brethren. Some steps have been taken to improve the handicraft workers' position; a special credit organisation has been set up, taxation reliefs have been granted, and early in 1955 health insurance benefits were extended to include them. But they need easier access to raw materials, the problem of easy credit for small home enterprises still remains, the taxation burden is often too great for them, and handicraft workers are still excluded from social insurance benefits apart from health.

FUTURE PROSPECTS

From the foregoing summary it will be seen that Italy's industry, starting out from the unpromising situation of 1945, would seem in many respects to have made a truly remarkable recovery. The 1954 index of industrial production was in fact 71 per cent above that of 1938, while the level of activity in the manufacturing industries was 65 per cent above. Moreover with some increase in domestic prosperity arising out of the Government's long-term development plans, especially for Southern Italy, there were by 1953 definite indications of growing consumption in the home market, the weakness of which had hitherto always proved a handicap. There is plainly a large potential market for consumer goods in the South, and though it will take time the gradual improvement in the standard of living there and elsewhere in Italy is bound to bring about an increase in demand for goods hitherto regarded as unattainable luxuries.

But certain inherent problems still remain. A major one is the need of larger capital resources if progress in industry is to continue its advance. On this depends another question, that of industry's capacity to provide employment for greater numbers. The spectre of unemployment and consequent labour unrest has undoubtedly hampered progress in the past. It made necessary the ban on staff dismissals in the first post-war years. Then, when dismissals were both permitted and in some cases unavoidable in view of overall reorganisation (such as has been described in branches of the engineering industries) strikes broke out and caused serious dislocation and loss of production. It is true that these strikes, and those for increased wages, were at least in part political in character, organised by the Communist-controlled trade union, the CGIL, and only rarely supported by the other unions—in June 1954, in fact, as has been seen,[1] the non-Communist unions and the Employers' Confederation arrived at a settlement of the long-standing wages dispute which the CGIL refused to recognise. But the fact remains that industry needs to find the means of increasing both opportunities for employment and overall productivity, and this can only be done by means of increased investment and expansion, especially directed towards the branches of industry which most nearly correspond to Italy's own needs and resources and where development is therefore most promising: natural gas, the light engineering industry, building, electrical power, and chemicals. The ten-year development plan outlined by Signor Vanoni at the beginning of 1955[2] offered the means of tackling seriously these problems of increased investment and employment.

[1] See above, p. 110. [2] See below, pp. 188 ff.

CHAPTER XVI

AGRICULTURE

CROPS AND FOOD

DESPITE the post-war trend towards an increased development and modernisation of her industries Italy, from her very geographical structure and situation and her shortage of industrial raw materials, must inevitably remain a country in whose economy agriculture plays a large part. In fact, though its share was steadily diminishing, in 1954 agriculture (including forests and fisheries) contributed 26 per cent to the national income (as against 40 per cent for all industrial activities); over 8 million people, or 42·4 per cent of the working population, were engaged in agriculture (as against 31·6 per cent in industry); and agricultural food products accounted for 24·6 per cent of the country's exports.

For a country so largely dependent on agriculture Italy's physical handicaps are considerable. Something like four-fifths of the country is mountainous or hilly, and the labour of centuries has built up the structure of elaborate terracing that alone makes cultivation possible in regions which in a more richly-endowed land would be left barren. Moreover much of the soil is poor; the torrential nature of the mountain rivers, especially in the South, brings the seasonal danger of floods, as well as producing soil erosion; and many of the coastal regions were till recently marshy and malarial and can only be kept in a healthy state by constant maintenance of land reclamation works and drainage.

Geographical reasons account for the very great variety to be found in the size of farms and the types of cultivation. The most prosperous region, from the agricultural point of view, is of course the great plain of the Po, once a fen, but reclaimed over a long period, and more especially in the last sixty years, by patient and costly canalisation, drainage, and irrigation. It is now one of the most highly cultivated regions of Europe, with big farms equipped on modern lines, raising dairy cattle for whose feeding the water-meadows provide fodder crops. This, too, is the main rice-growing region.

Throughout the North there is mixed farming, with dairy herds grazing on the mountain slopes and corn, fruit, and vines on the foothills. But as one moves further south livestock becomes sparser, with sheep and goats predominating. The sheep are grazed on the plains in winter, moving up to the hills for the summer along the centuries-old tracks—the *tratturi*—which are still used today. In the Tavoliere, formerly a famous sheep-farming region though now largely given over to extensive wheat cultivation, part of the ancient track used for the *trasumanza*, or seasonal migration of the flocks, runs side by side with the modern highway past the Foggia airfield.

The main cereal crop is wheat, which is grown on something like 1½ million farms throughout the country, of which about 1,200,000 market all or part of their produce. The total area under wheat, forced up to 5,300,000 hectares in the pre-war years of Mussolini's 'Battle for Wheat', now averages 4·6–4·8 million hectares. But there are considerable regional variations in methods of cultivation and in yield: on Northern farms, with good soil and using modern methods, yields are high, reaching an average of 20·7 quintals per hectare in 1948–52, whereas in the South, where extensive cereal cultivation on poor soil predominates in the *latifundia* regions, yields are only about half that figure, averaging 10·3 quintals per hectare in 1948–52.[1]

The importance of wheat in the nation's economy can hardly be exaggerated, providing as it does the staple food of the people, whose diet consists of up to something like 60 per cent of cereals.[2] There are, of course, considerable regional variations in the extent to which Italian diet consists predominantly of bread and *pasta*, the generic term for the varieties of spaghetti, ravioli, tagliatelle, and so on which can be made increasingly delicious according to their condiments. In fact, pre-war annual per capita cereal consumption ranged from

[1] National statistics, quoted in ECE, *Economic Survey of Europe in 1953*, p. 135.

[2] UNRRA, *Survey of Italy's Economy* (Rome, 1947), states (p. 41) that 'in terms of total per capita consumption of cereals Italy surpassed all other countries of Western Europe. . . . Conversely, it had the second lowest level of potato consumption in all of Continental Europe'.

186 kg. in Liguria to 225 kg. in Lucania (1937–9 average),[1] consumption in the South being accounted for almost entirely by wheat, while in the North rice and maize are also included. The latter is also extensively used for animal-feeding.

In the immediate pre-war years of the 'Battle for Wheat' Italy achieved about 95 per cent self-sufficiency in wheat. But this was only brought about by the utilisation of land fundamentally unsuited for wheat-growing, and by the sacrifice of fodder crops. Since the war this trend has been reversed, and the whole tendency is now towards a more varied type of farming, with greater accent on livestock and hence on fodder crops. Consequently Italy now imports more wheat than before the war, being dependent on imported wheat for something like 11–12 per cent of her total needs.

Though meat consumption is gradually increasing, it still remains exceptionally low by Western European standards; meat forms perhaps 3 per cent of the average diet, consumption of both meat and milk being very much higher in the North than in the South. Thus though Italy's livestock population is relatively small, she is nevertheless not far from self-sufficiency in meat. This is now also true of sugar, which partly for climatic reasons is another item of low consumption, though now on the increase. Sugar-beet is widely grown in the Veneto and Polesine regions, where its cultivation and refining form one of the main industries, and where, consequently, the serious floods in the Polesine in the autumn of 1951 meant a great setback not only to local economy but to the whole country's sugar supplies. Protective tariffs have enabled this industry, an important one for the region, to compete with the much more cheaply-produced imported cane-sugar; but the system of taxation makes the retail price of sugar very high, and this accounts to some extent for the low consumption.

Climatic reasons also account in part for the low consumption of fats and edible oils, represented mainly by animal fats in the North and by olive oil in the South. Here, though Italy is one of the largest world producers of olive oil (second only to Spain), home production is not sufficient for consumption; before the war it covered about three-quarters, the difference

[1] See Paolo Vicinelli, 'Italian Food Problems', in Banco di Roma, *Review of the Economic Conditions in Italy*, Vol. III, No. 2, March 1949.

being made up by imports of seed oils which are in part offset by exports of olive oil. This may seem an anomalous position, but Italian refined olive oil is still so important an export item that the home market must suffer when, as in bad harvest years, there is not enough to go round. Olive cultivation occupies a special place in Italy's agricultural economy: olive groves cover some 800,000 hectares of specialised plantations, of which three-quarters are in the South, especially in Apulia and Calabria, where they occupy respectively a quarter and a third of the cultivable land. Much of the land so used is of very low productive value, and but for the olive groves would be merely uncultivated grazing ground. Thus, despite the competition from imported seed oils, which can be obtained in their place of origin at much lower cost, every effort is being made to maintain the market for domestic olive oil by means of protective tariffs. These are much higher on extracted seed oils than on the groundnut, sunflower, and other seeds themselves, in order to encourage the importation of the raw materials, thus assuring work for the well-equipped Italian pressing, refining, and extracting industries.

Vine-growing is another most important aspect of Italian agriculture throughout the country. Domestic consumption of wine is said to be declining with the increased popularity of beer and even, since the war, of Coca-Cola! Wines, vermouths, and table grapes are all important export items. So too, of course, are tomatoes and their products, citrus fruits from the orange and lemon groves of Sicily and the Southern Tyrrhenian coast, peaches from Emilia, Liguria, and Venetia, cherries and almonds from the fertile Adriatic coast round Bari and elsewhere, and a variety of market-garden produce.

By no means all the fruit and vine cultivation is on specialised plantations; indeed an outstanding feature of Italian agriculture is the high proportion of arable land on which fruit trees also grow among the crops, sometimes even attaining to a 'third degree' of cultivation with vines trained from branch to branch of the trees.

Among industrial crops, apart from sugar-beet which has already been mentioned, the main crop is hemp of which Italy is the largest European producer apart from Russia, and which grows principally in Emilia and Campania. Tobacco, which is a State monopoly, is grown in considerable quantities in the Salentine peninsula round Lecce (where it forms the principal industry), and also to a lesser extent in Venetia and the Benevento province of Campania. Sericulture, formerly an important activity (and Italy still ranks as the largest producer of raw silk in Europe), is now on the decline, with the rising popularity of artificial textiles and the increasing industrialisation of the North, where the majority of the mulberry trees grow on whose leaves the silkworms are fed.

LAND TENURE

Although there are more than 9 million farm properties in Italy, the vast majority of them are very small. According to post-war (but pre-land reform) statistics,[1] among privately-owned farms those of under half a hectare accounted for 35·6 per cent of the total number but for only 4 per cent of the total area thus owned, while all farms of up to 5 hectares accounted for 93 per cent of the total number and 31 per cent of the privately-owned area. At the other end of the scale, some 1,900 very large farms of from 500 to over 1,000 hectares, representing 0·1 per cent of all holdings, together accounted for an area of over 1¾ million hectares, or 8·7 per cent of the total farm area. It is, of course, as to these large estates that the pattern has changed somewhat since the introduction of the land reform of 1950.[2]

Smallholdings exist throughout the country, but their greatest importance is in the areas of intensive cultivation. The very large properties, on the other hand, are to be found, roughly speaking, at two extremes: the large commercial farms of the Northern Plain, and the *latifundia* of the Southern mainland and the Islands.

Among the farms not worked directly by their owners the systems of tenure are complicated and variable. Management of the bigger estates is generally entrusted to *fattori* (stewards or managers), who in some cases may also be tenants, while parts of the estate are sublet in smallholdings to peasant families. These may be either (*a*) cash tenants; or (*b*) share tenants, or

[1] See Giuseppe Medici, *Politica Agraria 1945–1952* (Bologna, Zanichelli, 1952), p. 24; and UN, *Progress in Land Reform* (New York, 1954), p. 13.
[2] See below, pp. 199 ff.

mezzadri, who pay no cash rent but divide all the produce of the farm with the proprietor or chief tenant on an agreed proportion (usually half and half in the North, but a much lower share for the tenant in the South); or (*c*) share-croppers, who divide a single crop in the same way. The contracts between landlord and tenant are variable and often insecure, and since the war have been the subject of much parliamentary discussion; proposals for a settlement were put forward by Signor Segni, then Minister of Agriculture, in 1950 but had not yet been fully adopted five years later.[1]

Finally, there is the large army of day-labourers, owning no land, renting a small plot only if they can afford it and if it is available—a big if—who are hired to work on the big estates. Something will be said about their situation in describing the operation of the land reform in the South,[2] a large part of whose purpose is to improve their conditions.

Signor De Gasperi, speaking at the Naples Congress of the Christian Democrat party in June 1954 and stressing the predominant interest of the country in agriculture, quoted figures which give an idea of the proportions of the various types of farmers in Italy. Some 12,502,000 of the electorate, he said,[3] were engaged in agriculture, divided as follows:

		Per cent
Medium and small operating owners	5,901,000	47·2
Mezzadri (share tenants)	2,500,000	20·0
Large landowners (of over 150 ha.)	138,000	1·1
Medium tenant-farmers	275,000	2·2
Agricultural employees and small tenants	375,000	3·0
Braccianti (day-labourers)	3,313,000	26·5
	12,502,000	100·0

GOVERNMENT ACTION SINCE THE WAR

Italian agriculture suffered severe damage as a result of the war, not only through direct destruction of farm buildings, vineyards, olive groves, and orchards, devastation of forests, and the fighting and minefields which rendered large areas unproductive, but also in indirect ways equally serious in

[1] See above, p. 115. [2] See below, pp. 196 ff.

[3] *Il Popolo*, 28 June 1954. The difference between this figure and that of around 8 million normally given as the number employed in agriculture is presumably to be accounted for by the inclusion of farmers' and peasants' wives and other dependents of voting age.

their effect. Maintenance of the elaborate drainage and irrigation works on which Italian agriculture so largely depends had been neglected during the war years, while shortage of fertilisers (Italy herself produces no natural phosphates or potash) and insecticides seriously affected the crops. Livestock numbers, which had been well maintained till 1942, had been reduced by 1945 in all species by from 20 to 35 per cent of the 1942 level;[1] these losses also included draft animals, still (and more particularly at that time) an important factor in Italian farming. Mechanisation was in any case at a low level in pre-war Italy—little over 10 per cent of the land was then ploughed with tractors and only 60 per cent of the harvest was threshed mechanically—and by the end of the war much of the farm machinery was obsolete or in bad repair.

Thus the first post-war years were largely devoted to repairing the damage wrought by the war. UNRRA imports of wheat and other foodstuffs, as well as of fertilisers, seed, and insecticides, filled the gap until normal production could be reorganised. Farms were restocked through purchases of livestock from abroad. Bread remained rationed for some time and the wheat pools (*ammassi*) were maintained as a means of ensuring basic food needs. Contributions to them remained compulsory in the first post-war years; they later became voluntary, providing a market at a guaranteed price for a part of the farmer's produce. During the period of acute shortage the black market in food flourished; apart from bread, rationing had ceased (even in the war it had never functioned very effectively) and such goods as were available went at astronomic prices to the rich, while the farmers made hay and the poor starved.

This situation was checked by the anti-inflationary measures of 1947 which resulted in a fall in agricultural prices and brought a return to more normal conditions. With the advent of Marshall aid and the possibility of obtaining equipment from abroad, State intervention, hitherto largely concentrated on repairing the ravages of war, could turn towards long-term planning. Between 1948 and 1951 measures were carried out with ERP aid for extending irrigation in the South, and for land reclamation and improvement, reafforestation, and

[1] UNRRA, *Survey of Italy's Economy* (Rome, 1947), p. 27.

mountain river conservancy. Anti-pest and anti-malaria campaigns were undertaken and work on experimental stations was revived, while agricultural credits were granted to farmers undertaking improvements.

The year 1950 witnessed the introduction of the two long-term schemes for the land which must be regarded as among the De Gasperi Government's major achievements: the land reform and the twelve-year Development Plan for the South operated under the Cassa per il Mezzogiorno. Both these schemes, concerned principally with the improvement of conditions in the backward South, will be described in detail in the chapter dealing with that region.[1]

The land reform is still at too early a stage to allow of an appraisal of its long-term effects on the country's social and agrarian structure. While its benefits to the landless peasant are too obvious to need stressing, its introduction inevitably created an atmosphere of uncertainty among landowners which caused them to hesitate to undertake improvements on land of which they might eventually be deprived. By 1954 expropriations had been completed in the South and the other main reform areas, but uncertainty still persisted as to the application of the general reform elsewhere, for the law governing it, introduced to Parliament in 1950, had still not been debated or approved. The Minister for Agriculture, Senator Medici, speaking in June 1954, announced the Government's intention to end the existing state of uncertainty by introducing a general reform for agriculture based on three fundamental principles: the fulfilment of social needs, increased production, and a wise use of the State's limited financial resources.[2] At the same time he emphasised the need to end the existing indiscriminate 'freeze' of farm tenancy lease contracts which, as he said, was equally harmful to production and to social peace in the countryside. From these statements it seemed likely that definite measures would soon be taken on these two questions[3] which, by the uncertainties they aroused, had for years impaired the farmer's confidence and willingness himself

[1] See below, pp. 199 ff. [2] *Il Popolo*, 26 May 1954.

[3] The question of farm tenancy leases became the subject of much political controversy early in 1955, and formed one of the main obstacles in the way of maintaining the four-party coalition; but no settlement had been reached when the Scelba Government fell (see above, p. 115).

to undertake improvements. Senator Medici in fact stressed the need for landowners' collaboration in carrying out, with State aid, such improvements on their properties.

In 1951 another long-term plan was introduced by Signor Fanfani, then Minister of Agriculture—a twelve-year plan for agriculture whose aim was to provide credits to farmers to help them to overcome the major obstacles to further development: insufficient mechanisation, and inadequate irrigation and farm buildings. Under this plan, approved by Parliament on 25 July 1952, farmers were granted credit at a low rate of interest —3 per cent—to assist them in purchasing farm machinery and in carrying out irrigation and farm-building improvements. The sum originally advanced by the Government provided in the first instance for a loan of 25 milliard lire a year for five years (1952–7); it was to be used as a revolving fund, including interest and amortisation, and farmers were themselves to provide a quarter of the amount they required. Special preference was given to the small and medium farmer and to co-operatives. The loan was widely applied for, responding as it did to one of the major obstacles hitherto hampering farm development—the difficulty of obtaining from the banks the long-term credit needed for operations involving a heavy capital outlay.

The effects of this scheme, as well as of the Government plans for Southern development, have been strikingly apparent in the sphere of increased mechanisation. The number of tractors, less than 39,000 in 1938, had by 1953 risen to over 119,000. The majority were still to be found in the North, where the big commercial farms had already introduced them before the war; but they are being extensively used by the State organisations operating the land reform in the South, and private farmers are now adopting them in the Tavoliere, a region whose flatness makes it more especially suitable for mechanised farming than some of the other regions of the South.

The serious floods of 1951 and 1953 in the Polesine and in Calabria respectively brought home the need for intensified mountain river conservancy measures, maintenance of which had lapsed during the war. Moreover, in addition to reafforestation, laws were introduced to control the felling of timber. Special laws were also passed providing for assistance to farmers in mountain areas.

By 1955 the agricultural situation could in many ways be regarded as encouraging, despite the persistent problems of low agricultural prices, insufficient markets abroad for Italian produce, and unemployment among the *braccianti*. Production had reached the pre-war level by 1950, and from then onwards steadily improved, surpassing the 1938 figure by 16 per cent in the exceptionally good year of 1953, when the wheat harvest reached the record figure of 90 million quintals. For operating owners (*coltivatori diretti*), numbering some 7 million, the decision reached in May 1954 to extend social assistance benefits to them meant a considerable advance in security. Moreover by mid-1954 the average wages of farm workers had by progressive stages increased to nearly 80 times the pre-war level (1938 = 100), an increase proportionately greater in relation to the cost of living than that for any category of industrial workers.

CHAPTER XVII

FOREIGN TRADE, FINANCE, AND PLANS FOR THE FUTURE

FOREIGN TRADE

ITALY is still one of the countries whose foreign trade contributes least to the national income; yet given the poverty of her natural resources she is highly dependent on imports. Raw materials in fact form a major proportion of her imports, which consist as to some four-fifths of essential goods that cannot at present be produced in Italy, so that to a considerable extent imports are inelastic. Exports, on the other hand, consist at least in part of luxury or at any rate non-essential goods, and are consequently more dependent on external fluctuations of demand. Italy's reaction against an imposed autarky, and her realisation of her dependence on the economy of other countries, has been an important factor in dictating her post-war policy of adherence to all plans for European integration. The Budget Minister Vanoni in 1954 expressed the view that a determining element in Italy's economic policy was 'the increasing consciousness that the country's further economic progress is to be sought . . . by means of her insertion and integration in ever wider economic areas of a supra-national character.'[1]

Given the essential character of her imports, as opposed to that of some of her exports, a deficit in her trade accounts is an almost inevitable and regular feature of Italy's balance of payments. This is, however, to some extent offset by the quite considerable income derived from the invisible items—freight, emigrants' remittances, and tourism.

After the war Italy's foreign trade had to restart practically from scratch, and during the first two years she was dependent on external aid to finance even her minimum import requirements. But from early in 1946, when controls were relaxed,

[1] In review of Italian post-war economy at Christian Democrat Party Congress, Naples, 28 June 1954 (*Il Popolo*, 29 June 1954).

BALANCE OF PAYMENTS

Currency Data 1953–1954 (million dollars)

	Convertible currencies		*EPU currencies*		*Other currencies*		*Totals*	
	1953	*1954*	*1953*	*1954*	*1953*	*1954*	*1953*	*1954*
Imports	445·5	378·7	1,473·9	1,587·8	198·2	254·5	2,117·6	2,221·0
Exports (including offshore purchases)	315·6	382·1	911·6	1,020·4	166·8	203·6	1,394·0	1,606·1
Trade balance	−129·9	3·4	−562·3	−567·4	−31·4	−50·9	−723·6	−614·9
Invisible transactions and transactions in transit	212·0	214·6	250·8	321·5	70·6	29·9	533·4	566·0
Dollar settlements with EPU	−79·7	−113·1	79·7	113·1	—	—	—	—
Transfers to EPU of existing resources	—	—	51·6	52·9	−51·6	−52·9	—	—
EPU Agreement consolidation and repayment	—	−43·3	—	43·3	—	—	—	—
Overall balance	2·4	61·6	−180·2	−36·6	−12·4	−73·9	−190·2	−48·9
Balance excluding economic aid and offshore purchases	−58·9	−70·9	−180·2	−36·6	−12·4	−73·9	−251·5	−181·4
Economic aid (MSA, FOA)	133·1	104·3	—	—	—	—	133·1	104·3
Offshore purchases	61·3	132·5	—	—	—	—	61·3	132·5
Balance available	135·5	165·9	−180·2	−36·6	−12·4	−73·9	−57·1	55·4

(SOURCE: *Relazione generale sulla situazione economica del Paese (1954)*. Rome, Istituto Poligrafico dello Stato, 1955.)

ITALY'S FOREIGN TRADE, 1938–54

Year	Imports			Exports			Percentage of exports to imports	Deficit (milliard lire)
	Value (milliard lire)	Indices (1948=100)		Value (milliard lire)	Indices (1948=100)			
		Quantity	Price		Quantity	Price		
1938	11·3	88	1	10·5	100	1	92·9	−0·8
1946*	91·5	..	..	64·6	..	..	70·6	−26·9
1947	936·9	..	..	341·4	..	..	36·4	−595·5
1948	844·3	100	100	575·9	100	100	68·2	−268·4
1949	883·0	115	94	641·3	110	94	72·6	−241·7
1950	926·4	127	89	753·0	138	91	81·3	−173·4
1951	1,354·5	145	115	1,029·5	158	109	76·0	−325·0
1952	1,459·7	162	111	866·5	142	102	59·4	−593·2
1953	1,512·7	175	102	941·8	150	97	62·3	−570·9
1954	1,501·6	180	101	1,022·5	163	101	68·1	−478·1

* figures incomplete.

(SOURCES: Italy, Istituto Centrale di Statistica, *Annuario Statistico Italiano, 1944–48, 1954;* U.N., *Monthly Bulletin of Statistics*, June 1955.)

trading responsibilities gradually returned to private channels; bilateral agreements were concluded with a number of countries, and exports, aided by the incipient revival of industry using such stocks of raw materials as could be obtained, made a remarkably rapid recovery even in that first year. In 1947 the purchase of the first batch of Liberty ships from the United States helped to form the nucleus of the new Italian merchant marine, which by the end of that year reached about half its pre-war tonnage.[1] From 1947 to 1950 trade developed steadily and contributed to the gradual reduction effected, with the aid of ERP, in the balance of payments deficit, including the very heavy dollar deficit. This reduction also reflected the cautious and anti-inflationary trend in the Government's financial policy which had been initiated by Signor Einaudi and pursued by Signor Pella since October 1947. It was accounted for in part by the rise of exports, but also by some limited restriction of imports; and it was this latter aspect which in 1949 called forth criticism from ECA which at the time caused a good deal of controversy, alleging as it did that the existing level of imports was 'too low to support a level of industrial activity consistent with full utilisation of capacity, a high level of investment, and a reasonable standard of living.'[2]

Whatever the pros and cons of this thorny subject—and there were at least two distinct schools of thought about it in Italy herself—the foreign trade pattern inevitably underwent a change in 1951 which reflected the long-term domestic development plans initiated during 1950–1.[3] Imports rose and included a higher proportion of capital equipment, and though exports also increased considerably the balance of payments deficit went up sharply.

In 1952, about the time when ERP aid came to an end, the position became even more acute, but now the deficit, nearly double that of 1951, arose not so much through rising imports as through a sharp fall in exports. This was due to a number of factors, some of them transitory, some long-term, which

[1] By the end of 1953 Italy had in service a merchant fleet of 3,720,000 tons, thus exceeding the pre-war figure of 3,500,000 tons. A ten-year shipbuilding programme introduced in 1954 planned to add a further 3 million tons.

[2] ECA, *European Recovery Program: Italy: Country Study* (Washington, February 1949).

[3] See below, p. 186.

combined to make 1952 an exceptional year. Of these the most important were: (i) Italian measures, introduced in October 1951, for the liberalisation of imports from EPU countries which had the effect of actively encouraging imports from those areas; (ii) the world textile crisis, which as far as Italy was concerned spelt a reduction to the tune of 178,000 million lire in her sales of textiles abroad,[1] thus accounting for most of the fall in exports; (iii) import restrictions adopted by other countries, notably the sterling area and France; (iv) facilities granted by other countries in favour of exports which were not matched by similar facilities in Italy; and (v) a deterioration in the terms of trade.[2]

The position improved in 1953, when the overall deficit was slightly reduced: the terms of trade improved, exports increased more than imports, and there was a considerable expansion in the visible items. An even more marked improvement took place in 1954. But certain problems which were thrown into relief in 1952 still remained unsolved. Given Italy's limited supplies of foreign currency, direct or indirect American aid must continue to be an essential need. Italy has firmly adhered to her original conviction that liberalisation of imports is the policy most nearly corresponding to the country's need for a high and permanent degree of freedom of trade; and she has in fact gone further than any other OEEC country in practically abolishing restrictions (up to 99 per cent) on all imports from those countries. But this policy has not always been matched by that of other OEEC countries, whose restrictions on imports affect some of the most characteristic Italian exports.

Commodities

The table on the next page shows the part played by the various commodity groups in Italy's foreign trade.

The steady increase in imports from 1951 onwards was especially noticeable in certain branches such as industrial finished goods, and above all in capital goods such as machinery needed for the country's development and reorganisation pro-

[1] The value of textile exports was 262,000 million lire in 1950; 385,000 million lire in 1951; and 207,000 million lire in 1952.

[2] See Giulio Pietranera, 'The Crisis in the Italian Balance of Trade', in *Banca Nazionale del Lavoro Quarterly Review*, No. 24, January-March 1953.

Italy's Foreign Trade by Main Commodity Groups

	Imports							
	Milliard lire				Per cent			
	1951	*1952*	*1953*	*1954*	*1951*	*1952*	*1953*	*1954*
Foodstuffs	257	251	280	215	19·0	17·2	18·5	14·3
Textiles	298	285	261	253	22·0	19·5	17·3	16·9
Metallurgical products	119	160	162	173	8·8	11·0	10·7	11·5
Mechanical engineering products	123	196	223	224	9·1	13·4	14·7	14·9
Coal and coke	140	119	102	93	10·3	8·2	6·7	6·2
Mineral oils	126	160	183	200	9·3	11·0	12·1	13·3
Others	292	289	302	343	21·5	19·7	20·0	22·9
Total	1,355	1,460	1,513	1,501	100·0	100·0	100·0	100·0

	Exports							
	Milliard lire				Per cent			
	1951	*1952*	*1953*	*1954*	*1951*	*1952*	*1953*	*1954*
Foodstuffs	204	197	227	252	19·6	22·7	24·1	24·6
Textiles	377	200	212	204	36·6	23·1	22·5	20·0
Metallurgical products	41	47	43	45	4·0	5·4	4·6	4·4
Mechanical engineering products	186	199	192	201	18·1	23·0	20·4	19·7
Coal and coke	—	5	2	1	—	0·6	0·2	0·1
Mineral oils	29	54	89	112	2·9	6·2	9·4	11·0
Others	193	165	177	207	18·8	19·0	18·8	20·2
Total	1,030	867	942	1,022	100·0	100·0	100·0	100·0

(Source: *Relazione generale sulla situazione economica del Paese* (*1954*.) Rome, Istituto Poligrafico dello Stato, 1955.)

grammes. Among exports, textile manufactures continue to be a major item, and, despite fluctuations, the growing importance of light mechanical engineering products is also apparent: in 1953 they accounted for more than a quarter of the total value of exports. As compared with the pre-war situation, finished and semi-finished goods and raw materials today represent a higher percentage of total exports, while the share of agricultural foodstuffs has fallen (from 33·2 per cent of the total in 1938 to 24·1 per cent in 1953). Indeed, the statistics given above demonstrate the fallacy of the widely held view that Italy is primarily an exporter of agricultural produce, for even in a good year such as 1953 foodstuffs (including those subjected to manufacturing processes) accounted for barely a quarter of total exports. The fallacy is understandable at a first glance, for it is the lemons and oranges, the early cherries, the succulent peaches, and all the many different tomato products that bring Italy constantly to the mind of the ordinary British purchaser, recalling in a flash the scent of citrus groves basking in a sun such as his own island seldom enjoys. But these visible reminders of Italy are far from being her only foreign-exchange earners.

Direction of Trade

The pattern of Italy's trade with other countries has undergone considerable changes since the war, as can be seen from the following table:

PERCENTAGE DISTRIBUTION OF EXPORTS AND IMPORTS

	Exports					*Imports*				
	1937	*1950*	*1951*	*1952*	*1953*	*1937*	*1950*	*1951*	*1952*	*1953*
US and Canada	8	7	7	11	11	12	24	23	23	15
Latin America	7	11	9	7	7	12	11	10	6	7
Continental EPU	33	40	37	41	42	36	28	27	30	37
Dependencies	1	1	2	2	2	3	3	2	3	3
United Kingdom	6	11	13	8	7	4	6	4	6	8
Dependencies	1	4	5	5	4	3	2	4	3	2
Other sterling countries	3	9	11	7	8	8	9	13	12	15
Rest of world	41	17	15	19	19	22	17	17	18	14

(SOURCE: *International Financial Statistics*, Vol. VII, No. 5, May 1954, p. 28.)

In the immediate pre-war years, Germany, followed at some distance by the United States and United Kingdom, was by far the most important trading partner for Italy, accounting in 1936–8 (together with Austria) for 26·8 per cent of her imports and 18·9 per cent of her exports.

The main feature of the early post-war years was Italy's dependence for imports on the United States, which in 1947, for example, provided over 40 per cent of her total imports. This dependence, and the considerable dollar deficit that went with it, gradually decreased to reach an average of nearer

15 per cent in 1953–4, when, with a marked increase in Italian exports to the United States, the position with the dollar area was becoming more normal (though it was still clear that to achieve anything like equilibrium Italian exports to the United States would need to increase by about 80 per cent above their existing level). This trend coincided with the progressive reduction of ERP aid which from 1952 onwards was to a limited extent superseded by offshore procurement orders.[1] It was also the result of Italy's efforts to purchase as far as possible from the EPU countries, which would be more likely to afford a market for Italian exports. By 1953, in fact, two-thirds of Italy's total trade was with the EPU area, imports from that area having risen from a value of $1,140 million in 1951 to $1,630 million in 1953. This policy brought about a sharp change in her position in relation to EPU, where from being a high creditor nation in 1951 she lost much of her credit during 1952 and by the end of 1953 had become a debtor to the tune of $312 million. For while her imports from both the OEEC and the sterling areas rose, her exports to the OEEC countries increased only slightly and those to the sterling area fell. This situation was to a great extent due to the import restrictions imposed in France and the sterling area, the latter accounting in 1953 for more than half Italy's deficit with EPU. In 1953–4 there were some signs of a relaxation of these restrictions, at any rate as far as the United Kingdom was concerned.

The other remarkable feature in the pattern of Italy's foreign trade from 1952 onwards was the return of Germany to her pre-war position as one of Italy's main trading partners. Already by 1952 she was second only to the United States as to both imports and exports, and in 1953 she came much nearer to the United States' level for imports and took first place among all Italy's clients for exports. Of the other EPU countries, France and Switzerland still, as in the past, play an important part in Italian trade, both for imports and exports. Among the sterling area countries, Australia takes a high place as supplier; Italy needs her wool, which accounts for some four-fifths of the total value of imports from Australia.

In recent years Italy has paid increasing attention to the

[1] See above, p. 159.

Mediterranean and Middle Eastern countries; in 1953 imports from this area represented 15 per cent, and exports to the area 14 per cent, of the total. After the settlement of the Trieste question there were hopes of a revival of trade with Yugoslavia.[1] Eastern Europe and China, which in 1938 together took some 7 per cent of Italian exports, in 1953 accounted for 4·2 per cent of the total. Among the Latin American countries Argentina and, to a lesser extent, Brazil are Italy's most important trading partners. Trade relations with both these countries are governed by bilateral agreements of 1952. The foundation of Italo-Argentine trade is wheat, of which Argentina has become an increasingly important supplier to Italy, since the United States and Canada require payment in dollars. In return Italy exports capital equipment to Argentina.

Finance

Post-War Inflation and its Check

When the war ended Italy's finances were in a parlous condition. Inflationary symptoms had already been apparent for more than a year, for since the division of the country after the Armistice of September 1943 there had been two separate Ministries of Finance, each with unbalanced Budgets, and two Central Banks each issuing quantities of new currency. By mid-1945 prices had become astronomical, the black market reigned supreme, and virtually the only goods purchasable with lire were those brought in by the Allies.

During the first post-war year following on the country's reunification there was some revival of confidence. The Budget deficit was still enormous, but was financed largely by a successful post-Liberation loan and by borrowing from the commercial banks. By mid-1946 prices had fallen slightly, but the unbalance between demand and available goods remained.

Between June 1946 and September 1947 prices rose by 150 per cent; the cost of living doubled; the issue of paper money continued to increase much faster than the increase in the national income, while by mid-1947 the lira had lost over 98 per cent of its pre-war value. Moreover, with continued need for high imports and the only gradual revival of exports, the foreign-exchange position was highly precarious. The Govern-

[1] See above, p. 134.

ment had to undertake heavy expenditure on repairs of war damage, especially to transport, and on subsidies, mainly to wheat prices.

It was at this point, at the end of the summer of 1947, that the decision was taken to adopt immediate measures to end the rapidly developing inflation. This decision was initiated under the aegis of Professor Luigi Einaudi, then Budget Minister, and of Giuseppe Pella, then Finance and Treasury Minister, with whose name the 'new line' then adopted was to be associated for the next five years. The importance of this change in policy can hardly be exaggerated: it marks a sharp dividing line between the two post-war periods of Italian economic history. By checking inflation it placed the country once more on the road to financial stability.

Briefly, the most important aspect of the new policy, as outlined in a Bill approved by Parliament on 4 August 1947, which came into operation on 30 September, was the imposition of new reserve requirements on the Italian banks. Each bank was permitted to lend up to 75 per cent of its deposits only, thus maintaining a compulsory cash reserve of at least 25 per cent of the total sums deposited. On a more long-term view, certain guiding principles were adopted which were adhered to throughout the next five years during which Signor Pella remained in charge of the country's financial policy. These included—to quote Signor Pella himself[1]—(i) a Budget policy which aimed at increasing revenue, controlling expenditure, and keeping the deficit within non-inflationary limits (i.e. of a size that could be covered by the spontaneous flow of savings in the form of Treasury loans on both short and long terms, without having to resort to the printing of paper money on the Treasury's behalf); (ii) a credit policy directed towards financing the country's expanding activities within the limits of money actually available for investment; (iii) a policy of imports and exports designed to improve the balance of payments; and (iv) the abandonment of direct restrictions and the direct control of consumption, and the limitation of price controls to certain basic sectors such as bread and essential public services.

[1] See Giuseppe Pella, 'Five Years' Struggle against Inflation', in *Italy: An Economic Survey*, published as a special Supplement to *The Statist*, 25 October 1952.

The effect of the new policy was immediately apparent and produced increasing stability during the following years. Bank deposits rose, and the increase in note circulation did not exceed the limits indicated by the increase in the national income, a principle which has been strictly borne in mind in post-war Italian finance. The Budget deficit was considerably reduced during the three years 1948–9 to 1950–1, though it began to increase again during the two following financial years, partly owing to the impact of the Korean war but also to the needs of rearmament under NATO (in 1952–3 defence represented more than a fifth of the total Budget) and the deficit remained high during 1953–4. But the lira withstood the shocks of the Korean crisis and in fact showed itself to be one of the most stable currencies in Europe. The following table shows the movement of wholesale prices and of the cost-of-living index during the period of emergence from inflation.

	Wholesale Price Index	*Cost-of-living Index*
	(1938 = 1)	
July 1947	57·79	48·05
December 1947	55·25	49·29
1948 (average)	54·43	48·44
1949 ”	51·69	49·15
1950 ”	49·05	48·49
1951 ”	55·81	53·20
1952 ”	52·70	55·46
1953 ”	52·50	56·54
1955 ”	52·93	58·06

In 1949 the lira exchange rate was fixed at 625 to the dollar and 1,749 to the £1 and has remained stable ever since.

Taxation Reforms

If the introduction of the deflationary policy constituted a landmark in the conduct of Italy's post-war finances, the other major outstanding feature was the taxation reform of February 1951. Unlike many countries, the main source of revenue in Italy is still derived from indirect taxation, which in 1952–3, for example, accounted for 78·2 per cent of revenue, while direct taxation represented only 16·1 per cent (comparable figures for the United Kingdom are direct taxation 54·7 per cent, indirect 45·3 per cent). One of the main ultimate aims of the Italian reform is to remedy this unbalance. In its initial stages, however, the reform affected only direct taxation: the unsatisfactory methods of income tax collection in Italy, leaving the way open to widespread evasion, had long been criticised as one of the main reasons for her unstable financial situation, while the inflation and chaotic conditions which followed the war had increased the phenomenon of tax evasion.

Moreover, inflation had brought about significant changes in the distribution of tax revenue, the most marked feature being the relative decline in the share of taxes on income and property, which in 1951–2 accounted for only 23 per cent of the total tax revenue, as compared with 32 per cent in 1938–9; while on the other hand revenue from turnover taxes increased from 20 per cent in 1938–9 to 38 per cent of the total in 1951–2.[1]

The law of 25 February 1951, put forward by Signor Ezio Vanoni (then and till January 1954 Finance Minister and subsequently Budget Minister) and described as 'Regulations for the Equitable Adjustment of Taxation and Extraordinary Fiscal Collection', was regarded as only the first step towards a wider reform which was to modify profoundly the whole Italian fiscal system. It was based first and foremost on the principle of the annual declaration of income. To the British taxpayer this may seem to go without saying: but in Italy in the past the absence of a declaration could be taken to mean that taxable income remained unchanged—or at any rate the onus of providing proof to the contrary had lain on the revenue authorities. The result was frequently a prolonged game of hide-and-seek between taxpayer and collector, in which each recognised and strove to forestall the moves of the other, and from which the taxpayer as often as not emerged victorious and unscathed. The new law, by its insistence on an annnal declaration, aimed at putting an end to the possibility of evasion and thus ensuring a more equitable distribution of the taxation burden. A lower limit, originally of 240,000 lire a year, subsequently raised to 480,000, was fixed for income tax exemption, while the tax-free basis was extended to include fresh categories. A later law reduced the rates of taxation, especially at the lower income levels.

The immediate result of the new law was to produce in

[1] See ECE, *Economic Survey of Europe since the War*, p. 76.

1951 nearly 4 million declarations of income. Some of these showed an income below the taxable level, but the remainder were found to have declared a total income more than twice as large as that assessed in the revenue offices. Naturally it was not to be expected that a new law would check evasion overnight, as some notorious cases have gone to prove. But the sport of evasion is undoubtedly now more difficult to pursue, and in the meantime the burden of taxation is being more evenly distributed. The same would seem to be true of the national income: in 1952 the average real per capita income had increased by 4·55 per cent since 1938, while real per capita tax receipts had increased only by 0·58 per cent, thus suggesting a more even distribution of wealth—though at the same time emphasising the difficulties of increasing the pressure of direct taxation in a country such as Italy where the average per capita income is extremely low (reckoned in 1953 at around 211,000 lire a year, or £120).

Further steps towards fiscal reform were taken in 1954, when the Finance Minister, Roberto Tremelloni, announced severe penalties for tax evasion, including imprisonment in cases of fraud, and put forward a Bill introducing for the first time taxation of the profits of joint stock companies. This measure aroused some protests in business circles, but was expected to bring in around 60,000 million lire a year.

Investment Policy

The first year of the deflationary policy coincided with the advent of ERP aid, which played an important part in Italian reconstruction both in its effect on the balance of payments and in the matter of investments. A fifth of ERP aid received[1] was used for the import of machinery and equipment (the remainder being used for imports of grain and essential raw materials), while the Counterpart Fund, totalling 664·4 milliard by the end of 1951, was devoted entirely to investments: the financing of industry, railway reconstruction, public works, agriculture, building, and the Southern Development Fund (Cassa per il Mezzogiorno).

[1] Totalling $1,515 million between 3 April 1948 and 31 December 1952 (see US Mutual Security Program, *Monthly Report of the Mutual Security Agency*, 30 November 1952.).

With ERP aid as a basis, the Italian Government was able to turn its attention to long-term planning and investment in the various directions that have been referred to: the schemes for the reorganisation of the steel industry, the development of hydro-electricity and natural gas, the plans for the development of the South, and those for tackling the housing and unemployment problems. As has already been mentioned,[1] the reproach was made by the ECA authorities at an early stage in the European Recovery Programme (1949) that Italy was making insufficient use of the funds thus made available. It is true that the spectre of a fresh relapse into inflation seems at first to have inhibited the planners from embarking on bold schemes of expenditure, and that there was a tendency to conserve resources. It is, however, equally true that, as an authority on Italian economic problems has expressed it, the structural difficulties of the country's economy 'have the tendency to keep the maximum level of investment in Italy that is consistent with the avoidance of outright inflation considerably below the optimum investment level which would correspond to the point of full or near-full employment.'[2]

In any case, the fact remains that from 1950 onwards bolder steps were adopted and the planning stage gave way to practical execution. In 1954 something like a fifth of the national income was devoted to capital investment, which totalled 2,350 milliard lire, as against 2,050 milliard in 1951. Signor Vanoni in his report to Parliament in March 1954[3] mentioned that private investment had an important share (more than half) in this total; and he cited, as an example of the stimulus exercised by public investment, the fact that during 1953 in Italy, unlike the majority of European countries, output in the metal-using industries had increased more rapidly than output as a whole.[4]

The problem of capital shortage and the need for investment, so serious at her present stage of development for a country with Italy's limited resources, was put in its long-term setting by Dr Menichella, the Governor of the Banca d'Italia, in his

[1] See above, p. 176.

[2] See Bruno Foa, 'The Italian Investment Problem Revisited', in *Banca Nazionale del Lavoro Quarterly Review*, No. 27, January-March 1951, p. 23.

[3] *Il Popolo*, 24 March 1954.

[4] See also ECE, *Economic Survey of Europe in 1953*, p. 3.

annual report at the end of May 1954.[1] Tracing Italy's advance through the years of post-war reconstruction, he pointed to the remarkable increases in agricultural and industrial production: in 1953 production in agriculture was 16 per cent, and in industry 56 per cent, above the pre-war level, while during the previous three years alone industrial production had increased by 34 per cent. Never in Italy's economic history, he said, had such rapid progress been achieved in so short a time. The present stage was one in which investment of capital was especially necessary, both in order to increase the productivity of the existing concerns through reorganisation and modernisation of plant, and for the establishment of new enterprises which would absorb fresh manpower. The proof of the need for investments lay not only in the very considerable increase in the production of capital goods (a rise of 53 per cent between 1950 and 1953) but also in the imports of machinery from abroad, to a value of 220 milliard lire, made possible in recent years through ERP aid.

But this 'thirst for investments', Dr Menichella said, could be regarded as transitory, and would diminish once the immediate phase of reorganisation and modernisation was over, and as the rate of increase in population slowed down. It was therefore important in this transitory phase that the highest possible proportion of the national income should be capitalised, and that the demand for consumer goods 'should not increase at the rate which rising production might seem to justify'. Italy's great need now was to increase her exports, if necessary even at the expense of home consumption; and the other need was for international co-operation, both in the form of investments from abroad and of trade liberalisation measures to match the steps which Italy herself had taken in that direction.

'Consume less today in order to consume more tomorrow': the words have an all too familiar ring to British ears, and are likely to be even less welcome in a country such as Italy where the standard of living of many is already very low. But, as Dr Menichella explained, the aim was not to restrict the incipiently rising demand for consumer goods among the

[1] *Relazione della Banca d'Italia, 31 May 1954*; summarised in Supplement to *Mondo Economico*, 5 June 1954. The same themes were emphasised afresh in Dr Menichella's report for 1954 (*Mondo Economico*, 11 June 1955).

poorest classes, where indeed it was to be welcomed, but rather to curb expenditure and encourage saving among the better-off and those who had profited by the concentrated wage increases of recent years, and by this means bring nearer the goal of a more equitable distribution of the country's wealth.

Plans for the Future

A few months later, Dr Menichella's advice was echoed and given more concrete form with the announcement early in January 1955 by Signor Vanoni, Minister for the Budget, of a ten-year plan for the development of income and employment in Italy. This plan had already been foreshadowed by Signor Vanoni at the National Congress of the Christian Democrat party in the previous June, and it had aroused interest during his visit to the United States in the autumn. In the meantime Italian experts, with the help of several foreign economists, had been at work on the draft of the plan. Signor Vanoni emphasised that the study in its existing form was only a basis for discussion: the measures it proposed would have to be debated in Parliament and embodied in legislation. He also made it clear from the outset that fulfilment of the plan must depend to a considerable extent on the degree of co-operation which Italy could obtain from other countries; and to this end he took an early opportunity of presenting the plan on 14 January 1955 to the Council of OEEC, where it was at once approved and assistance was promised from other member countries.

Briefly, the plan,[1] envisaged to cover the ten years 1955–64, aimed at increasing the national income by raising investment in all sectors of the economy and thus creating 4 million new jobs by 1964, which it is estimated would virtually wipe out unemployment (the figure of 4 million jobs needed is calculated on the basis of the number of existing unemployed and under-employed, plus new workers coming on to the labour market and those likely to be displaced by technological processes, over the ten-year period). National income, it is stated, increased between 1951 and 1954 at an annual rate of just

[1] The draft plan was entitled *Schema di sviluppo dell'occupazione e del reddito in Italia nel decennio 1955–1964* (Rome, January 1955). English version: *Outline of Development of Income and Employment in Italy in the Ten-Year Period 1955–64* (Paris, OEEC, January 1955).

over 5 per cent—a rate of expansion among the highest recorded in Italian economic history—while the average annual increase in gross investment was 6·6 per cent. It is essential for the plan's fulfilment that this rate of increase in the national income should be maintained over the ten years. It is believed that such an increase should be sufficient to ensure the estimated capital requirement for new investment, but only on condition that a substantially larger proportion of the increase in national income than hitherto is used for that purpose. In fact, 'investment should absorb more than one-third of the total income increment for the entire ten-year period', leaving less than two-thirds for consumption. New investments in 1954 accounted for about 14·4 per cent of the national income, but it is reckoned that this figure must be increased to nearer 20 per cent if the plan in its present form is to succeed. The necessary restrictions on consumption should fall on those already employed and 'the increase in resources available for consumption will have to go . . . to the newly employed'.

Every encouragement was to be given to private investment. At the same time the Government proposed to intervene directly in three particular 'impulse sectors', namely agriculture, public utilities and services, and public works, and also in housing. Total investment in the key sectors during the ten-year period should amount to 10,600,000 million lire, as compared with a net investment of 630,000 million lire in those sectors in 1954; while total investment in all branches of the economy was estimated at 35,000,000 million lire (about £20,000 million). It was reckoned that the impulse to the country's economy thus provided should be sufficient over the ten years to create the 4 million new jobs needed to eliminate unemployment.

This is, of course, a highly ambitious scheme, still in its infancy and which may have to be altered in detail. Its success must obviously depend on a variety of contingencies, both domestic and international: first and foremost, it presupposes a long spell of stable government and efficient administration. The effects of such stability would be felt abroad as well as at home, in producing the atmosphere of confidence needed to further foreign investment. In this connection encouraging signs during the first half of 1955 were the International

Bank's loan of $70 million to the Cassa per il Mezzogiorno[1] and loans from Switzerland totalling over 300 million Swiss francs to various Italian concerns. Legislation was to be introduced with a view to facilitating a larger flow of private capital from abroad, including, in particular, the abolition of existing limitations on the transfer of profits.

[1] See below, p. 204.

CHAPTER XVIII

THE SOUTHERN PROBLEM

CENTURIES OF NEGLECT

FREQUENT references have already been made to the fundamental differences, both economic and political, between the North and South of Italy which geography and history have combined to produce, and which have coloured the whole development of the country ever since the unification.

In climate, while Northern Italy on the whole resembles other countries of the European continent, the South—corresponding roughly to the regions south of a west-east line drawn from Rome to, say, Termoli on the Adriatic—possesses all the Mediterranean characteristics of climate and vegetation. Much of the country is mountainous and there is no large fertile plain to correspond to the Po Valley, for even the Apulian plain of the Tavoliere, round Foggia, is waterless and a limestone crust lies near the surface of the soil. Rainfall is confined to the autumn and winter, while the summers are scorching and arid. On the Ionian shore the rivers of Calabria and Lucania are torrential when swollen by the winter rains; in summer they dry up entirely, leaving only their stony beds and the wreckage of their floods. On the Adriatic there are no rivers at all south of the Ofanto, which enters it north of Barletta. Deforestation in the Sila mountains of Calabria and in Lucania has produced soil erosion. The soil itself is poor, except on the fertile coastal strips between the Gargano spur and the heel on the Adriatic, and round Naples and along the Tyrrhenian coast of Calabria. Much of it is intractable slatey clay; where limestone is near the surface, stones and outcroppings mottle the red fields with white flecks.

The histories of North and South have been no less different. To go no further back than the Middle Ages, while the Northern towns became the centres of flourishing city-states with a form of local self-government in each Commune, the South was under the rule of foreign invaders. Separated by

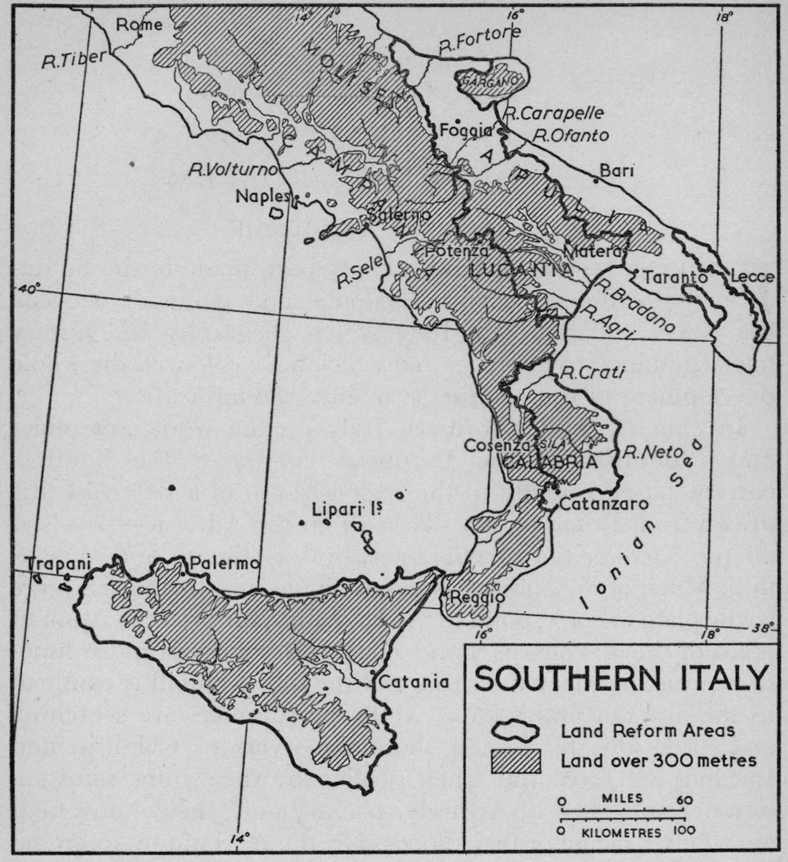

the central belt of the Papal States, the two halves of the peninsula led lives subjected to quite different influences. Bourbon rule persisted in the Southern Kingdom of Naples and the Two Sicilies until the unification; and with it went a quasi-feudal social framework which has lasted almost till today.

The unification of Italy bore hardly on the South. Capital tended to be concentrated in the already much more prosperous North; tariffs, till then low in the South, were adjusted to the much higher level of those of Piedmont; and the early growth of Southern industry was nipped in the bud.

In the years that followed, communications and industry

went hand in hand to further the rapid development of the North. But the industrial tide left the South high and dry to make what living it could out of agriculture. Politicians of the day were not unaware of this unbalance in the new Kingdom's economic structure, and from 1900 onwards efforts were made, under the impetus of a few ardent protagonists of the South such as Franchetti, Colajanni, Fortunato, De Viti De Marco, and Nitti (to be joined later by Salvemini), to raise the level of Southern economy. A series of special laws between 1901 and 1906 provided for public works, tax exemptions, and other forms of assistance for particular areas in the South, and between 1906 and 1911 a parliamentary inquiry on the condition of the peasants in the Southern Provinces produced an immense report running to eleven volumes. But progress was slow—how slow can be seen from the example of the Apulian aqueduct, the major and most needed public works undertaking for the region, designed to bring water from the mountain source of the Sele, above Eboli, right across to the Adriatic and down to the heel of Italy; begun in 1906, it was completed only in 1938.

This first period of special legislation for the South coincided with a large-scale effort to deal with another aspect of the Southern problem: that of over-population. The Southern provinces contain something under a third of Italy's total population (in 1952 their population totalled 17·6 million of the nation's 47 million). The rate of natural increase has risen steadily in the South till the last decade, whereas in the North it has been gradually falling for the past forty years. Given the South's economic poverty, its own soil could not hope to support the whole of its growing population. The solution found was emigration, and between 1900 and 1910 an average of 603,000 Italians migrated each year to the Americas or to other European countries, of whom a large proportion came from the South.[1] Italian emigration to the Americas, especially to the United States, had in fact begun as early as the 1890s, and from then onwards was to provide an important outlet for the country as well as a substantial source of income in

[1] See below, pp. 208, 226. In 1901–11 net emigration from the South accounted for 6·8 per 1,000 of the total population, from the North 3·8 per 1,000; net emigration included migration to the other part of Italy (*Atti della Commissione parlamentare di inchiesta sulla disoccupazione* (Rome, 1953), Vol. III, Pt. I, pp. 24–5).

emigrants' remittances home, until domestic legislation on the part of the reception countries closed the doors in the 1920s. But by that time Fascist autarkic policy was already striving against Nature to keep Italians at home and force native resources to provide them with a livelihood.

The Fascist régime paid relatively little attention to the South. It was in any case the Cinderella of the State, and it was not the Fascists' habit to focus attention on intractable problems which could not quickly show a spectacular dividend. Instead, they sent their political prisoners to *confino* there —as readers familiar with Carlo Levi's *Christ Stopped at Eboli* will know. But in one cherished Fascist scheme the South could play a part: this was the 'Battle for Wheat', which was to render Italy self-sufficient in this staple food. So the South, already largely given over to extensive wheat cultivation on the big *latifundia*, was encouraged to extract even more grain from its poor soil, mainly at the expense of fodder production. At the same time some serious attempts were made to tackle the problem of land reclamation in the marshy, malaria-infested coastal areas: the Sele delta round Paestum was effectively drained and made fertile (the show piece in this connection was the Pontine Marshes, nearer Rome), and further plans for land reclamation were set on foot under the Serpieri law (so called after its promoter) of 1933; but these had made little progress when the war broke out. Another scheme interrupted by the war was that for land settlement, especially of ex-servicemen, in the *latifundia* districts of Sicily and the Tavoliere.

It has been seen how wartime experience divided anew the two halves of Italy, already committed by the past to such differing outlooks and ways of life. If the South suffered less through fighting and material damage than the Centre and parts of the North, its inherent economic weakness nevertheless made it more vulnerable than the rest of the country. In particular, the damage to electrical installations and the prolonged separation from Northern sources of industrial supplies were disastrous factors in dislocating Southern economy. Moreover the end of the war, bringing with it the return of men from the forces and from the former colonies, laid bare the old Southern problem of over-population which Italy's wars (in Abyssinia and Spain as well as the major war of 1940–5) and colonial migration had served in some measure to disguise. The need for work expressed itself in a cry for land for the peasants; and the Communists, as can now be seen in retrospect, had already realised how great an opportunity for expansion the South, hitherto little touched by their propaganda, could offer them.

More than half the population of Southern Italy is still dependent on agriculture for its livelihood. Figures for 1952 show the following pattern of occupational distribution in the South and the North:

OCCUPATIONAL DISTRIBUTION OF ACTIVE POPULATION, 1952
(*per cent*)

	South	*North*
Agriculture	53·0	37·3
Industry and transport	27·4	39·2
Trade and other	19·6	23·5

(SOURCE: ECE, *Economic Survey of Europe in 1953*, p. 124.)

On the other hand, the agricultural land available in the South has been reckoned at 0·45 hectares per capita—the lowest of any Southern European country except Greece, where the figure is the same.[1] Much of that land, as has already been said, is of poor quality and in hilly or mountainous regions, but poverty and land hunger have necessitated the cultivation of even the most unrewarding and inaccessible plots. Implements and methods of cultivation were till recently of the most primitive, and crop rotation was generally confined to alternating years of wheat and fallow. The average yield per hectare, forced up to 10·9 quintals during the 'Battle for Wheat' in the 1930s, again reached that level in 1952; but it still remained only about half the yield of the North (19·1 quintals per ha. in 1935–9, 20·7 quintals in 1948–52).[2] Even on the big estates there is little livestock, and the sacrifice of fodder crops to wheat in the 1930s is only now gradually being remedied to some extent.

There are, of course, considerable regional differences in the agricultural pattern of the South. In striking contrast to the big *latifundia* of Calabria and the Tavoliere, largely given

[1] ECE, *Economic Survey of Europe in 1953*, p. 76.
[2] ibid., pp. 135, 139.

over to extensive cereal cultivation, the Adriatic coastal strip north and south of Bari appears a radiant and fertile oasis. Here are vast stretches of vine and olive cultivation, as well as fruit and almond trees; and further south, in the Salentine peninsula round Lecce, tobacco is grown. A similar fertile region of vines, olives, and citrus fruits lies along the Tyrrhenian coast of Calabria.

The forms of land tenure vary too. In the *latifundia* regions about a third of the land is leased out by the landlord or his middleman to peasant tenants who may also work on the estates as day-labourers; the contracts are precarious, sometimes reckoned in money against daily wages, sometimes of the share-cropping kind (*mezzadria*), with the tenant getting far less than the half share of the produce which is customary in the North. The same system is found on the medium-sized estates. On all these estates, both large and medium, there is little capital outlay on improvements or implements; on the big *latifundia* the landlords seldom live on their estates, and take little interest in their management. In the fertile coastal areas, on the other hand, where cultivation is intensive, the amount of capital invested in the soil is high even by world standards.

From the foregoing brief account of an intricate situation it will readily be seen that the peasant's opportunities for work are highly restricted. They amount, in fact, to two: he can work as a labourer (*bracciante*) on the big estate, either attached to the estate by complicated ties of tenancy or as a day-labourer; and in his spare time he can work his hired plot of land. In practice, neither of these alone can supply a livelihood, and even in combination they barely provide enough to reach the lowest subsistence level. Day-labouring is seasonal, supply far exceeds demand, and the wages till recently were around 100 lire a day—in 1954 they were raised to 150 lire; normally a peasant can expect day-labouring employment for only about a third of the year. From the land he rents (and of course only a proportion of *braccianti* can afford, or even find, land to rent) the small amount he makes bears no relation to the labour he must expend on this thankless soil; moreover his plot may very well be situated as much as 12 or 14 kilometres distant from his home, and two or three hours of the day must then be spent in journeying to and from his work. The peasant's morning exodus and evening return, accompanied by his donkey, if he can afford one, to carry his tools or produce, is a regular feature of the Southern countryside.

For the peasants do not live in the country near their work, but crowded together in swollen villages, almost towns in size, but so completely lacking in normal urban amenities as to make the word appear a misnomer. There were in the past sufficient reasons for this traditional way of living. The coastal areas were avoided because of pirates and malaria (and in consequence they became still more unhealthy through neglect); instead, living centres grew up inland, and frequently on hilltops, where people herded together for protection against bandits and marauders. Now both of those reasons are no longer valid—for since the war DDT measures have virtually suppressed malaria, and recent progress in land reclamation, if maintained, should prevent its recurrence. But the town-dwelling habit persists, partly because of water shortage in the countryside, and also largely because of the fragmentation of land-holding which has now reached such a point that a peasant may sometimes have to make do with two or three small strips of rented land, each in a different direction, and therefore most easily reached from a central living point. Yet overcrowding in these huge villages is such that families of eight or ten frequently live in a single room.

It might be thought that life in these urban communities would offer some possible alternative employment to agriculture. But, as we have said, these are 'towns' (of 30,000 inhabitants and over) in little more than size; and it has been estimated that on an average only 5·5 per cent of their population is engaged in industrial activities, as compared with 16·4 per cent of the town-dwellers in the North.[1] One has only to think of some of the Apulian towns, such as Andria, Candela, or Cerignola (the home town of the Communist trade union leader Di Vittorio), to realise what bleak prospects they offer. The main street is flanked by low white, flat-roofed houses; the side streets, often not even cobbled, become quagmires in the rainy season; shops are few and poor, for most purchasing is done in the market place, and in any case there is no money

[1] 1951 Industrial Census.

to buy with; there is no industry proper, traditional handicrafts are on the wane, and their place is only taken to some extent by the newer crafts of the bicycle and motor-repair shops. The only trades that afford some employment are the small-scale businesses catering for strictly local customers, such as the miller, the shoemaker, the tailor, the carpenter, the blacksmith, and the ubiquitous barber. The rest must find what work they can on the land. How many of them fail to do so can be guessed from the numbers that crowd the market places of a summer evening during harvest when the *fattori* come in to engage day-labourers for the next day's work.

The possibilities for employment are, of course, quite different in the few large towns and their surroundings—Naples, with its port and extensive related and other industries; Bari, a well-equipped modern town where, though the port's traffic has declined since the war, there are huge oil-refineries, a branch of Fiat, and other industries; and to a lesser extent Foggia, the centre for the relatively prosperous agricultural area further South. How large a part Naples plays in the share of Southern industry as a whole can be deduced from the industrial employment statistics: Campania (which in this connection means chiefly Naples and Salerno) accounts for 63,000 of the South's industrial workers, as against 47,000 for all the rest of the Southern mainland, and 42,000 for Sicily and Sardinia. Apart from the more diversified industries of Naples and Bari, the main Southern industries are connected in one way or another with food-processing—flour mills, *pasta* factories, olive oil refineries, factories for preserving and canning tomatoes and fruit—and wine-making.

Public utilities and transport afford a good deal of employment, for this is a field where demand had to be met by local resources. Transport has expanded considerably since the war, and, with new roads and improvements to existing ones, local bus services now do much to supplement the railway system which, in this difficult mountainous country, had hitherto left many inland regions quite inaccessible.

To complete this brief sketch of the Southern background, a word must be said about education. Elementary education presents a quite special problem in such a region of poverty, immense distances, and still inadequate communications. In the past illiteracy was widespread in the South, and even in the immediate pre-war years was reckoned at 39 per cent of persons over 10 years of age; by 1951 it had fallen to 24 per cent (as against 11 per cent in the North). Southern school-teachers, especially in the smaller centres, have a task calling for genuine self-sacrifice. Not necessarily Southerners themselves, they are poorly paid and housed, with small opportunities for distraction or for pursuing their own studies. School buildings are often woefully inadequate; the children may have to come long distances on foot; their very shoes and clothing present a problem; and the teachers have to instil some knowledge against a background of overcrowded houses and, in many cases, near starvation.

Yet at both secondary-school and university level a marked preference is shown for the kind of training that will lead to 'white-collar' jobs rather than for technical training. In the secondary schools of the South pupils who choose the *licei* and *magistrali* schools are more than double the number of those attending technical schools; and the same pattern appears in the Southern universities, where the favourite faculties are law and medicine, with engineering, agriculture, and economics at the bottom of the scale. This is no doubt largely a reflection of the same employment problem, at a higher level, that has already been discussed: in the absence of industry, the openings for a man with some scholastic qualifications are largely confined to law, medicine, teaching, or . . . the vast army of the civil service. Moreover, the Southerner who has acquired some learning is traditionally unwilling to squander it on a non-intellectual occupation which lacks prestige. So each year the universities turn out more and more Southern lawyers, who, if they fail to find employment in their already overcrowded profession in their home towns, must swell the lower ranks of the civil service or starve.

Government Plans for the South

Land Reform

The Government which Signor De Gasperi formed after the Election of April 1948 had included among its electoral promises a pledge to introduce land reform. It had always been understood that this measure would benefit in particular the peasants of the South, for this was the region of the greatest land hunger and agricultural unemployment. Some special laws to assist the South had already been introduced in 1947: these included fiscal and Customs privileges, credit facilities, and a programme of public works. But the rising tide of discontent there, fomented by Communist propaganda, had already strengthened the conviction that drastic measures were needed, and when in the autumn of 1949 peasants began to occupy land illegally on some of the big estates in Calabria and Sicily, the Government realised the urgency of speeding up the land reform measures which had already been presented to Parliament.

It was therefore decided to put into effect at once the parts of the general land reform law which concerned the South; and a special law governing land reform in the mountainous Sila region of Calabria was passed on 12 May 1950, while similar legislation known as the *stralcio* law, to apply to other considerable areas of the South as well as to some other selected regions, came into force on 21 October 1950.[1]

The Sila law was, so to speak, the pilot project for land reform elsewhere, and it is therefore worth while examining it in some detail. The Sila region of Calabria was chosen for this first experiment because it was a particularly necessitous area of great poverty, large estates, and neglected land. The law provides for the expropriation, against compensation to landowners, of land on estates exceeding 300 hectares (750 acres) which are capable of improvement. The amount to be expropriated is calculated on the rateable value of the property as a whole, taken in conjunction with the average income per hectare. (This method, though extremely complicated, avoids the pitfalls of the two simplest criteria—expropriation based on either acreage or total income alone. The acreage standard would have left out of count such factors as yield and investment in the land, while expropriation carried out on a criterion of income might have left untouched large areas of land with a low yield, such as the typical *latifundia*). The land thus obtained by expropriation is allocated to the peasants for a trial period

[1] The *stralcio* or 'partial' law was so called because it was a part of the general land reform law, then in draft, which was envisaged for the country as a whole. This general law had not yet been approved by mid-1955, and it now seems likely that it will be considerably modified—see above, p. 170.

of two years, after which the peasants pay for the land in annual instalments of about £10 a year over thirty years, when it becomes their own.

The *stralcio* law differed in one or two respects from the Sila law: notably, it fixed no lower limit of land-holding beyond which estates became liable to expropriation (the Sila law had fixed 300 hectares); and it exempted from expropriation so-called 'model farms' provided they fulfilled certain conditions connected with modernisation of equipment, number and conditions of workers employed, and high production. This law applied to large areas in the Southern provinces of Apulia, Lucania, Molise, and also to certain other parts of Italy—the Tuscan Maremma and the Fucino basin; the Po Delta; parts of Campania near the Volturno and Sele rivers; and Sardinia. In Sicily special land reform legislation had been set on foot with State aid in 1948 under the island's regional government. In both Sicily and Sardinia the land reform affects the whole area of the island.

Special agencies were set up in the different regions to apply the reform. In the case of the Sila, where the coming of land reform had been envisaged as early as 1947, such an agency had already been at work for two years preparing land surveys and determining from the cadastral registers the often highly complicated ownership of land. It was thus possible, once the law was passed, to work out fairly rapidly where the expropriation cuts should be made. Peasants who wanted land were then asked to apply for it, the only qualification required being that they must be solely dependent on agriculture for their livelihood; and as there was not enough land to go round the names of those who were to receive it were decided by lot. Once the expropriations had been approved by Government decree, it was then possible to go straight ahead with the formal distribution of the land to the peasants; and the first of many similar allocation ceremonies took place on 24 September 1950 at the hilltop village of Santa Severina in the Sila.

It was not, however, the intention of the reform that the peasants should be left without aid or guidance to cultivate their new properties. For one thing, in many cases the land was in no fit state for cultivation without a good deal of prior improvement; and under the supervision of the reform organisation's technicians the next stage was to prepare the ground for deep ploughing. On this poor and neglected soil it was often necessary to use bulldozers to root up rocks and bushes, and these mammoth machines and the tractors that went with them, making their first appearance on the Calabrian hillsides, probably did as much as anything to convince peasant scepticism that the reform really meant business.

At the same time the reform planned to relieve congestion in the overcrowded towns by starting new villages in the countryside where peasants could live nearer to their work. Some of these centres had already been established by 1954, often in combination with one of the reform organisation's tractor centres. These are run under the supervision of technicians, who also advise the peasants on new methods of cultivation, distribute seed and fertilisers, and in general help the new smallholders during the initial period of acclimatisation.

By May 1955, five years after the reform was inaugurated, the expropriation stage had been completed both in the Sila and the *stralcio* areas, and of the total of 700,000 hectares of land expropriated, 500,000 hectares had been distributed to 92,389 peasant families, who thus obtained holdings averaging 4–5 hectares (around 10 acres), the size varying according to the quality of the land. By that time over 18,000 new houses had been built, and more were under construction; 32 farm village-centres had been established, 4,600 km. of roads constructed; some 4,000 tractors were operating in the reform areas; and over 2,000 technical training courses had been held.[1]

It was not to be expected that a reform of this kind, striking at the heart of feudal privilege, would go through without opposition, and in fact it came under attack from both Right and Left. The landowners naturally objected to being deprived of part of their land, and they also attacked the method of the reform, urging, rather belatedly, that the same ends could have been achieved more satisfactorily through the granting of credits for direct purchase of land to be arranged between owner and tenant. The politicians of the Left attacked the reform on quite different grounds: they claimed that it went nothing like far enough, and advocated instead something

[1] Report of Signor Fanfani at Congress held at Foggia for all the new smallholders established under the land reform (*Il Popolo*, 9 May 1955).

resembling the much more far-reaching land reforms carried out since the war in the Eastern European countries. They lost no opportunity of pointing to the mistakes, whether real or imaginary, of the reform organisations, and found an easy field for propaganda among the local jealousies and dissatisfactions inevitably aroused by the initial impact of such an innovation in a society whose structure had remained static for centuries.

Mistakes have, of course, been made—many of them of a technical character which it would take too long to discuss here. On the landowners' side, it can probably be argued that the reform as first conceived and applied did in some instances tend to sacrifice unjustifiably those properties where genuine efforts had been made to introduce improvements—the 'model farm' exemption clause in the *stralcio* law, for example, was said to impose such stiff conditions that practically no estate could qualify. Among other criticisms, it is probably true in some instances that the avowedly paternalistic approach of the technicians—an approach which was unavoidable if such a scheme was to succeed in these backward areas—was not always accompanied by sufficient attention to the need to educate the new peasant-smallholders, not perhaps so much on the technical side as in the development of a small-farmer mentality, with all its responsibilities. Finance, too, may prove something of a problem in the future. Understandably, the expenditure in the initial years was exceptionally heavy, but it was disquieting that a large proportion of the original ten-year allocation of 350 milliard lire had been spent by 1955.[1]

But the experiment is still only in its early stages, and the fact remains that something had been achieved in five years where in the past no appreciable improvement had been made in the peasants' lot in as many centuries.

The Plan for Southern Development

If the land reform had been launched in isolation it is at least doubtful whether it could have succeeded as far as it did within only five years. But in the spring of 1950 another Government-sponsored scheme was initiated, of an even more

[1] See Aldo Pagani, 'Il bilancio degli enti di riforma', *Mondo Economico*, 18 June 1955.

far-reaching character, for improving conditions and combating unemployment throughout the depressed areas of the country, and particularly in the South. This was a ten-year plan (subsequently extended to twelve years) which envisaged an expenditure of 100,000 million lire a year in the South, and of 20,000 million lire a year in the North. A special organisation, known as the Cassa per il Mezzogiorno, or Fund for the South, was set up to administer the scheme, which in its first two years, 1950–1, was financed up to two-thirds by Interim Aid and the ERP lire fund. Subsequently the Fund has been financed in a variety of ways which include special medium-term credits and the establishment of a revolving fund for Southern industrialisation. Moreover the International Bank for Reconstruction and Development granted two preliminary loans of $10 million each to the Cassa in 1951 and 1953, followed in May 1955 by a loan of $70 million, with the prospect of further loans on a similar scale in the next two years. This last sum—the biggest development loan hitherto made by the Bank in Europe—was to be devoted to specific agricultural and industrial projects in Sicily and the Southern mainland, chosen by the Bank from a number of suggestions put forward by the Cassa and selected because they seemed particularly likely to improve the region's productive capacity.[1]

The Cassa organisation is directed by a committee of Ministers (responsible for the various economic Ministries concerned), who jointly draw up its plans. It therefore has a considerable degree of autonomy, and can act more quickly than would be the case if all plans had to be submitted individually to the Ministry concerned. The largest proportion of its investments are directed towards measures calculated to assist agriculture: land reclamation and improvement, irrigation, and mountain conservancy, as well as land reform itself; the rest is to be spent on public works such as road-building and improvement and the construction of aqueducts, dams, hydro-electrical installations, and other water works, with a small allotment for tourism.

The practical significance of these plans in such a region as

[1] They included an extensive scheme for hydraulic works in the plain of Catania, eight hydro-electric installations with a total capacity of 220,000 kwh, and seven new factories for cement, fertilisers, insecticides, wood pulp, etc.—all, be it noted, commodities related to local needs or production.

Southern Italy can hardly be exaggerated, and one needs only to visit some of the areas where they are being carried out to realise how the countryside is already being transformed and given new potentialities. For example, along the Ionian shore, a deserted region till lately malaria-ridden, backed by soil-eroded hills where the four or five main rivers alternately flood or dry up according to the season, dams are now being erected across the rivers—the Agri, the Sinni, the Bradano, and the Tara—which will make possible the conservation of waters from the torrential streams further up and their utilisation for irrigating large areas of the surrounding country. On this irrigated land it will be possible to introduce a variety of new crops, such as fodder crops, tobacco, tomatoes, and vegetables, in addition to extending cultivation and improving yields of cereals, olives, and vines, as well as building up the exiguous livestock population. Similar irrigation works are being undertaken further north on the Ofanto, the one large river which, rising in the Lucanian mountains, flows through Apulia south of the Tavoliere. This is a region of large and medium estates, mostly given over to extensive wheat cultivation and poor pasture, where there is much unemployment and where the land reform has already begun to install peasant proprietors. Here too it is expected that the new irrigation measures will make possible a considerable increase in livestock and in fodder crops.

These are only a few of the most striking examples of what is being done in the South. Other important developments are the building of new roads, aqueducts, and power stations, re-afforestation or other soil conservation measures, and measures for mountain river conservancy—these last made doubly necessary by the floods which devastated Calabria in the autumns of 1951 and 1953. All these 'public works', besides their long-term benefits to the land, are providing employment for large numbers of the local population; it was estimated that about 100,000 persons were employed by the Cassa in 1953.

In the years since its inception the Cassa has also begun to turn its attention towards the need for establishing some localised forms of industry in the South. The public works now being undertaken are, it is felt, the necessary prerequisite for any industrial development, which would be impossible without adequate communications, water and electricity supplies, and freedom from flood menace. But plans are already on foot for starting factories for the preserving and canning of agricultural products; other projects for industries associated with local needs include the production of fertilisers (a plant for superphosphates was started in 1953 at Porto Empedocle in Sicily) and of cement, factories for which have already been opened near Naples and in Sicily; and, as we have seen, a part of the International Bank loan is to be used for the development of such industries. At the end of 1954 the United States Foreign Operations Administration also allocated $20 million towards the development of Southern industry. Moreover by 1955 some long-established Northern concerns (e.g. Fiat, Pirelli, Olivetti) were beginning to establish branches in the South.

The Cassa has encountered far less criticism than its companion scheme, the land reform: quite understandably, for it will obviously benefit rich and poor alike—the landowners cannot but welcome basic improvements which will have repercussions on their own estates, while the peasants have in the immediate present new possibilities of work, with the prospect of a tremendous improvement in their whole condition in the future. The rising prosperity which the Cassa's works are bringing to the South can in fact already be seen in the increased purchase of consumer goods there since 1953. Such criticism as there has been is of the kind so frequently levelled at any big new undertaking, especially in a Southern country; it can be summed up in two words—graft and waste. The political impact of the reforms has been discussed elsewhere.[1] But if circumstances allow of the peaceful development and completion of these plans, there seems every reason to hope by the mid-1960s a great change will have come over the face of Southern Italy.

[1] See above, pp. 76–7, 93–4.

CHAPTER XIX

POVERTY, HOUSING, AND UNEMPLOYMENT

The most serious and permanent domestic problems which have confronted Italy's post-war Governments have been of a social character: the basic poverty of large strata of the population, and the widespread unemployment which accompanies it. Every succeeding Government, whatever its other preoccupations, has realised the inescapable need to alleviate these conditions: and the full-scale Parliamentary Inquiries into the problems of poverty and unemployment which were set on foot under the chairmanship of two Social Democrat Deputies, Ezio Vigorelli and Roberto Tremelloni, in 1952 bear witness to the seriousness with which the Government regarded these perennial diseases at the root of the country's economic well-being.[1]

POPULATION AND POVERTY

Italy is often described—and not least by Italians themselves—as a poor country and one with an expanding population. Both these generalisations need some qualification. As to poverty, Italy is poor in natural resources, that is to say in practically all of the most essential raw materials; and owing to the mountainous nature of the country much of her land is unsuited for cultivation. Moreover her national production, and therefore her national income, are unduly low, and this means a shortage of capital to invest in productive schemes. But within the country there is a great inequality in the distribution of wealth, both regionally, as we have already discovered in discussing the fundamental unbalance between North and South, and also socially; one needs only to make the

[1] The findings of the Inquiry into Poverty, conducted under the chairmanship of Ezio Vigorelli, were published as *Atti della Commissione Parlamentare di Inchiesta sulla miseria in Italia e sui mezzi di combatterla*, 13 vols. (Rome, 1953). The findings of the Inquiry into Unemployment, conducted under the chairmanship of Roberto Tremelloni, were published at the end of 1953 as *Atti della Commissione Parlamentare di Inchiesta sulla disoccupazione* (Rome, 1953; referred to below as 'Tremelloni Report').

brief transition from the glittering shops and cars of Rome to the hut dwellings outside the city to realise how great the extremes of wealth and poverty can be.

As to population, too, while it is true that Italy has a high rate of natural increase and consequently a larger population than she can support,[1] statistics show that, at any rate in the North, the downward trend has already set in.

POPULATION MOVEMENTS, 1871 TO 1951
(Annual Rates per 000 of total population)

Period	SOUTH		NORTH	
	Natural Increase	*Net Emigration*	*Natural Increase*	*Net Emigration*
1871–1881	7·9	0·2	7·0	2·2
1881–1901	10·5	4·0	10·0	3·3
1901–1911	10·9	6·8	11·8	3·8
1911–1921	8·0	7·1	4·7	2·3
1921–1931	13·7	3·1	9·2	2·3
1931–1936	13·6	4·9	7·7	0·3
1936–1951	13·2	4·2	5·9	0·02

(SOURCE: Tremelloni Report, Vol. III, Pt. I, pp. 24–5. Net emigration includes emigration to the other part of Italy.)

From the above figures it is clear that, particularly in the South, up to 1921 the rate of natural increase was to an appreciable extent offset by emigration. Subsequently the Fascist régime encouraged Italians to be prolific—there was even a tax on bachelors then; but at the same time the possibilities of emigration abroad were greatly reduced.[2] Moreover the movement of the birth rate was very different in the two regions; the North appears to have resisted Fascist encouragements more successfully than the South, for while in the North between the first world war and the present time the birth rate fell from 31 to 17 per thousand, in the South the reduction was only from 34 to 27. Consequently we find that in the North,

[1] According to the 1951 census, Italy, with an area of 111,228 sq. miles, had then a population of nearly 47 million. This gives a population density of 155 persons to the sq. km., which is lower than that of Holland (317), Britain (207), or Western Germany (196), but much higher than that of another predominantly agricultural country, France (77). For geographical reasons the distribution of population in Italy is very uneven.

[2] See below, p. 226.

with a declining rate of natural increase, emigration is gradually disappearing, while Southerners, since large-scale emigration abroad is no longer possible, have tended increasingly to migrate to the North of Italy. In fact, even as early as 1931, more than 1 million persons born in the South were living in the North, whilst only 160,000 persons born in the North were living in the South.[1]

Italy's relative wealth or poverty is perhaps best gauged by means of her consumption of certain basic commodities. It has been reckoned that her total consumption in 1950 was only 47 per cent of that of the United Kingdom (comparable figures for other countries are: France 80 per cent; Western Germany 64 per cent; the United States 152 per cent).[2] The table on the next page affords some standards of comparison between Italy, France (another country largely dependent on agriculture), and the United Kingdom (a highly industrialised country where the comparison therefore has less force).

The Vigorelli Commission, in the course of its inquiry into standards of living during 1952–3, reached the conclusion that 11·7 per cent of Italian families must be classified as having a 'very low' standard and 11·6 per cent as 'low', while 65·7 per cent could be said to be in modest conditions and 11 per cent in easy circumstances. Of the 1,357,000 poorest families, 1,161,000, comprising 4,600,000 people, came from the South and the Islands, while of the 1,349,000 families with a low standard of living, 925,000, or 4,226,000 persons, were from the same region. On the subject of housing, it was found that 232,000 families, or 2 per cent of the population, were living in cellars, attics, or warehouses, while 92,000 families were housed in huts or caves. Over 9 per cent of Italian families were living in overcrowded conditions, with more than three people to a room: and here again the situation is most acute in the South—in 1951 the number of rooms per 100 inhabitants was reckoned at 54 in the South, as against 83 in the North.[3] Similar regional disparities are to be found in the estimated average annual income per head, which varies from a maximum of 271,000 lire in Lombardy, Piedmont, and

[1] 1931 census.

[2] OEEC, *An International Comparison of National Products and the Purchasing Power of Currencies*, by Milton Gilbert and I. B. Kravis (1954).

[3] ECE, *Economic Survey of Europe in 1953*, p. 124.

STANDARDS OF CONSUMPTION, HEALTH, EDUCATION, AND TRANSPORT

	ITALY		S. ITALY ALONE		FRANCE		U.K.	
	1934–8	*1951*	*1934–8*	*1951*	*1934–8*	*1951*	*1934–8*	*1951*
CONSUMPTION								
Total calories per day	2,510	2,485	..	..	2,830	2,750	3,125	2,990
Textiles (kg. per capita per year)	3·8	4·9	..	..	7·4	7·4	11·9	12·4
Electricity (non-industrial; kwh per head per year)	38	118	21*	54*	50	103	147	423
HEALTH								
Infant mortality (per 1,000 live births)	106	67	125	81	71	51	55	31
Hospital beds (per 10,000 persons)	56	80	29	41	..	112	..	117
EDUCATION								
Apparent consumption of newsprint (kg. per capita per year)	1·6	2·3	..	..	7	8	26	12
Wireless sets per 1,000 persons	22	80	13	..	115	175	181	245
TRANSPORT								
Railway—tons-km. per capita	218	240	..	..	700	1,075	576	761
Road—passenger cars and buses per 1,000 persons	6·8	9·3	3·2	4·5	44	46	43	50
Motor trucks per 1,000 persons	2·1	5·7	0·8	2·7	11	19	10	19

*ECE Estimate.

(SOURCE: ECE, *Economic Survey of Europe in 1953*, pp. 78–9.)

Liguria to a minimum of 75,000 and 70,000 respectively in the two poorest Southern provinces of Lucania and Calabria.[1]

Social insurance, which is compulsory for industrial workers in Italy, covers a wide field. Its benefits include family allowances, unemployment insurance, assistance during illness and accidents at work, old-age pensions, and a variety of special funds for certain classes of workers. Since 1946 the whole cost of contributions has been borne by the employer, an arrange-

[1] ibid., p. 123.

ment which has been criticised as much for its psychological effect on the worker as for the burden which it places on the employer's production costs.[1]

The Italian State since the war, and particularly since 1949, has spent very considerable sums (averaging well over 1,000,000 million lire a year since 1951)[2] on social assistance, pensions, and family allowances. But social legislation in Italy still suffers from lack of co-ordination, both in its past development and in its present organisation. Social assistance in the past, and still to a great extent today, has depended not only on the State but also on private charitable institutions, many of them sponsored by the Church. Thus a multiplicity of different and often overlapping organisations has grown up to deal with the various aspects of social assistance. The public welfare authorities in the Communes, which form the backbone of local welfare work, receive State grants, but these are often insufficient to meet particular local needs, and in any case the work of these bodies is hampered by bureaucratic complications and formalities, and by the lack of a guiding overall plan. The Vigorelli Commission strongly recommended a complete reorganisation of the machinery in order to avoid waste or overlapping, and to make the best use of the existing bodies. It considered that the real difficulties at present arose not so much through shortage of funds as through the lack of a satisfactory organisation to apply them. It also stressed the need for better housing, improvements in care for the aged and for children, and greater facilities for vocational training. When the Commission's Report was discussed in May 1954 it was decided as a first step to extend health insurance benefits to State pensioners (numbering 2,200,000) and to the 7 million independent farmers; and early in 1955 these benefits were also extended to workers in handicrafts industries.

HOUSING

The contrast between rich and poor in Italy is nowhere more apparent than in the homes in which they live. The eighteenth-century palazzi and country villas still bear witness

[1] See Ezio Vigorelli, *L'italiano è socialista e non lo sa* (Milan, Mondadori, 1952). This book, published before the Vigorelli Commission's report, discusses in detail various aspects of the social assistance question.

[2] Statement by Signor Vanoni, *Il Popolo*, 24 March 1954.

to the most glorious period of Italian domestic architecture and the prosperity that went with it; but at the other end of the scale come the cellars, attics, warehouses, huts, and caves. The contrast is, of course, the more spectacular because of the magnificence of the rich man's 'castle': and times are changing fast, for the 'castle' is rapidly becoming a burden for the owner which he can no longer afford to sustain, while the poor man at his gate, though still housed in little more than a hovel, may be able to afford a 'Vespa' motor-scooter on which to go to work. But even if he could pay for better accommodation, the chances are that he could never find it, given the size of his family, at a rent within his means.

For, as a result of war-time destruction and the almost complete suspension of new building in the war's latter years, Italy in 1945 was faced with a most serious housing shortage. It was calculated that some 1,800,000 rooms had been destroyed, 1,100,000 heavily damaged and 2,700,000 less severely damaged,[1] while according to Government estimates some 854,000 persons were homeless and nearly 3½ million were living in rooms too badly damaged to be really habitable.

In the first post-war months the Italian Government had all it could do to tackle the problem of restoring communications and repairing damaged roads, railways, and bridges. A special organisation under UNRRA auspices, known as UNRRA–CASAS, was therefore set up in the spring of 1946 to deal with the housing situation in the regions of Emilia, Tuscany, Lazio, and the Abruzzi which had suffered most severely during the prolonged fighting on the Gothic and Gustav Lines. Between 1946 and 1949 UNRRA–CASAS, which was financed through the Lira Fund (a fund created by the sale in Italy of UNRRA supplies delivered free to the Italian Government), confined itself to the most urgent problems of house repair in these areas and to building new dwellings, as far as possible with the co-operation of the homeless themselves. From 1950 onwards, when some ERP funds became available, a fuller housing policy was undertaken and the sphere of operations extended to include Southern Italy.

[1] UNRRA, *Survey of Italy's Economy* (Rome, 1947). The word 'vano', or room, is always used in Italian estimates of living space; as so many Italians live in apartments in blocks, or in rooms in divided houses, this is the most practical way of reckoning.

Between 1946 and the beginning of 1954 over 50,000 new rooms had been built under UNRRA–CASAS, and 310,000 damaged rooms repaired;[1] this work has been carried out in some 750 communes, mostly in mountainous districts and difficult of access.

In some instances UNRRA–CASAS has even helped to establish new villages. Perhaps the most outstanding example is the village of La Martella, in Lucania, built with funds from UNRRA–CASAS and the Cassa per il Mezzogiorno. Inaugurated in May 1953, La Martella is to provide accommodation for families from the 'Sassi', the cave-dwellings of Matera, whose plight is described in Carlo Levi's *Christ Stopped at Eboli*. The 'caves' of Matera seem at first glance not so far removed from normal houses: but their façades, built to look like house-fronts around their narrow doors, are deceptive, for the single living-room within is no more than a grotto, one of the hundreds of natural cavities created by erosion in the limestone formation of the hillside. Here generations of families have lived, giving their cave-dwellings a semblance of normality with the furnishings of a poor household. There is, indeed, something to be said for the caves, for they are warm in winter and cool in summer, and that is an asset in the torrid climate of this exposed Lucanian town. But by modern standards they are hopelessly insanitary, lacking light, water, and drainage; and in the cave's further depths beyond the living room the family's livestock is housed—a few fowls, and the donkey that accompanies the peasant on his daily journey to and from his work. Since the war journalists and others, as well as Levi, had drawn attention to the living conditions of these cave-dwellers, who numbered some 15,000, or half the population of Matera. Signor De Gasperi himself visited the town in July 1950, and soon afterwards a law was passed to speed up measures for providing alternative accommodation for the inhabitants of the 'Sassi'. La Martella, the new village built in the countryside six miles outside Matera, can only house a proportion of them, 167 families, and the most necessitous families were moved first; but work on two other similar villages was begun in 1953, and families are gradually being moved out from the 'Sassi' as the new houses

[1] *Il Popolo*, 4 March 1954.

are ready to receive them, while the vacated caves are being sealed off to prevent their being used again as dwellings.

UNRRA–CASAS was only the first of the organised schemes for tackling the housing problem. Other building schemes financed in part through State credits or concessions have been carried out by provincial and other local authorities, the Institute for Civil Servants' Housing, and various co-operative organisations. But the main State-organised scheme was the so-called 'INA-Casa' Housing Plan, introduced in February 1949 for a seven-year term by Amintore Fanfani, then Minister of Labour, and subsequently extended till 1958. This plan[1] aimed at building a large number of low-priced *case popolari*, or workers' dwellings, while at the same time providing work for the unemployed.[2] Some 850,000 rooms were to be built between 1949 and 1956 in areas covering more than half of Italy's 7,765 communes; a third of the new building was to be in the South. Financing is covered by contributions alike from the State, from employers, and from the workers themselves: workers contribute a small proportion of their wages varying from 0·3 to 0·6 per cent, employers twice that amount, while the State subscribes a sum equal to 4·3 per cent of the total of these two contributions together, plus 3·2 per cent of the cost of each dwelling built, for twenty-five years. Those eligible for the new dwellings are chosen according to precise criteria: first priority is given to applicants who are homeless or who occupy uninhabitable premises such as hovels or caves; next come families threatened with eviction, and then those living in unhygienic conditions of over-crowding, with one or more families sharing the same dwelling. Rents are low, around 4,500–4,700 lire (about £2 10*s.*) a month for a three-roomed dwelling with kitchen and bath-room, while tenants who wish eventually to become owners pay monthly instalments of 7,000–7,500 lire over twenty-five years, at the end of which the property becomes theirs. By the end of October 1954 nearly two-thirds of the Plan's target had been fulfilled; 111,470 new dwellings had been built, with 566,021 rooms, and the weekly output averaged 2,800 rooms a week, equal to the accommodation for 560 families.[3]

[1] Text in *Gazzetta Ufficiale*, 7 March 1949. [2] See below, p. 221.
[3] See *Italian Affairs* (Rome, Documentary Centre), March–May 1955.

Thus by the end of 1954 something towards alleviating the housing shortage had been accomplished through UNRRA–CASAS, INA-Casa, and other State-aided schemes. But the need still remained very great, as was demonstrated by the impressive statistics on inadequate housing conditions produced by the Vigorelli Commission.[1] The Scelba Government placed the provision of better housing in the forefront of its programme, and in April 1954 the Social Democrat Minister for Public Works, Romita, put forward a new eight-year plan to provide housing for the most necessitous families. This plan, the cost of which (estimated at 168 milliard lire) was to be borne entirely by the Government, aimed at building 120,000 dwellings, or 480,000 rooms, over the eight years, which it was reckoned would provide for about a third of the 324,000 families regarded by the Vigorelli Commission as inadequately housed. Government subsidies to the various housing organisations were also to assist in stimulating the building of a further 835,000 rooms over a six-year period, while the INA-Casa scheme, due to end in 1956, was to be prolonged for another two years. Rents in all cases were to be low, and there were easy terms for owner-tenant purchase by instalments.

Nothing has so far been said about private building. This has been extensive, as anyone visiting Italy, and in particular Rome, since the war will have seen for himself. But a criticism constantly levelled against the Government in this connection is that too little has been done to check speculation in land, which has 'raised the cost of building to the skies', as the critics say. The cost of building sites has increased fantastically since the war, particularly in Rome but also throughout the country, and by 1954 represented something like 40 per cent of building costs. Private builders have therefore tended to concentrate on the construction of luxury flats which can bring in high profits, to the almost total exclusion of building for more modest purses. The type of luxury construction to be seen in, for example, the Parioli quarter of Rome would certainly seem to bear out this contention. Rome, indeed, is something of a special case. There, in the last eighty years, the population has grown from 200,000 to 2 million (in the past fifteen years alone it has risen by something like half a

[1] See above, p. 209.

million), and the shortage of building sites, coupled with the concentration of land in the hands of a few owners, has led to widespread speculation—an outstanding example was that associated with the name of Ugo Montagna, which came to light during the Montesi scandals in the spring of 1954.[1]

Hitherto the housing problem has been discussed from the angle of the poorly-housed tenant or the would-be tenant unable to find a home. But there is another aspect of the question which bears hardly upon landlords—that of frozen rents. In Italy, as in Britain and other countries, rents were frozen after the war: the same thing had happened after the first world war, when they remained frozen for fifteen years. But in Italy they were frozen at their pre-war figures, whereas by mid-1947 the lira had lost more than 98 per cent of its pre-war value—with the result that a month's rent might in fact be worth little more than a packet of cigarettes. It was therefore decided to permit periodical increases to the basic rent; but these increases were always so small that rents still remained far below their real value in post-war lire.[2] In 1954 there was some talk of decontrolling rents altogether, but instead it was decided in June of that year to retain the 'freeze' until the end of 1960, while at the same time permitting annual increases on a sliding scale. This decision naturally brought relief to the many who had for years been living at a purely nominal rent and who feared the sharp rise that would inevitably take place when prices became normalised; but in the meantime the landlords of such properties have sustained heavy losses over a number of years, only slightly alleviated by the unofficial agreements which have in some cases been reached between landlords and tenants.

UNEMPLOYMENT

In pre-war days unemployment did not present the acute problem in Italy which it does today. A number of factors combined to disguise the population pressure. Young men

[1] See above, p. 108.

[2] In 1951, after several increases to basic rents had taken place, it was reckoned that rents still averaged only 9 times the pre-war figure (1938 = 1), whereas the cost of food had increased by 61 times and that of clothing by 67 times (see Libero Lenti, 'Inquilini privilegiati contro inquilini reietti', in *Mondo Economico*, 17 March 1951).

went into the army or the militia, and long years of mobilisation kept them there; for example, the 20-year-olds who went to the colours in 1909 stayed in the army for eleven years, throughout the Balkan Wars and the first world war, while in the 1930s much the same thing happened through the rapid succession of the wars in Abyssinia and Spain and the second world war. Fascist public works schemes, the swollen bureaucracy, and the colonies all provided employment, while emigration, though not on the scale of the early years of the century, still reduced the population pressure to some extent.

After the war all this was changed. Italy was disarmed, and under the peace treaty the total personnel of all her forces, including Carabinieri, was restricted to 330,000. While the colonies had formerly provided some outlet, the reverse was now true, and the numbers of those returning from the forces and seeking work were further swelled by colonists repatriated from Africa, as well as by refugees from Venezia Giulia. Moreover during the war emigration had been at a complete standstill. The young men seeking work had in many cases had no previous training, for their youth had been spent in the army; and the factories were already over-staffed as a result of the expansion of industry to meet war-time needs.

Ever since the war the number of unemployed in Italy has in fact been reckoned, in very general terms, at around 2 million. An examination of the labour statistics and of the Tremelloni Commission's findings makes it possible to qualify this figure to some extent. Comparison of the figures for the months of highest and lowest unemployment, January and September, disclose a seasonal fluctuation of some 400,000–500,000. Nevertheless, the Ministry of Labour statistics for September 1953, based on the number of those registered at the Labour Exchanges, showed a total of 2,048,520 unemployed, an increase of 1·1 per cent over the annual average of 1947. This figure includes probably something like 200,000 persons who want to change to a new job or supplement their main occupation. Where, as in Italy, there is much under-employment it is difficult to arrive at precise figures, and the Central Institute of Statistics figures, calculated on a different method, regularly show lower returns than those of the Ministry of Labour. One must also take into consideration, on the one hand, an uncertain number of workless people who do not bother to register, and, on the other hand, some who register but are not really unemployed. Probably the safest indication is that of the Tremelloni Commission which, conducting its investigations in 1952–3, reached the conclusion that a figure between 1,300,000 to 1,400,000 must be taken as the index of structural unemployment in Italy. This would mean a percentage of 2·7 in relation to the total population of 47 million, or 6·6 per cent of the working population, reckoned at something over 19¼ million.

Moreover owing to the unusually high proportion of the population in Italy which is not employed—reckoned at 59 per cent—the degree of dependence on each worker is high too. It is reckoned that about a quarter of the unemployed are heads of families, with an average of one dependant for each worker in the North and two in the South. Statistics suggest that something like 9 per cent of Italian families include at least one member who is unemployed.

Employment in the various sectors is divided as follows: agriculture, 7½–8 million; industry, over 5½ million; trade, banking, and insurance, around 1,890,000; civil servants, 1,044,000; transport and communications, some 660,000; others, nearly a million. The number of registered unemployed is highest among industrial and unskilled workers; but under-employment, due to seasonal factors, is also very high among agricultural workers, who are without adequate employment for around 34 per cent of the total of their working days.[1] Under-employment in industry was a frequent phenomenon in the early post-war years, when, owing to the ban then existing on dismissal of workers, factories were compelled to keep on their pay-rolls a number of supernumerary employees for whom only part-time work could be found. The complete ban on dismissals came to an end in July 1947, and since then dismissal of workers has been carried out according to a procedure established by agreements (of 7 August 1947 and 18 October 1950) concluded between the Employers' and Workers' Confederations.[2] Owing to high costs, structural reorganisation,

[1] Tremelloni Report.

[2] See Maurice F. Neufeld, *Labor Unions and National Politics in Italian Industrial Plants* (Cornell University, 1954), p. 66.

and modernisation of plant, factories in certain branches of industry have found it necessary to dismiss some of their workers or even, in some cases, to shut down altogether;[1] and this has had some effect in increasing the number of totally unemployed. The Tremelloni Commission reckoned the rate of under-employment in industry at 11–12 per cent. Another category of workers where unemployment is high is among 'intellectuals', men and women with university qualifications. We have already met this phenomenon in the South. In 1952 some 4·71 per cent of male 'intellectuals' were reckoned as unemployed, though only 1·97 per cent among women graduates, since women's work in this field is still in its early stages.

The civil servants form a category in themselves. They include not only employees of the various Ministries, and of local government organisations, but also teachers and the innumerable officials of the post office, public transport, and other services. Between 1910 and 1950 their numbers rose from 7·6 to 23·2 per thousand of the population and in 1950 represented 7·8 per cent of the total labour force, including employees of local administrations. Their salaries in relation to the cost of living have risen far less than have wages in industry or even in agriculture.[2] Yet between 1945 and 1952 there were on an average 28·5 applicants for every post open to competition in the lower grades of the civil service.[3]

There are considerable regional variations in unemployment which in the North is mainly industrial, in the South agricultural. The number of registered unemployed in 1952 varied from a minimum of 1·55 per cent of the province's population in Trentino and 1·65 per cent in the Val d'Aosta to a maximum of 5·06 per cent in Apulia and 4·34 per cent in Campania and in Reggio Emilia.[4] These three latter regions are the main centres of surplus labour, followed by the Veneto, Friuli, and Calabria.

A particularly serious feature of the situation is the difficulty encountered by young people in obtaining their first jobs. In September 1952 such candidates, according to the Tremelloni Report, numbered 600,000–700,000, representing 29·2 per cent of the total unemployed; but in some regions,

[1] See above, p. 159.
[2] *Bollettino Mensile di Statistica.*
[3] Tremelloni Report.
[4] ibid.

e.g. Venezia and Campania, the proportion was nearer 40 per cent and in Lombardy they accounted for two-fifths of the total. Nearly four-fifths of them were unskilled. The reason for this particular aspect of the unemployment problem is in part demographic. Between 1936 and 1951 the population of working age increased by about 270,000 a year, whereas the population actually working increased, on an average, by only 47,000 a year; and whereas up to 1900 about three-quarters of the new age-groups regularly found employment, between 1900 and 1951 only about a third did so. There is thus by now a constant backlog which is never worked off. Other more immediate causes for the failure to absorb the new age-groups lie in the insufficiency of employment in agriculture, and also in technological progress in industry. In the latter field, while the volume of industrial production increased by 40 per cent between 1936 and 1951, the increase in industrial employment amounted to only 5 per cent.

These causes, of course, apply also to unemployment as a whole, as well as among young people. Other long-term reasons are the high birth-rate, already referred to above; the tendency of workers to transfer from agriculture to industry; the reconversion of industry to a peace-time footing, and the subsequent reorganisation in certain branches; the growing entry of women into the labour market; the 'immobility' of labour, i.e. the difficulties in the way of transferring from one trade or branch of industry to another; the deficiency of technical training; the suspension of large-scale emigration; and, last but not least, the low degree of capital investment. Among the more immediate causes of unemployment, the Central Institute of Statistics places first the dismissal of workers from industry, accounting for 46·4 per cent of the total unemployed in 1952.[1] Seasonal fluctuations accounted for 16·3 per cent, about half of which was in agricultural employment; and 14·8 per cent was attributed to the closing down of factories. On the other hand only 3·3 per cent of unemployed workers were found to have left of their own free will.

The next few years are likely to be the most difficult in dealing with the unemployment problem. For while the declining birth-rate will eventually bring some alleviation, this

[1] Tremelloni Report.

difference will not make itself felt until around 1970; and in the meantime the particularly large age-groups of 1939–40 will be coming on to the labour market.

According to the Tremelloni Commission, during the four years 1953–7 some 137,000 new workers, i.e. young people seeking their first jobs, might be expected each year, and it was calculated that employment could be found for a total of 500,000 new workers, or 125,000 a year. This calculation was based on the hypothesis that the transfer of workers from agriculture to industry (of the order of 50,000–100,000 workers a year) would continue, that industry would provide employment for 50,000–100,000 more workers a year through increased production and building schemes, and that other activities could employ some 100,000 a year.

GOVERNMENT ACTION

In the years since 1948 a number of measures have been inaugurated with the express aim of providing more opportunities for employment. Italian Governments have proved resourceful in evolving dual-purpose schemes that will be of use in themselves as well as in the provision of work. The earliest such scheme was the INA-Casa Housing Plan, introduced by Fanfani in 1949,[1] which aimed at tackling simultaneously two of the country's most serious problems, unemployment and the housing shortage. After five and a half years it had proved so successful that in December 1954 it was decided to prolong its term (due to end in 1956) until 1958. This decision was taken as a part of the measures designed to put into effect the recommendations of the Vigorelli and Tremelloni Commissions.

Another plan of Signor Fanfani's launched in 1948 was for labour training centres—*cantieri di lavoro*—where the unemployed are given technical instruction in some particular branch of work on which they are at the same time employed. For this they receive 300 lire a day in addition to their unemployment benefit. The *cantieri* were started in depressed areas of Apulia, Sicily, and Sardinia, and have since been extended to other regions. Their work has consisted mainly of road-building, land clearance, and reafforestation, the latter

[1] See above, p. 214.

particularly necessary in conjunction with the Government's plans for combating soil erosion in the South. During 1952–3 the *cantieri*, which then numbered 8,290, gave work to 441,000 unemployed.[1]

A tremendous impetus to employment came in 1950 with the Government's ten-year plan for the development of the South, organised under the auspices of the Cassa per il Mezzogiorno.[2] It has already been seen how far-reaching those plans are, and what possibilities they afford for providing employment on the great variety of public works which are being undertaken. This was hitherto the Government's major effort in the direction of combating unemployment, as well as in its primary aim of improving Southern conditions; and its effects will be felt increasingly in the next few years, now that the planning stage is passed and more and more undertakings are getting under way. The land reform, too, with its emphasis on land transformation and improvement, is doing much to provide fresh employment in the regions where it operates. Finally, the Vanoni ten-year plan for economic development announced at the beginning of 1955[3] had as one of its main objects the creation of 4 million new jobs during the decade 1955–64, and its emphasis on the need for establishing training facilities was an indication of its realistic approach.

In all these schemes, indeed, stress had been laid on the need for technical training. The high proportion of unskilled workers among the new recruits has been noted as one of the main barriers to their obtaining their first jobs, and both the Vigorelli and the Tremelloni Commissions emphasised the need for improving the possibilities for vocational training and for apprenticeship. This is no new cry in Italy: for years since the war such private bodies as, for example, the Società Umanitaria in Milan, under the devoted leadership of the well-known anti-Fascist Riccardo Bauer, have been directing public attention to this need and providing for it as best they could themselves. The high cost of apprenticeship training in industry has hitherto been a bar to its widespread adoption in factories which, as we have seen, are already burdened with surplus manpower. But it is now realised how shortsighted a

[1] *Il Popolo*, 22 May 1954. [2] See above, pp. 203 ff. [3] See above, pp. 188 ff.

policy it would be to disregard the need, in view of the increasing numbers of new workers coming on to the labour market; and in the course of parliamentary discussions on the Tremelloni Commission's Report in May 1954 it was decided to speed up further means of vocational training, as well as to facilitate apprenticeship in factories by granting a four-year exemption from social assistance taxation in factories giving employment to young people in their first posts. It was also decided to restrict overtime to cases where no new workers could be taken on. Many concerns have already started training centres of their own (e.g. Fiat, Olivetti), and State-aided centres under the Ministry of Labour exist in some of the main towns such as Genoa, Venice, and Florence—the latter is an outstanding example, organised by the enterprising Christian Democrat Mayor, La Pira, in conjunction with the Ministry of Labour. In November 1954 it was decided to open nearly a hundred agricultural training schools in the South, and early in 1955 special training centres were being opened in fourteen communes scattered throughout the country in areas where unemployment was particularly serious (e.g. Muggia, near Trieste, and Minervino in Apulia).

The need for tackling the problem of unemployment among the young is too obvious to need emphasis. On the political side alone, it is among the young and dissatisfied unemployed that extremist propaganda finds its readiest recruits. A hopeful aspect is that, as the Tremelloni Commission found, the standard of education is higher among the younger unemployed than among the older men; but this also makes it the more necessary to make use of the young quickly, before they become disgruntled. As the Commission noted, the longer a man is unemployed the more difficult it becomes for him to find work. Official statistics suggest that a quarter of the unemployed had had no work for more than a year, and most of those questioned during the Commission's Inquiry had been unemployed for periods totalling more than three years. As might be expected, their health deteriorated—nearly half of those questioned were found to be ill in one way or another—and thus their difficulty in obtaining employment increased. For all these reasons, as well as for the country's own productive development, a sounder utilisation of its manpower is a first priority for the Government. This was fully recognised in the Vanoni Plan of 1955 which, with its proposals for tackling the problem by increased capital investment in key economic sectors, held out high hopes that the next ten years might witness a vast change in the employment situation.

CHAPTER XX

EMIGRATION

Some years ago an Italian film, *Il Cammino della Speranza*, told the story of a village in the sulphur-mining region of Sicily. The mines were going through a bad period and work had dwindled to practically nothing; the villagers were starving. Then there came on the scene a plausible and smooth-mannered individual from the mainland who offered to take volunteers through Italy and over the frontier to France where work would be plentiful: he drew a convincing picture of a promised land: all he needed from them was the money for their fares. Immediately hope sprang up, savings were scraped together, and at last the party set forth in a lorry for the coast amid the cheers and good wishes of their less fortunate friends and relatives left behind. They got as far as Naples, and there the smooth-mannered type went to buy the tickets for France—and vanished. He had simply made off with their savings. Some of the party turned back at once to Sicily and starvation: that at least was familiar. The tougher ones decided not to give up, but to try to work their way up through Italy to the frontier. The rest of the film describes their Odyssey—a job here and there, interspersed with countless rebuffs; some fall by the wayside; and at last a handful reach their goal.

The story is not, of course, entirely typical. The case of the Sicilian sulphur industry is an extreme one;[1] speculators do not inevitably spring up from nowhere to fleece despairing peasants of their last lira; and the majority of Italian peasants, however great their need, would probably prove less gullible than those of the *Cammino della Speranza*. But the point is that the situation is perfectly possible: where there is no work to be found and no money to buy bread, the Italian who has hardly been beyond the bounds of his own village is prepared to try anything, to make a complete leap into the unknown,

[1] Besides lacking modern plant and equipment, it is highly dependent on the fluctuations of external demand.

if the unknown holds hope of work for himself and bread for his children.

In this readiness to set forth to a wider world Italians are only following a tradition now familiar for generations. In the past, indeed, the main safety-valve for Italy's superabundant population lay in emigration. Between the 1880s and the first world war the numbers leaving Italy to seek work abroad grew by leaps and bounds, and went far to offset the steady increase in the population: between 1901 and 1913 they averaged from 550,000 to 650,000 a year, and in the peak year of 1913 reached 872,000, or 246 out of every 10,000 inhabitants.

Emigrants from the South were always far more numerous than from the more prosperous North. The majority of Southerners went overseas, mainly to the United States or Latin America: in the early 1900s, for example, some three-quarters of Italy's emigrants to overseas countries came from the South. Northerners, on the other hand, preferred if possible to find work in the nearer European countries, and much of the migration from the North has always been for seasonal work in Switzerland and France.

In the inter-war years two factors combined to check the flow of Italian emigration overseas. The first and most important was the new policy of the receiving countries. The United States Immigration Act of 1921, which imposed severe restrictions on immigration, closed the door of one of Italy's main outlets, and this legislation had its counterpart in the post-war years in Brazil, Uruguay, Argentina, and Australia. Secondly, Fascist demographic policy tended to discourage Italians from leaving the country—the very word 'emigrants' was discarded and replaced by the term 'Italians abroad'. The only exception to the policy of keeping them at home was the encouragement given to would-be emigrants to the Italian colonies in North and East Africa. But despite lavish expenditure on the development of these colonies, the difficulties of making a living there remained very considerable, and according to Italian estimates the pre-war (1938) Italian population of the African colonies, Libya and East Africa, amounted to less than a quarter of a million. It is only fair to add that the schemes for developing Ethiopia and, more particularly, the grandiose plan for the colonisation of Libya[1] had not had time to develop fully before the war broke out.

After the second world war, as has been seen, the problem of Italy's surplus population became acute, and from 1947 onwards, when the country resumed freedom of action in the conduct of her foreign affairs, considerable efforts were made to revive emigration to the traditional reception countries. The result is that Italian emigration of recent years has averaged 150,000 persons annually, or about two-thirds of the increase in population of working age.

EMIGRATION FROM ITALY, 1901–52

(Annual averages in 000)

	1901–10		1924–8	1934–8	1949–52				
					Total	of which to			
						USA & Canada	Latin America	Other overseas countries	Europe
Non-seasonal:									
Gross*	603	Europe 251 / Overseas 352	255	65	196	23	97	20	56
Net*		Overseas† 180	99	26	163	19	80	17	47
Seasonal	..		..	..	115	—	—	—	115

.. = not available.
* Includes seasonal migration, 1901–38.
† 1902–10. No figure for Continental repatriation available.

(SOURCE: ECE, *Economic Survey of Europe in 1953*, p. 193.)

Emigration to European countries was more easily arranged than to countries overseas, and had in fact already been resumed as early as 1946. The main receiving country was France, to which between then and the end of 1952 more than half the total number of Italian emigrants to European countries went. Next came Belgium, which offered special facilities to Italian miners and their families, and which over the whole period 1946–52 received 165,694 Italian emigrants. Britain followed with smaller numbers (the peak year was 1951, with 9,000),[2] and some other European countries, e.g.

[1] Described by Martin Moore in *Fourth Shore: Italy's Mass Colonisation of Libya* (London, Routledge, 1940).

[2] It was in 1951 that the scheme for recruitment of Italian miners to work in Britain was launched. It was unfortunately suspended in June 1952 owing to the intransigence of the British trade unions—see above, p. 129.

Sweden, took a small number of specialised Italian workers. Throughout this period seasonal migration to France and Switzerland took place on a large scale, reaching peak figures of 21,210 to France and 132,935 to Switzerland in 1952.[1]

Considerable efforts were made to revive emigration to overseas countries, and to this end from 1948 onwards a number of bilateral agreements were concluded. The main outlet of the past, the United States, in continuation of its pre-war policy still offered very little hope to would-be emigrants. The annual quota for Italy remained at under 6,000 until 1953. Then, however, under the Refugee Relief Act of 3 December 1953, it was decided to admit special quotas of immigrants for a limited period, and Italy received a quota of 60,000, an additional 10,000 being allocated for Trieste, which presented a particular problem with the refugees congregated there from Venezia Giulia and Yugoslavia, as well as from Eastern Europe. Applications flowed in, and the intention was to admit the new immigrants under the quota gradually over the next two years. But owing to the stipulations as to the classes of immigrants prescribed under the McCarran Act it seemed doubtful whether either of Italy's quotas could be fully utilized.

Latin America was the other main traditional destination of migration from Italy. Here in the past large numbers of Italians had settled, especially in Argentina and Brazil, and at first great hopes were placed on a revival of this trend, the more so since the post-war development policies of the Latin American countries seemed likely to favour an inflow of foreign labour. Argentina's five-year plan, for instance, appeared to offer almost unlimited possibilities, and an agreement signed in January 1948 provided for extensive immigration of Italian workers thither—the very high figure of 100,000 a year was mentioned, and was in fact nearly reached in 1949. But difficulties soon arose in the fulfilment of General Perón's ambitious plans—with corresponding repercussions on the Italian immigrants. Arrangements about contracts proved highly unsatisfactory, there were delays in sending home remittances, and the number of emigrants diminished, while many returned home dissatisfied with conditions. A further agreement in 1952, once again providing for 500,000 workers, mainly agri-

[1] ILO, *Industry and Labour*, Vol. XI, No. 1, 1 January 1954, p. 47.

cultural, to emigrate to Argentina over the next five years, did not in its early stages seem likely to be much more productive.

Even more serious difficulties were encountered in Brazil, to which plans for large-scale Italian emigration were directed not only through a bilateral agreement of 10 October 1950 but also under the scheme launched by the Inter-Governmental Committee for European Migration, to which Italy adhered in 1952. The latter plan aimed at sending out 40,000 Italian emigrants to Brazil during 1953, to be followed by further contingents. But here too conditions often proved unsatisfactory; there were insufficient guarantees against the arbitrary action of employers, contracts were in some cases not fulfilled, and numbers of emigrants asked to be repatriated. Of the other Latin American countries, Venezuela was the only one to take large numbers (over 22,000 in 1953); while nearly all of them at one time or another propounded grandiose immigration schemes, these came to be viewed with caution in the light of past experiences.

Great hopes were placed on the prospects of large-scale emigration to Australia opened up by the five-year agreement of 29 March 1951. This got off to a very poor start, for by the time formalities had been completed the slump of 1952 was at its worst, and piteous tales were told of Italian immigrants herded together in the camp of Bonegilla without prospect of work or accommodation—a fate they temporarily shared with immigrants from other countries as well, including Britain. Nevertheless, some 26,000 Italians went to Australia in 1952, of whom something like 1,000 returned home. Emigration from Italy was then temporarily suspended, but with improving conditions there seemed reasonable prospects that Australia might provide a solution for a steady number of Italian immigrants in the coming years, and early in 1955 their annual quota was reckoned to be 15,000. Of the other Commonwealth countries, Canada has regularly received a number of immigrants from Italy, and for 1954 a quota of 25,000 was planned. Some Italian farmers have also settled in Rhodesia, while Italian investment in South Africa—for example, the establishment of a Snia Viscosa factory in Durban—has brought with it a small migration of skilled Italian workers and technicians. An Italian mission visited many countries of Africa in the early spring of 1955 to discuss emigration possibilities, and its leader, the Under-Secretary for Foreign Affairs, Badini Confalonieri, stated on his return that while mass emigration to any of the countries visited appeared out of the question, there were excellent prospects for the employment of specialised manpower.[1]

As far as international efforts towards assisting migration are concerned, Italian representatives have consistently put forward their country's case at the various emigration conferences of the ILO and on the Manpower Committee of OEEC. Italy places great hopes on the creation of a European community in which labour will flow freely from one country to another, and here a beginning has been made with the European Coal and Steel Community. But the international organisation directly concerned with the migration problem is the Inter-Governmental Committee on European Migration already referred to. Under ICEM, to whose administrative funds Italy contributes at the rate of 9 per cent, some 50,000 Italians had already emigrated during the first two years February 1952–April 1954, while in the whole year 1954 Italian emigrants numbered 48,000, or more than a third of the total organised under ICEM.

Thus through international schemes and bilateral agreements migration from Italy was by 1955 providing prospects of a livelihood abroad for an average of some 150,000 workers a year. Remittances in 1954 amounted to 71,000 million lire, by far the larger proportion coming from emigrants in European countries. Nevertheless, despite all the efforts to place Italians abroad, emigration was still providing for only some 7½ per cent per annum of the 2 million unemployed, let alone the annual quota of new workers coming on to the labour market.

There are a variety of reasons for the relative failure of emigration to provide a more complete answer to Italy's population problem. From what has already been said it should by now be clear that there can be no single 'complete' answer to a problem of such dimensions: any solution will have to be reached by a patchwork of measures, both

[1] *Corriere della Sera*, 25 March 1955.

domestic and international, each one of which can only hope to make a partial contribution. But among such measures emigration must clearly play a considerable part and Italian views are often sharply divided as to the reasons why it has not hitherto been more effective.

The cause is, of course, in part to be found in the post-war international situation, where, with thousands of literally homeless refugees still to be provided for, preference in international legislation has not unnaturally been given to them rather than to the nationals of a country which cannot assure a livelihood for all its own people. Here, as Italian spokesmen have never tired of repeating, Italy is in a quite special position —comparable only with that of Greece, the other country of Southern Europe where population pressure is at its greatest. The Italian Government is inclined to feel that more could, and should, be done through international measures; and in the meantime, in their anxiety to provide for at least some of the unemployed, they have in the past seized upon offers from possible reception countries which have not in the event come up to expectations. In some instances, notably Argentina and Brazil, offers to accept immigrants from Italy have been the more readily accepted because the Italian side of the financing could be covered, at any rate in part, by Italian blocked funds in those countries.

The Government's emigration policy has been criticised not only, as was to be expected, in Left-wing circles, but also, and from a more serious standpoint, in circles closely concerned with the whole question of emigration and unemployment. The Società Umanitaria of Milan, for example, in its fortnightly bulletin the *Bollettino Quindicinale dell'Emigrazione* has consistently pointed out with chapter and verse mistakes that have been made and possible ways of improving emigration policy as a whole. In a debate on emigration in the Chamber on 2 October 1953[1] a Christian Democrat Deputy, Antonio Dazzi, himself closely concerned throughout his life with emigrants and their problems, made some detailed suggestions for improvements. Describing emigration as 'the Cinderella among our policies', he pointed to the need to increase the efficiency of the existing emigration services—'other countries

[1] Reported in *Bollettino Quindicinale dell'Emigrazione*, 25 October 1953.

make difficulties', he said, 'but in the meantime we should eliminate our own difficulties at home'.

The conduct of emigration affairs is in fact at present divided between the Ministry of Foreign Affairs and the Ministry of Labour, whereas in pre-Fascist days the whole administration was concentrated in a High Commissioner's Office which, created in 1901, successfully carried out the country's emigration policy during the peak pre-first-world-war period. This office was abolished by the Fascists in 1927, and replaced, as to the financial side, by an Istituto di Credito per il Lavoro italiano all'Estero (ICLE), which still remains the financial organ, operating with funds from the Treasury and, in recent years, from ERP. Dazzi and other critics suggest that this cumbersome divided control should cease and that the conduct of emigration affairs should once more, as in the past, be concentrated in a single autonomous organisation endowed with the necessary funds and empowered to frame and carry out the whole of the country's emigration policy.

Another point frequently raised, and one on which there is general agreement, is the need to provide better training for would-be emigrants. It is now realised that the days are past when reception countries could be expected to welcome unskilled immigrants in large numbers. In the European countries, apart from seasonal agricultural workers, the demand has for some time past been almost exclusively for workers with some specialised skill—miners for Belgium, builders for Switzerland, and so on. But in the overseas countries too there is now small prospect of success for the wholly unqualified worker, and the Government is urging local Chambers of Commerce to start training courses for would-be emigrants where they will not only be taught a trade but also given some rudimentary knowledge of the language and customs of the country to which they hope to go.

Some of these points were made by an Italian Consul, Adolfo Crescini, who after three years' experience as Consul in Venezuela broadcast on the Italian radio some advice to prospective emigrants among his compatriots which is reproduced here because it seems to sum up many of the difficulties involved in emigration.[1] The country in question is Vene-

[1] Text in *Bollettino Quindicinale dell'Emigrazione*, 25 May 1954.

zuela, but much of what the Consul says can be applied to other countries as well.

Doubtless some of you who are listening to me are preparing to set out to Venezuela, or are turning it over in your minds as a remedy for all the ills and difficulties that have harassed you at home. To you I would like to give some advice, in the light of my experience as one who for years has had to listen to the confessions of less fortunate or disillusioned emigrants.

1. Before you decide to leave, think seriously of the step you are taking, weigh the pros and cons, and, above all, make sure that the document asking you to come over, or the labour contract, is signed by someone who is genuinely prepared to look after you from the moment that your ship touches the quay at La Guaira. Too many people set out armed with a document that has all the appearance of authenticity, but which has no real validity, with the result that once landed on the other side they find themselves alone and abandoned in a country whose language they do not know, without any idea where to sleep or to turn for their first job.

2. Be sure about your own capacity for work, your health, and your adaptability to work in a climate which is sometimes temperate, sometimes tropical, but always humid and liable to produce a feeling of exhaustion in anyone not in the soundest health.

3. Be sure that you are really versed in your trade. Venezuela is a young, generous, and hospitable country, ready to believe anyone who says that he is skilled in some particular trade. Italians who really possess such skill at once find good and well-paid jobs, but those whose qualifications go no deeper than words are destined to find endless disappointment and bitterness. They get a job today but are dismissed tomorrow, and then wander from one workshop to another, always sinking lower, until at last, discouraged and embittered, having used up their last reserves, they turn up at the Consulate and ask to be repatriated. And believe me, there is nothing sadder than to see a young, strong, healthy man presenting himself at the Consulate or the Assistance Committee to ask for board and lodging, and to hear that to get his passage to Venezuela he sold his cottage or his plot of land or, worse still, mortgaged them or borrowed the money.

4. Be prepared, especially if you have no particular qualifications, to go and work in the interior, anywhere where there is the chance of employment, often in the open country miles from the nearest habitation. This is not exceptional—it is the usual condition of work for tens of thousands of our labourers employed on road-making or on the railways that are still in their infancy.

5. Be perfectly clear in your mind that in Venezuela you have got to *want* to work, and that it is not a country where money drops from the sky. Unless you are prepared for hard sacrifices, for life in the open under a tropical sun and storms of a violence

unknown to us at home, you had better save your fare and stay in Italy.

6. In any case, I would most strongly dissuade anyone from setting out without a watertight labour contract in hopes of working in an office. The builders' yards in Venezuela are full of accountants, surveyors, and men with university degrees who in order to get a daily meal are serving as bricklayers or working pneumatic drills or digging trenches. During my three years in Venezuela I have managed to get a good many industrial or agricultural workers taken on, but only by using all my personal influence did I succeed in getting work for a couple of clerks—not more.

In conclusion: the simple peasant or labourer, or anyone who is not in perfect health, had better not go to Venezuela. On the other hand, it is the place for a man with a definite trade who is prepared to live far from a town and work hard.

Given those conditions, I would advise my own son to emigrate to Venezuela. And in fact I have a son there now.

CHAPTER XXI

EDUCATION

THE question of education has cropped up at intervals throughout this book, whether by implication in considering the slow development of political maturity in a recently unified country, or more directly in the discussion of such problems as the backward South and the need for more vocational training among unskilled workers.

Education at all levels has been the subject of frequently recurring controversy in Italy. Perhaps in no sphere of Italian life has the influence—and burden—of past inheritance made itself so deeply felt. Successive reformers have striven to prune the aspirations towards encyclopaedic knowledge, coupled with the emphasis on classical learning, which Italian education inherited from the early teaching Orders. Yet in 1922 we find Professor Gaetano Salvemini proclaiming that 'Our whole educational system is based on the fatal conception that a pupil must learn at school everything that would be in any way necessary, or even merely useful, to him in after life'.[1] And a brief perusal of the highly comprehensive school syllabuses of today suggests that in thirty troubled years this particular aspect of Italian life has not changed much.

It was in an attempt to get away from this conception, and more particularly from the rhetoric and sterility in teaching that went with it, that the Idealist philospher Giovanni Gentile, then Minister of Education, introduced in 1923 the most radical reforms which Italian education had known since the country's unification. Briefly, these reforms aimed at making education less remote and abstract and evoking the pupil's own innate intelligence through a direct study of the great authors and of basic principles, so that the subject studied would itself become the major consideration, rather than the textbooks which imparted it. Unfortunately the liberal spirit which animated these reforms—introduced, paradoxically

[1] Gaetano Salvemini, *Problemi educativi e sociali dell'Italia d'oggi* (1922).

enough, by one who was later to become the accredited philosopher of Fascism[1]—was soon extinguished by the progressive invasion of educational life by Fascist influence.

Education was to be even more closely tied to the Fascist party line by the *Carta della Scuola*, or School Charter, introduced in 1939 by the then Minister of Education Giuseppe Bottai, which replaced the Gentile law of 1923. A current witticism described this reform as the *Scuola della Carta* rather than the *Carta della Scuola* (not the School Charter but the School of Paper). New regulations abounded, all tending towards the subordination of learning to Fascist nationalistic and militarist ideals. The Charter did however contain one innovation which reflected the transformation already at work in society as a whole, in its inclusion of labour (in the sense of technical and manual work) as an essential part of school education.

In the event, the new Charter had barely got under way when war broke out, and its effects proved to be only one of the many problems with which the post-war educational reformers were faced in their efforts to restore its former liberty to Italian education. On the material side, damage to school buildings (insufficient even before the war) had been considerable, while many more schools were still requisitioned. There was a great shortage of all school equipment, and the need to eliminate the Fascist school textbooks was complicated by the virtual impossibility of speedily obtaining other books to replace them. War and military occupation had had their demoralising effects on the country's youth: with the breakdown of transport and shortage of classsroom many children, especially of primary and elementary school age, received practically no schooling during the latter war years, and instead roamed about free to become camp followers or infant black marketeers in the way made familiar in such films as *Sciuscia*. Meanwhile illiteracy had risen alarmingly, and in the first post-war years was reckoned to be near the 7 million mark at which it had last stood in 1931. Yet on the other hand the number of qualified teachers far exceeded the posts available,

[1] One of Gentile's last public actions was to make an oration on behalf of Fascism in June 1943, only a month before Mussolini's downfall. Gentile was shot dead in Florence in April 1944.

with the result that many of them had to take posts as part-time or extra assistants, combining this with any other work they could pick up in order to gain an insufficient livelihood, while many others remained totally unemployed. The difficulty of finding work, as well as the influx of men returning from the forces, brought about a tremendous increase in the number of students at the universities. Registered students in 1946–7 reached the peak figure of nearly 190,000, or 4·2 per cent of the total population (as compared with 77,000, or 1·8 per cent, in 1938–9); and though the numbers gradually fell in succeeding years there were still nearly 139,000 in 1951–2.

The organisation of Italian education is somewhat complicated, and a brief sketch of the framework may be useful as a prelude to outlining the post-war measures undertaken towards its reconstruction.

The Italian Constitution of 1948 lays down (Art. 34) that 'Education is open to all' and in its lower grades, covering eight years (6–14), is free and compulsory.[1] Secondary education falls into two parts. The lower grades (ages 11–14) are catered for by the *Scuola media unica* (intermediate school) or the *Scuola di avviamento professionale* (vocational training school), while for the higher grades (from 14 upwards) there are four alternative types of school, the *liceo classico* and *liceo scientifico*, the *Istituto Magistrale* (for elementary school teachers' training), and the *Istituto Tecnico*, or technical school.

State examinations (*esami di Stato*) mark the end of each grade, with the *esame di maturità*, or school-leaving certificate, at the end of the whole classical and scientific curriculum.

There are both State and private schools in Italy. In the elementary grades by far the largest proportion of pupils (some 93 per cent in 1946–7) attend State schools. The majority of the private schools are in the hands of the religious teaching orders. Private schools can if they wish qualify to be 'State-recognised' (*parificate*), in which case they are eligible for State aid and are in other respects on the same footing as the State schools; but in fact only about a fifth of the private elementary schools are so recognised. In secondary education

[1] Elementary education in Italy has in fact been free ever since the Lex Casati of 1859, and compulsory since the Lex Coppino of 1877.

the proportion of pupils attending private schools is much higher: in 1951–2 they represented some 27 per cent of the total. Pupils of private schools must take the State examinations.

The majority of Italian universities come under the State (among the few exceptions are the Catholic University of the Sacred Heart and the Bocconi University, both in Milan). Teachers and unversity professors in all State establishments count as civil servants, and their appointments are governed by the Ministry of Public Instruction.

POST-WAR GOVERNMENT ACTION

In the first year or two after the war the main problem was to restore the ordinary groundwork for education, while at the same time ridding it of Fascist influences. Reconstruction of damaged school buildings was the first need, and by 1947 a good deal had been done in this direction, though there was still a great shortage of classrooms, and classes often had to be carried on in barns or cellars or other makeshift buildings. The revision of the Fascist textbooks was carried out hurriedly, but on the whole effectively; but in the new atmosphere of free discussion there was considerable disagreement about the scope of more fundamental changes. Extra teaching staff had to be taken on to cope with the influx of pupils as conditions became more normal. Numerically this presented no difficulty, since unemployed teachers already abounded; but the qualifications of those who had taken their examinations in the last chaotic years of the war often left much to be desired. Moreover the enrolment of many teachers on a temporary basis, far in excess of the number of established paid posts, which the sudden post-war influx of pupils made unavoidable, created the problem of a vast army of unestablished teachers (*insegnanti incaricati fuori ruolo*) whose continued livelihood was highly uncertain since they never knew from year to year whether their appointments would be renewed. Although each year a few of them succeed in passing the competitive examinations for established posts, this problem still remains today, especially among secondary school teachers, more than half of whom are still *fuori ruolo*.

The need for a basic revision of the Italian educational

system was widely felt in the atmosphere of liberation which prevailed immediately after the war, and it was to meet this view that Guido Gonella, the prominent Christian Democrat publicist who became Minister of Education in July 1946, instituted in April 1947 a National Commission of Inquiry on Educational Reform. Questionnaires were sent out to teachers, parents, and others connected with education in its every stage and form, including the private schools. Throughout the five years of Gonella's term of office as Minister of Education 'la riforma' pervaded the educational background. Hundreds of findings were tabulated and assessed, hundreds of grievances aired and suggestions made. It was not till the middle of 1951 that Gonella finally presented his reform proposals to Parliament, and almost immediately afterwards he ceased to be Minister of Education. By that time the original proposals had been considerably pruned, and even their name had been changed from 'School Reform' to 'General Regulations on Education'. The vast conception of a basic reform of Italian education had dwindled to a series of unexceptionable precepts; the rest was quietly shelved.

Thus if Gonella (and with him the five years of education under Christian Democrat rule for which he stood) is to be judged as a reformer, he must be said to have failed. Nevertheless, as even some of his critics would admit,[1] some progress was made in certain directions under his régime. He succeeded in obtaining a higher proportion of public expenditure on education, which in 1951–2 represented over 10 per cent of the total Budget expenditure, as against only 5 per cent before the war. He brought about improvements in the status and pay of many categories of teachers, a most important question for this poorly-rewarded branch of the civil service (and despite these improvements theirs is still one of the professions in which salaries have most noticeably failed to rise sufficiently in relation to the post-war cost of living[2]). By taking on more teachers, too, Gonella reduced the size of the overcrowded classes from

[1] e.g., Giovanni Ferretti, 'Il bilancio del Ministro Gonella', in *Il Ponte*, November 1951.

[2] In May 1955 secondary school teachers throughout the country went on strike for several days—an unheard-of step in this most conscientious profession—in protest against the delay in introducing promised improvements in their pay and status.

the immediate post-war average of 50 to something nearer 30. He also tackled the question of growing illiteracy by instituting from 1947 onwards 'Popular Schools' (*Scuole Popolari*), which provided special courses for adult illiterates and semi-literates all over the country, and especially in the more remote parts of Southern Italy where the need was particularly great.[1] Between 1947 and 1953 over 3½ million were said to have attended these courses, and the number of illiterates was reckoned to have fallen from the immediate post-war estimate of 7 million to around 3 million. Efforts were also made to improve conditions in the many remote country schools where 'compulsory attendance' had become a dead letter, at any rate beyond the pupil's first three years (6–8), owing both to the inadequate provision of classes and to the difficulty of inducing parents to release their children from work in the fields and on the hillsides.

Some attempt was made to tackle the question of the shortage of school buildings, and under a law of 1949 grants were allocated for this purpose to the Ministry of Public Works (under which at that time school building came—another source of complication). But it was left for the Scelba Government in 1954 to introduce really far-reaching measures towards removing this fundamental stumbling block. By that time education had at last, after nearly eight years, passed out of the hands of a Christian Democrat Minister to a Liberal, Professor Gaetano Martino, formerly Rector of Messina University; and this event was hailed by the secularists as the opening of a new era in Italian post-war education (though their rejoicings were to be short-lived, for in September 1954 Professor Martino replaced Signor Piccioni as Foreign Minister and the Ministry of Education reverted to Christian Democrat hands[2]). The times certainly seemed favourable for a more energetic and realistic policy; and Professor Martino's emphasis on school-building needs, as an essential preliminary for wider improvements, could be compared with the practical approach of his colleagues Vigorelli and Tremelloni towards

[1] In this connection mention must also be made of the fine pioneer work of private organisations such as the Associazione Nazionale per gli Interessi del Mezzogiorno, under Umberto Zanotti Bianco, and the Unione Nazionale per la Lotta contro l'Analfabetismo.

[2] But it went to a Social Democrat (Paolo Rossi) under the Segni Government.

the problems of poverty and unemployment.[1] In mid-1954 it was reckoned that, despite the restoration of over 19,000 war-damaged school premises, in the elementary grades alone there were still 64,000 too few classrooms; and in describing the desperate need for more schools Senator Umberto Zanotti Bianco stated[2] that even in the North the number of classrooms was 22 per cent below the needs, in the Centre 46 per cent, and in the South 59 per cent—the worst place of all was Avellino, with a shortage of 72 per cent. Zanotti Bianco, who has himself devoted a lifetime to Southern problems, went on to describe how in some Southern districts children often had to walk 10 kilometres to and from school—'a school, maybe, without windows, or in a disused stable or farm building with no light except from the door'.

The financing of school premises is primarily a charge on the local authorities (i.e. the commune), not on the State, and it can readily be understood how impossible it is for poor communes with no wealthy rate-payers to meet the expenses involved in building or enlarging a school; even if they could borrow the capital they could not hope to raise the interest. The school building plan approved by Parliament in August 1954 provided for State contributions, over a ten-year period, of a percentage of the cost (6 per cent in the South, 5 per cent in the rest of Italy) towards the building of elementary and vocational schools, and of a slightly lower percentage in the case of all other types of schools. By this means it was hoped to build 300,000 classrooms over the next ten years; and prefects were urged to see that the local *cantieri di lavoro*[3] were employed as far as possible on school building—thus serving the dual purpose of keeping down expenses and giving the *cantieri* worthwhile employment. To meet the cost of these State contributions, reckoned at a total of 15 milliard lire, fees in all the paying (i.e. *medie* and *superiori*) schools were to be raised slightly; these fees are very low, and have hardly risen since the war.

Thus at least a beginning had been made towards remedying the shortage of accommodation which had retarded educa-

[1] See above, pp. 207 ff.

[2] In the Senate on 24 October 1953—see *Per l'edilizia della scuola primaria* (Rome, Tipografia del Senato, 1953).

[3] See above, pp. 221–2.

tional development ever since the war, and which threatened to become more acute if the proposal to raise the school leaving age of 15 should be carried out. But other long-standing problems remain. Among those most frequently mentioned is that of the *esame di Stato*—the State examination—and in particular of the *esame di maturità*, the examination for entering the university. The root of the long-standing trouble summed up in the words *esame di Stato*, a nightmare to Italian pupils and a King Charles's head to their preceptors, lies not so much in the examination itself as in all that it implies in the preceding curriculum. To gain the certificate pupils of the *liceo classico* have to pass not only in Italian, Latin, and Greek, but also in mathematics, physics, chemistry, natural sciences, history of art, political history, and economics. For the *liceo scientifico* pupils there is at least no Greek, but instead a foreign language, and more advanced physics and mathematics in addition to all the other subjects. It is small wonder that in a questionnaire on schools conducted by the Communist paper *Unità* in 1953 the predominant criticism alike from teachers, parents, and pupils was 'La scuola è troppo pesante' (school weighs too heavily); and the Education Minister Martino himself summed up the situation in the words 'In Italia si studia molto e male' (in Italy we study much and badly).

In this same connection another constantly recurring criticism is that of the failure of education to meet the needs of modern times. The continued emphasis on Latin, even for the much wider range of pupils now receiving a secondary education (and their numbers have nearly doubled since 1938–9), and the importance still attached to a classical education, is condemned by the critics on the ground that such an education merely turns out students who, while they rapidly forget their classics, are unfitted for, and scornful of, practical occupations. It is certainly true that in the South, in particular, a classical education still exercises an almost mythical appeal and prestige value. While in Northern Italy the number of students attending the technical schools has risen considerably since the war, in the South the proportion is still very low—and yet it is precisely here, with the particular Southern problem of unemployment among 'intellectuals', coupled with the new openings for technicians now arising through the region's development, that the need for more engineers and agrarian economists and fewer unemployed *avvocati* leaps to the eye. But the swollen faculties of law and medicine, especially in the Southern universities, which account for nearly half the total number of law students, continue to bear witness to the traditional appeal of these professions; on the other hand engineering and agrarian economy are among the least popular faculties.

University Students according to Faculties

Faculty	*1946–7* Registered students (000)	*1946–7* Percentage of women	*1951–2* Registered students (000)	*1951–2* Percentage of women
Law	23·6	7·8	28·3	13·9
Economy	30·1	9·6	20·1	15·3
Letters	19·4	67·3	13·3	75·7
Education	13·1	64·5	9·4	56·7
Science	24·1	35·0	21·6	37·4
Agrarian economy	3·5	3·4	2·4	3·3
Medicine	35·3	7·8	22·9	9·5
Veterinary science	3·3	0·2	1·7	0·3
Pharmacy	9·6	57·4	8·9	57·6
Engineering	15·1	0·7	7·8	0·4
Architecture	2·4	18·0	2·2	17·6

(Source: 'Cifre sulle Università', in *Mondo Economico*, 19 June 1954.)

A long-standing controversy of a quite different kind is that relating to the private schools and the influence of the Church in Italian education. While in Italy this does not now perhaps present a burning question to the extent that it still does in France, it has in the past been one of the most sensitive points in the relations between Church and State. At the time when Fascism came to power education in Italy was completely non-confessional. This position altered after the Concordat of 1929 which established a compromise whereby religious teaching was to be provided in all State schools: in the private schools run by the religious orders it had of course in any case been customary. After the war the new Italian Constitution of 1948, by its specific adherence to the Lateran Pacts (Art. 7),[1]

[1] Article 7 of the Constitution affirms that 'the relations between State and Church are regulated by the Lateran Pacts'.

tacitly continued to accept this obligation, while making no specific mention of religious instruction. There is in fact a period of religious instruction each week in all State schools, from which pupils may absent themselves if their parents wish. The instruction may be given either by the class teacher or by an ecclesiastic called in for the purpose.

In the early post-war days, when anti-clericalism was quiescent, these provisions on the whole aroused no particular controversy. But during the five years of Gonella's tenure of the Ministry of Education some of his critics reproached him with unduly favouring the private (i.e., in most cases, the specifically Catholic) schools at the expense of the State schools. This accusation is denied by the critic already mentioned,[1] who says, 'I believe his intention was to administer Italian education fairly'. Statistics in fact show that whereas the number of pupils in State schools increased by 42 per cent between 1945 and 1951, those in private schools increased by only 20 per cent—which does not suggest that the influence of the latter was in any way artificially extended during the Gonella period. The Liberal Education Minister Martino, speaking in the Senate on March 1954, declared that the State 'had no philosophical or scientific creed to affirm', and explicitly recognised the principle of the 'libertà della Scuola'—the freedom of education.

[1] Giovanni Ferretti, in *Il Ponte*, November 1951.

CONCLUSION: TEN YEARS AFTER

LOOKING back over the ten years of Italy's post-war story which this book has attempted to survey, the swift overall impression is one of an amazing recovery. No one, recalling the chaos of 1945, can fail to be impressed by the order and, in many respects, the prosperity of today, or to contrast that state with what might have been if Italian administrations had proved unable to play so skilfully the difficult hand they were dealt. The resilience of the Italian people has shown itself, too, in other spheres which it has not been possible to touch on here but in which Italy's achievements have done much to enhance her reputation abroad. Many a foreigner who knows little or nothing of Italy's political or economic situation can talk knowledgeably and enthusiastically about, for example, the films of De Sica (and their stars—I imagine it is incontrovertible that the Italian name most familiar abroad in 1955 was that of Lollobrigida), the novels of Alberto Moravia, Italian fashions and industrial design, and even Italian football and tennis teams.

The new Italy, in fact, is making a place for herself in the world of today in all sorts of ways that were probably not envisaged by the founding fathers of the Constitution.

Yet while many Italians may be prepared to rest content with things as they are so long as they can continue to air their grievances and indulge their propensity for inveighing against the Government, more reflective judgements on the past ten years would probably differ very widely. It so happens that the tenth anniversary of the end of the war and the culmination of the Resistance struggle, commemorated in the last days of April 1955, provided the occasion for a number of such assessments. This thinking-back to the latter days of the war and to the manner in which it came to an end in Italy inevitably brought into relief the crucial factor of the Resistance and its significance, not only then, but throughout the succeeding ten years.

For it is, ultimately, in the light of their attitude towards the Resistance—and, to go back a further remove, towards the Fascism that it fought—that Italians give their judgements on the past decade. Some of them would disagree with this, saying the Resistance was only an episode, that it directly affected only the few, that its so-called heroes and martyrs were young hot-heads who effected little and brought much misfortune to innocent citizens, or that it opened the way for Communism: but in so saying they would already have crystallised their attitude—which is, indeed, the attitude of the many who in 1945 desired little beyond an end of strife and a return to 'normal' conditions. Measured by that standard, the decade 1945–55 may not have fallen too far short of their expectations.

The active opponents of what the Resistance stood for naturally adopt a much more positive line. Fascists who had believed their régime the right one for Italy, monarchists for whom a Republic spelt disaster, are alike bound by their convictions to believe that Italy took a wrong turning in 1945–6. And in their strictures on the State that has emerged, much of what they find to censure is attributed to the residue of 'Resistance' ideology which influenced the framing of the Constitution and of governmental policy.

The Government, in its tenth-anniversary surveys, tended, as was inevitable, to stress the régime's positive achievements —the re-establishment of law and order and of financial stability, progress in social reforms and in Southern development, and the respected place now held by Italy in international affairs. Tribute was of course paid to the Resistance, and its decisive role in the struggle against Fascism was fully recognized; but in these tributes there was no great sense of shortcoming in relation to the ideals for which the Resistance fought. The aim of the Resistance, as it was understood by the vast majority of Christian Democrats and Liberals who supported it, was to overthrow Fascism and evict the Germans: once that turning-point had been reached, the next step was to be a restoration, if in modern dress, of the pre-Fascist liberal-democratic State. Progressive Liberals and Christian Democrats who had been directly associated with the Resistance—and foremost among them Signor De Gasperi—have always spontaneously recognized the genealogical descent of the

Republic from Resistance ideals; yet those ideals included, for many, a much more positive break with the past than the Republic has been able to achieve.

Thus it was in relation to those wider hopes, and in the Resistance circles that entertained them, that the sense of shortcoming was most strongly felt ten years after. Here one has to differentiate sharply between the attitude now adopted towards the Resistance in Communist and Socialist circles, and that of thoughtful progressives of the kind formerly associated with the Action Party. By and large, both these groups, as the war drew to an end, entertained not only the immediate military aim of defeating the Germans and Fascists but also the further political aim of establishing a new form of State in Italy; though within the Action Party opinions differed as to the lengths to which insurrection should go.[1] It was this aspiration towards a 'rinnovamento'—a complete 'renewal' of the State—which at the end of the war prompted the bitter struggle of the Left-wing anti-Fascist parties to maintain intact the powers of the Committees of National Liberation,[2] which they regarded as the instrument through which their aims could best be carried out.

In the Resistance days the differences between the form of 'new State' envisaged by the Communists and by the Actionists were not clear; indeed the Actionists in those days were by far the more explicit on the subject. During the post-war period of the Communists' collaboration in the Government (1945–7) the revolutionary aspects of their ultimate aims were kept in abeyance. But once in opposition there was no longer any need to prevaricate, and the Communist attitude towards the Italian State of today is broadly speaking critical from A to Z. And among these criticisms some of the most frequent all-purposes reproaches made against the Government concern its 'betrayal' of the Resistance and of the Constitution.

It is at least doubtful whether the Communists seriously entertained hopes of founding their ideal State in Italy in 1945. But the Actionists for a few short months did, and their disillusionment has been correspondingly the greater. Yet it is

[1] See Leo Valiani, 'Ricordi personali e documenti sul C.L.N.A.I. e l'insurrezione di Milano', in *Il Ponte*, April–May 1955.

[2] See above, pp. 10–11.

among them that the most enlightened criticism of the present State's shortcomings is to be found, often coupled with an understanding of the reasons for the failure to carry into effect their own ideals. The Resistance leader Ferruccio Parri explains a large part of this failure when he says:

How much of Italy had remained remote, both materially and psychologically, from the Resistance struggle? How many had experienced the misery of war but not the moral impetus of insurrection? The administrative Italy that Fascism had built, the conformist Italy that it had trained up through twenty years, had been set free from the institutions of the régime but not from its mental attitude and acquired habits. The buildings above ground had been destroyed, but who could gauge how much had been changed and renewed beneath the surface?[1]

And another critic from the same background, Leo Valiani, recalling how Croce refuted the accusation that the Italy of 1870 had not lived up to its mission, says that the now widely accepted view of Fascism as a 'malattia morale'—a 'moral sickness'—fails to account for the fact that tendencies towards totalitarianism still persist in Italy:

The truth is that there are not two distinct case-histories of Italy in the past forty years, one of sickness and the other of health lost and regained. . . . The cynical slogan coined by the victors of the last war—'90 million Italians, 45 million Fascists and 45 million anti-Fascists'—may wound our pride, but it also strikes home, with the salutary effect of making us feel that the Italian people is a single whole. It is the same country that is at the same time Fascist and anti-Fascist, sick and sound.[2]

The political story of the past ten years in Italy is, indeed, largely that of the struggle to build up a truly democratic form of government and to ward off totalitarianism, in whatever form. With the deterioration of East–West relations and the soon-established strength of the Left-wing parties, Communism early came to be regarded as the main opponent, and Christian Democracy as the chief bulwark against it: and indeed some have seen the struggle in straight terms of militant Communism versus the Church militant. The danger from the Right was perhaps less clear-cut but it was none the less insidious: it has

[1] Ferruccio Parri, '1945–1955', Preface to Liberation number of *Il Ponte*, April–May 1955.

[2] Leo Valiani, 'Il problema politico della nazione italiana', in *Dieci anni dopo, 1945–1955* (Bari, Laterza, 1955).

lain not so much in the direct revival of a Fascist party as in the residue in some quarters of a mentality bred in Fascist days which it will take long to eliminate. Some have even feared that the need to fight totalitarianism by means of controls and restrictions might lead to a form of clerical counter-totalitarianism among the Christian Democrats and within the Government itself, eventually producing a régime of the Salazar type. Though such fears were already being voiced during the latter days of Signor De Gasperi's lifetime, such a régime was in fact the antithesis of the Catholic-secular democracy for which he strove and in support of which he consistently fought to maintain the four-party coalition of Catholic and secular forces. It is a measure of the vitality of this idea that it should, despite all the inherent difficulties, have survived its author and been continued through both the Scelba and the Segni régimes.

Looking further ahead, it is hard to say for how long this particular four-party Centre combination may continue to be regarded as the most effective medium for maintaining stable government. The three great problematical factors remain—as indeed they have been ever since the post-war political alignments settled into a pattern—the unity and policy of the Christian Democrats; the potentialities for further advance of the Communists; and the ultimate intentions of the Nenni Socialists.

As to the unity of the Christian Democrats, enough has been said in earlier chapters to make clear how difficult this will be to maintain. As to their policy, the accentuation of Left-wing trends towards social reform has been apparent ever since the party's Naples Congress of 1954, and was made plain again both in the choice of Signor Segni as Prime Minister and in his programme, with its stress on the need to complete the lacunae of the Constitution, on the equality of all citizens before the law, on the importance of education, the restriction of monopolies, and the intention to pursue the land reform. Such policies would certainly seem to be consonant with the wishes of a large proportion of the electors who in 1953 still returned the Christian Democrats as the strongest party in the country. Yet if pursued with vigour they might, judging by the *Concentrazione* fraction's revolt from the party line around the time of the Presidential election in 1955, lose the party its Right wing; and while this might eliminate some tight-rope walking for party leaders, it would probably merely produce a stalemate in the political situation as a whole.

The possibilities of further advance for the Communists depend on a variety of factors, both domestic and international. At home, while the Government's social reform measures in the South did not pay the rapid dividends that some had hoped for, those measures have undoubtedly done much to check the advance of Communism in that particularly susceptible region, and their effect should be cumulative as prosperity increases, especially if the Vanoni Plan can succeed in bringing more and more workers into secure employment. Yet so long as the striking disparity between rich and poor persists, and with it the problem of the workless labourer with his large family, the Communists will not have to search far for adherents. The process of whittling away their allegiance is bound to be a gradual one, while a false step can add to it overnight. It is even more difficult to speculate on the possible effects which an international détente might have on this largest of the Western European Communist Parties: even if the outer bonds of the Cominform should loosen, it seems highly unlikely that, given Italy's strategic position in Western defence, the USSR would be prepared to relax its hold over Italian Communist Party policies. Another unknown factor, and one that is in part bound up with Signor Togliatti's leadership, is the outcome of the struggle for power between the moderate and the 'tough' (or Moscow) factions within the party itself.

Any striking change in the Communist Party's situation would obviously have far-reaching effects on the other Italian problem-party, the Nenni Socialists. But leaving out of count that hypothetical consideration, enough has already been said about the much-discussed 'apertura a sinistra' to suggest that an independent policy on the part of the Socialists, such as might eventually lead to a genuine *rapprochement* with the Centre parties, still lies in the distant future. Yet the cautious moves on both sides following on Signor Nenni's latest offer at the Turin Congress of February 1955 seemed to bring this possibility a trifle nearer. The choice of a new President with Signor Gronchi's earlier record of belief in this connection, the common ground for action afforded by the Vanoni Plan, and, once again, the prospects of an international détente, might all help to provide the conditions in which hitherto rigid party positions might become more flexible.

The Italian party political framework has indeed remained surprisingly static, apart from minor fluctuations—surprisingly, certainly, as compared with that of France—since 1948. This was of course in large part due to the predominance of the Christian Democrat party under Signor De Gasperi's leadership. It is still too soon to see whether that situation will continue under new leaders such as Fanfani, Segni, and Scelba (all, be it noted, men of the party's Left or Left-Centre). The only departure from the pattern of the four-party Centre combination under Christian Democrat leadership was Signor Pella's short-lived administration, which was virtually a single-party Christian Democrat Government relying on Right-wing support. We have probably not heard the last of Signor Pella as a politician, and if a Rightward swing were to occur—as it still might, for Italian politics are capable of providing surprises—it might well take this form again.

But until new elections are held under a new electoral law (and they were being spoken of for 1956, and must in any case take place by 1958) it will be impossible to break away from the mathematical restrictions imposed by the present relative party strengths in Parliament. The De Gasperi-*quadripartito* era survived beyond the setback it received in the 1953 Election; it survived, too, the death of its author. It remains to be seen whether the smaller Centre parties can summon sufficient strength to enable that particular combination to prove itself afresh the one most nearly corresponding to the needs of this country which, though so widely Catholic, yet retains some of the anti-clerical traditions of the Risorgimento.

Yet whatever new pattern of Government may come to the fore, the raw materials for it to fashion remain the same. It is a country of tremendous contrasts: of benefits lavished by Nature on the one hand and withheld on the other; of a people capable of resilience, resourcefulness, and hard work yet still lacking sufficient channels into which to direct their energies; of a ruling class grown cynical and indifferent through centuries of privilege; of a peasantry barely emerging from utter poverty and ignorance. The Governments of the past ten years have striven to reconcile some of these contrasts; and perhaps the greatest of their achievements may be found to lie in their efforts towards improving the lot of the South, where the contrasts exist in their most acute form, and thus laying the foundations for an Italy no longer consisting, in Disraeli's phrase, of two nations, but a unified whole.

It is a country still uncertain, after wars and political adventures, as to its basic direction. On the political plane alone, parliamentary democracy is bound to be a slow growth where a tradition of rhetoric still vies with intense individualism and philosophical hair-splitting; and its progress will often be fraught with disillusionment. Yet Italy's history goes to show that it is under free institutions that her finest qualities emerge; and, in Sismondi's words, she 'might justly glory in the fact that wherever she was free, she was always found constant in the road to virtue.'

APPENDIX

Italian Governments since the Fall of Fascism

Duration	*Prime Minister*	*Composition etc.*
26.7.43–8.9.43	Pietro Badoglio	In Rome; non-party.
1.10.43–17.4.44	Pietro Badoglio	In Southern Italy; non-party.
20.4.44–5.6.44	Pietro Badoglio	In Southern Italy; six CNL parties.
9.6.44–26.11.44	Ivanoe Bonomi	In Rome (and henceforth); six CNL parties.
10.12.44–12.6.45	Ivanoe Bonomi	CD, Lib., Lab.Dem., Com.
20.6.45–24.11.45	Ferruccio Parri	Six CNL parties.
10.12.45–1.7.46	Alcide De Gasperi	Six CNL parties.
12.7.46–20.1.47	Alcide De Gasperi	CD, Com., Soc., Repub.
1.2.47–31.5.47	Alcide De Gasperi	CD, Com., Soc.
31.5.47–23.5.48	Alcide De Gasperi	CD, plus some non-party 'technicians'.
23.5.48–12.1.50	Alcide De Gasperi	CD, PSLI, Lib., Repub. (PSLI Ministers withdrew in November 1949).
27.1.50–16.7.51	Alcide De Gasperi	CD, PSLI, Repub.
26.7.51–29.6.53	Alcide De Gasperi	CD, Repub.
15.7.53–28.7.53	Alcide De Gasperi	CD.
15.8.53–5.1.54	Giuseppe Pella	CD, plus some non-party 'technicians'.
18.1.54–30.1.54	Amintore Fanfani	CD.
10.2.54–22.6.55	Mario Scelba	CD, PSDI, Lib.
6.7.55–	Antonio Segni	CD, PSDI, Lib.

Heads of the State and Presidents of the Italian Republic, 1946–1955

Enrico De Nicola	(28.6.46–11.5.48)
Luigi Einaudi	(11.5.48–11.5.55)
Giovanni Gronchi	(11.5.55–)

BIBLIOGRAPHY

The following list is in no sense a complete bibliography, but merely an indication of some useful books and periodicals. Among the latter, specialist periodicals have been listed in the appropriate sub-section; but particular mention should perhaps be made of two more general periodicals which reflect interesting (and frequently critical) views on current Italian topics—*Il Ponte* (monthly; Florence, La Nuova Italia), edited by Piero Calamandrei, and *Il Mondo* (weekly; Milan, Domus), edited by Mario Panunzio.

General

Background and War, 1940–45

Badoglio, Pietro. *L'Italia nella seconda guerra mondiale.* Verona, Mondadori, 1946. English version: *Italy in the Second World War.* Oxford University Press, 1948.

Battaglia, Roberto. *Storia della Resistenza Italiana.* Turin, Einaudi, 1953.

Binchy, Daniel. *Church and State in Fascist Italy.* Oxford University Press for Royal Institute of International Affairs, 1941.

Grindrod, Muriel. *The New Italy: Transition from War to Peace.* London, Royal Institute of International Affairs, 1947.

Jemolo, Arturo Carlo. *Chiesa e Stato negli ultimi cento anni.* Turin, Einaudi, 1948.

Macartney, Maxwell H. H. *One Man Alone: The History of Mussolini and the Axis.* London, Chatto & Windus, 1944.

Monelli, Paolo. *Roma 1943.* Rome, Migliaresi, 1945.

Mussolini, Benito. *Storia di un anno.* Verona, Mondadori, 1944. English version: *Memoirs 1942–3* (ed. Raymond Klibansky). London, Weidenfeld & Nicolson, 1949.

Pentad (*pseud.*) *The Remaking of Italy.* London, Penguin Books, 1941. Four anonymous Italians and an Englishman outline plans for post-war Italy in the light of her past.

Salvadori, Max. *Brief History of the Patriot Movement in Italy, 1943–45.* Chicago, Clemente & Sons, 1954.

Sforza, Count Carlo. *Contemporary Italy: Its Intellectual and Moral Origins.* London, Muller, 1946.

Sprigge, C. J. S. *Development of Modern Italy.* London, Duckworth, 1943.
From the unification of Italy to beginning of Fascism.

Wiskemann, Elizabeth. *Italy*. (*The World Today* series). Oxford University Press, 1947.
A general survey of modern Italy.

Wiskemann, Elizabeth. *The Rome-Berlin Axis*. Oxford University Press, 1949.

Italy Today

Battaglia, Achille, and others. *Dieci anni dopo, 1945–55: Saggi sulla vita democratica italiana*. Bari, Laterza, 1955.
Essays on various aspects of Italian life by Resistance leaders, published on tenth anniversary of the end of the war.

Calamandrei, Piero, and Levi, A. *Commentario sistematico della Costituzione italiana*. Florence, Barbera, 1950. 2 vols.

Documenti di Vita Italiana. Monthly from 1950. Rome, Centro di Documentazione della Presidenza del Consiglio dei Ministri della Repubblica Italiana.
Useful documentation and statistics on a wide range of current domestic Italian topics.

Falzone, V., and others. *La Costituzione della Repubblica Italiana*. Rome, Colombo, 1948.
Text of the Constitution, with parliamentary discussion on each Article.

France: Présidence du Conseil: Direction de la documentation. *Chroniques étrangères: Italie*. Monthly from 1949. Paris, Documentation Française.
A monthly bulletin on principal current topics in Italian affairs, based on a wide reading and citation of the Italian press.

Garosci, Aldo, and others. *Il Secondo Risorgimento: nel decennale della resistenza e del ritorno alla democrazia, 1945–55*. Rome, Istituto Poligrafico dello Stato, 1955.
The counterpart of *Dieci anni dopo* (see above), issued under Government auspices.

Hughes, H. Stuart. *The United States and Italy*. Cambridge, Mass., Harvard University Press, 1953.
An excellent survey of the situation in Italy today, by an American.

Italian Affairs: Documents and Notes. Bi-monthly from 1952. Rome, Documentation Centre.
In English, on lines similar to *Documenti di Vita Italiana* (see above).

Italy: Consiglio dei Ministri. *Italy Today*. Rome, Documentation Centre of the Presidency of the Council of the Republic of Italy, 1955. illus.
Useful information about many aspects of present-day Italy.

Foreign Affairs

Adstans (*pseud.*). *Alcide De Gasperi nella politica estera italiana (1944–53)*. Verona, Mondadori, 1953.

Esteri. Fortnightly, Rome, Atlante.

A semi-official publication on foreign affairs.

Great Britain: Foreign Office. *Treaty of Peace with Italy, Paris, 10th February 1947*. Cmd. 7481, Treaty Series No. 50 (1948). London, H.M.S.O., 1948. Maps annexed to the Treaty, Cmd. 7482.

Relazioni Internazionali. Weekly. Milan, Istituto per gli Studi di Politica Internazionale.

Articles and documentation on international topics with a good and reliable coverage on Italian foreign policy.

Rivlin, Benjamin, *The United Nations and the Italian Colonies*. New York, Carnegie Endowment for International Peace, 1950.

Sforza, Carlo. *Cinque anni a Palazzo Chigi: La politica estera italiana dal 1947 al 1951*. Rome, Atlante, 1952.

Trieste

De Castro, Diego. *Il Problema di Trieste: Genesi e sviluppo della questione giuliana in relazione agli avvenimenti internazionali (1943–1952)*. Bologna, Cappelli, 1953.

Great Britain: Foreign Office. *Memorandum of Understanding between the Governments of the United Kingdom, Italy, the United States of America, and Yugoslavia regarding the Free Territory of Trieste, London, October 5, 1954*. Cmd. 9288. London, H.M.S.O., 1954.

Reports of the Administration of the British-United States Zone of the Free Territory of Trieste. Quarterly 1947–9, then annually.

POLITICS, PARTIES, AND ADMINISTRATION

Compagna, Francesco, and De Caprariis, Vittorio. *Geografia delle elezioni italiane dal 1946 al 1953*. Bologna, *Il Mulino*, 1954 (reprint from *Il Mulino*, January 1954).

Einaudi, Luigi. *Il Buongoverno*. Bari, Laterza, 1954.

Einaudi, Mario; Domenach, Jean-Marie; and Garosci, Aldo. *Communism in Western Europe*. Cornell University Press, 1951.

Einaudi, Mario, and Goguel, François. *Christian Democracy in Italy and France*. University of Notre Dame Press, 1952.

Ferrara, Marcella and Maurizio. *Conversando con Togliatti*. Rome, Edizioni di Cultura Sociale, 1953.

Biography of Togliatti and history of the Italian Communist Party.

Gramsci, Antonio. *Lettere dal carcere*. Turin, Einaudi, 1947.

Origins of Italian Communist Party, by its founder.

Hilton-Young, W. *The Italian Left: A Short History of Political Socialism in Italy*. London, Longman, 1949.

Rossi, Ernesto. *Il Malgoverno*. Bari, Laterza, 1955.

Collected articles, many dealing with administrative problems, by a well-known critic of the Government.

Tupini, Giorgio. *I Democratici Cristiani: Cronache di dieci anni*, Milan, Garzanti, 1954.

Vigorelli, Ezio. *L'Italia è socialista e non lo sa.* Verona, Mondadori, 1952.

Economic and Social Questions

Atti della Commissione Parlamentare di Inchiesta sulla disoccupazione. Milan-Rome, Istituto Editoriale Italiano, 1953. 5 vols.

The Tremelloni Report on unemployment.

Atti della Commissione Parlamentare di Inchiesta sulla miseria in Italia e sui mezzi di combatterla. Milan-Rome, Istituto Editoriale Italiano, 1953. 13 vols.

The Vigorelli Report on poverty.

Banca Nazionale del Lavoro (Rome). *Quarterly Review.* In English. Articles on a variety of Italian economic topics.

Banco di Roma (Rome). *Review of the Economic Conditions in Italy.* Bi-monthly. In English.

Great Britain: Board of Trade, Commercial Relations and Exports Department. *Italy: Economic and Commercial Conditions in Italy.* By E. J. Joint. London, H.M.S.O., 1955.

Italy: Istituto Centrale di Statistica. *Annuario Statistico Italiano.* Rome, Istituto Poligrafico dello Stato.

Italy: Ministero del Bilancio. *Relazione generale sulla situazione economica del Paese* (1954). Rome, Istituto Poligrafico dello Stato, 1955.

Report on economic conditions in 1954, presented to the Senate by the Budget and Treasury Ministers on 18 March 1955.

Italy, Ministero del Bilancio. *Schema di sviluppo dell'occupazione e del reddito in Italia nel decennio 1955–1964.* Rome, January 1955. English version: *Outline of Development of Income and Employment in Italy in the Ten-Year Period 1955–64.* Paris, OEEC, January 1955.

The Vanoni Plan.

Lo sviluppo dell'economia italiana nel quadro della ricostruzione e della cooperazione europea. Rome, Istituto Poligrafico dello Stato, 1952.

Medici, Giuseppe. *Politica agraria, 1945–52.* Bologna, Zanichelli, 1952.

The Statist (London). Special Supplements on Italy: *Italy, an Economic Survey* (25 October 1952); *Italy's External Trade* (1 May 1954).

Thomas, Ivor. *The Problem of Italy: An Economic Survey.* London, Routledge, 1946.

United Nations: Dept. of Economic Affairs. *Economic Survey of Europe since the War.* Prepared by the Research and Planning Division, Economic Commission for Europe. Geneva, 1953.

—— *Economic Survey of Europe in 1953, including a Study of Economic Development in Southern Europe.* Geneva, 1954.

Contains a special section on Southern Italy.

UNRRA, Italian Mission. *Survey of Italy's Economy.* Rome, UNRRA. June 1947.

U.S.A.: Economic Cooperation Administration. *Italy.* (European Recovery Program Country Study). Washington, U.S.G.P.O., 1949.

Southern Italy

Centro Nazionale di Prevenzione e Difesa Sociale. *Proceedings of the International Congress for the Study of the Problem of Under-developed Areas, Milan, 10–15 October 1954.* Milan, Giuffrè, 1954.

The volumes of this Congress's proceedings, issued in Italian, English, French, and German, contain a great deal of valuable material on social and economic conditions in Southern Italy.

Vöchting, Friedrich. *Die italienische Südfrage.* Berlin, Duncker & Humbolt, 1951.

Rodanò, Carlo. *Mezzogiorno e sviluppo economico.* Bari, Laterza, 1954.

Rossi-Doria, Manlio. *Riforma agraria e azione meridionalista.* Bologna, Edizioni Agricole, 1948.

Publications of SVIMEZ (Associazione per lo Sviluppo dell'Industria nel Mezzogiorno), the Cassa per il Mezzogiorno, and the various Enti di Riforma Agraria (Land Reform Organizations).

INDEX

INDEX

INDEX

INDEX

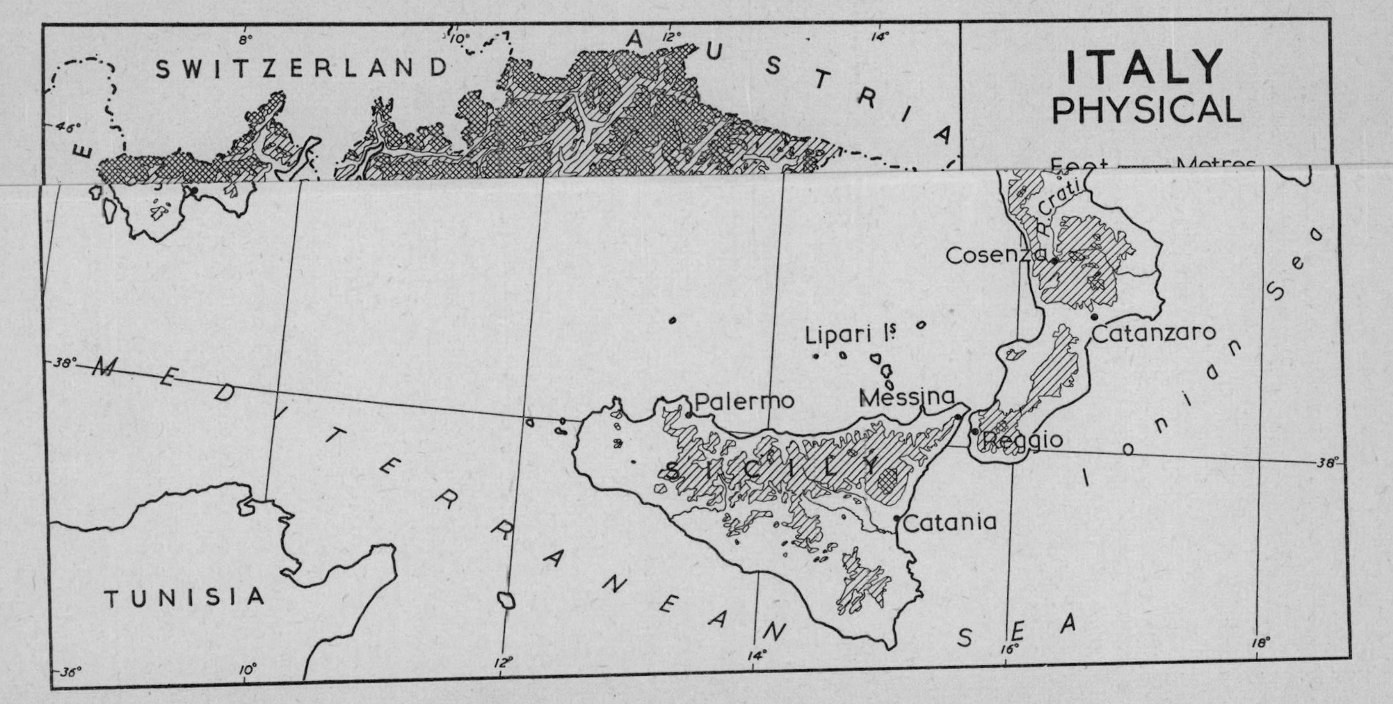
ITALY
PHYSICAL
SWITZERLAND
AUSTRIA
TUNISIA
MEDITERRANEAN SEA
Ionian Sea
SICILY
Lipari Is
Palermo
Messina
Catania
Reggio
Catanzaro
Cosenza
R. Crati
8°
10°
12°
14°
16°
18°
46°
38°
36°